The Masculine Woman in America, 1890–1935

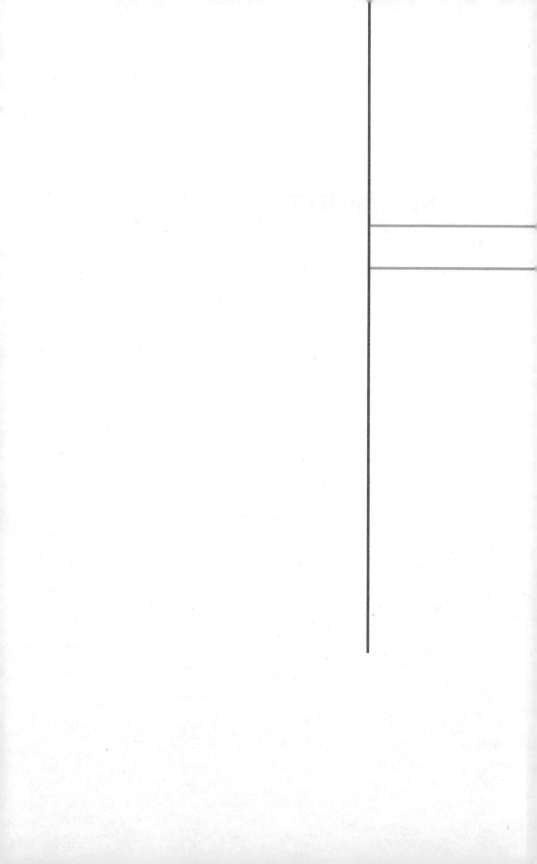

The Masculine Woman in America, 1890–1935

Laura L. Behling

University of Illinois Press
Urbana and Chicago

Library of Congress Cataloging-in-Publication Data
Behling, Laura L., 1967–
The masculine woman in America, 1890–1935 / Laura L. Behling.
p.   cm.
Includes bibliographical references and index.
ISBN 0-252-02627-6 (cloth : acid-free paper)
1. Women's rights—United States—History. 2. Women—Suffrage—
United States—History. 3. Women—United States—Public opinion.
4. Lesbianism—United States—History. 5. Masculinity—United
States—History. 6. Women in literature—History. 7. Women in popu-
lar culture—History. 8. Sex differences—United States—History.
9. Public opinion—United States—History. I. Title.
HQ1236.5.U6B45   2001
305.42'0973—dc21   00-009894

C 5 4 3 2 1

Contents

Acknowledgments

In the summer of 1993, my sister and I visited the Huntington Library, Art Collections, and Botanical Gardens in San Marino, California. By happenstance, we discovered the special exhibit "From Allegory to Activism: Changing Images of Women in American Illustration, 1890–1920" and were particularly drawn to the illustrations and descriptions of the turn-of-the-century "New Woman" and the social, cultural, economic, and political spheres she threatened. We were two highly educated professional women in the late twentieth century; our careers, lifestyles, and attitudes were possible only because of the commitment these women had to achieving equality, opportunity, and respect. That visit was the source for this project, in both focus and interdisciplinary format, and the beginning of my appreciation for women who challenge the status quo.

I am grateful to a number of people for their careful comments, critical insights, thoughtful advice, and support of my ideas: Wendy Martin, Constance Jordan, and Lori Anne Ferrell from the Claremont Graduate School and Frances Pohl from Pomona College. Emily Rogers was unfailing in her work as my first editor at the University of Illinois Press, a job ably assumed by Willis Regier. Most especially, thanks are due to Ellen Caldwell for her generosity of space and spirit and for her faith in me and my work.

Some of these chapters have appeared in various periodicals. I thank the editors of the *Journal of Modern Literature, Women's Studies,* and *American Literary Realism* for allowing me to use them in modified form for this book.

Introduction

When the American woman suffragists demanded, as Pauline Kellogg Wright Davis wrote in an editorial in the suffrage magazine *Una* in 1853, "to be regarded, respected and treated as human beings of full age and natural abilities" (n.p.), they certainly could not have dreamed that in the early decades of the twentieth century their call for political equality would be used as evidence of their desire to become "female men." These same woman suffragists, who, despite their wish for voting rights, were so careful to project an image of domesticity and femininity, would never have guessed their movement would spark profound changes in traditional attitudes about sex, gender, and sexuality. Nor could they have known that the psychology of sex and sexual behavior would, at the beginning of the twentieth century, seize both scientific and popular imaginations and link the woman suffrage movement to what was then called "viraginity" or "female sexual inversion."[1] My focus in this study is on late-nineteenth- and early-twentieth-century American society, where the beginnings of modern sexuality and psychology intersect with the foundations of modern womanhood, a time Judith Halberstam characterizes as holding "momentous negotiations about gender . . . [that] produced particular forms of femininity and masculinity and clearly showed that femininity was not wed to femaleness and masculinity was certainly not bound to maleness" (48). Specifically, I explore how the U.S. woman suffrage movement's emphasis on securing social and political independence for women was translated by a fearful society, in American literature and the popular press, into a movement of women whose assumption of the prerogative to vote was perceived to have altered them into "masculine women" and female sexual inverts.

My work follows Halberstam's *Female Masculinities* in that it examines the concept of masculinity exhibited in bodies that are not male and begins to rectify what Halberstam calls the "collective failure to imagine and ratify the masculinity produced by, for, and within women" (15). Unlike Halberstam, who focuses on the contemporary production of masculinity that is dependent on female versions and "actually affords us a glimpse of how masculinity is constructed as masculinity" (1), I explore the early twentieth century as a site for a construction of masculinity that accrued solely to female bodies. Although I would agree that the suffragists' rendition of masculinity has not been incorporated into contemporary theories of masculinity—in Halberstam's words has "been blatantly ignored" (2)—it was clearly visible to much of the American public during the years of the U.S. suffrage movement. Parades, protests, and pickets led to verbal and visual demonstrations of the suffragists' supposed abandonment of femininity for political power and hence masculine prerogative.

Sexologists, social commentators, authors, and illustrators alike remarked on the dangers of independent women who had acquired masculine traits. Richard Le Gallienne, writing in *Vanity Fair* in 1924, wondered if the modern woman, as a result of her independence, was "becoming more of a man, or less of a woman" (27). Ten years earlier, the same magazine displayed an advertisement for women's clothing that succinctly captured the dual-gendered nature some women were thought to have assumed; the suit of clothing promised "The Ways of a Maid with the Modes of a Man." Robert Benchley's 1925 *New Yorker* piece went one step further by satirically surmising that "sex is out" because the gender markings of feminine and masculine were so easily manipulated (16).

The confusion about femininity and masculinity, however, was clearly connected to the woman suffragists, and because they worked for political enfranchisement, a heretofore male domain, they were considered masculine. Antisuffragists worried that women's maternal duties would be abandoned once they gained access to the ballot box and, even more worrisome, that women's femininity would be lost and they would become, in the words of Horace Bushnell, an ardent antisuffragist, "large-handed, big-footed, flat-chested, and thin-lipped." Bushnell, in his 1869 treatise entitled *Women's Suffrage: The Reform against Nature*, declared, "Women having once gotten the polls will have them to the end, and if we precipitate our American society down this abyss, and make a final wreck of our public virtue in it, that is the end of our newborn, more beneficent civilization" (31).

These changes ran far deeper than alterations in the economic sphere and superficial physical characteristics. Aided by the developing theories of sexology that attempted to classify and order human sexual behavior, some began to look at U.S. woman suffragists and "see" masculinization and female sexual inversion. Dr. H. W. Frink wrote, "A certain proportion of at least the most militant suffragists are neurotics who in some instances are compensating for masochistic trends, in others are more or less successfully subliminating sadistic and homosexual ones" (quoted in Macy 62). Havelock Ellis cited emancipation as a cause of increasing sexual inversion in women ("Sexual Inversion in Women"), while the physician James B. Weir Jr. even went so far as to warn of a "matriarchy" if women were allowed the vote.

Cultural critics have contributed to a substantial body of research on the U.S. woman suffrage movement and female sexuality,[2] including sexual "aberrancy," but rarely has the link between the two been fully explored. George Chauncey Jr. concurs: "The implicit concern about challenges to the sex-gender system" that pervaded medical accounts of "inversion" "linked the apparent rise in sexual inversion to the influence of the women's movement" (104). The ancient topos of *mundus inversus,* the world turned upside down, to which Carroll Smith-Rosenberg alludes (286), illustrates the social tensions embedded in both the woman suffrage movement and sexological theory. Those fearful of political power wielded by women thought woman suffrage assaulted the traditions of political and economic power and destroyed social conventions. They also predicted that the enfranchised women's physical identity would be altered—women turned into freaks. The social disorder of these suffragists who did not adhere to traditional gender categories specifically manifested itself as masculine womanhood and female sexual inversion. The world of the heterosexual status quo was thus turned upside down—the suffragists who rallied for their voting rights were perceived to be, essentially, sexually "inverted." Just as important, this alleged sexual inversion of the suffragists was scientifically and publicly authorized.

This study's focus on the "masculine woman," a character who is both female sexed and masculinely gendered, begins with an extension of current gender theory that reads gender as a marker of not only sex but also, vital for purposes here, sexuality. Sexualities—both heterosexuality and homosexuality, or to use the late-nineteenth- and early-twentieth-century term *sexual inversion*—are implicitly and explicitly defined by gender. Since females have traditionally been gendered as feminine and males traditionally gendered as masculine, the explicit sex binary is female/male, and the implicit gender binary is feminine/masculine. Heterosexuality has thus traditionally been defined not only by the different sexes but also by the different genders. Conversely, female homosexual relationships have depended on the presence of a masculine woman and a feminine women—the homosexual couple is constructed on the heterosexual model.

It is crucial to recognize, however, that this equation is built on rigidly defined binaries—"women" and "men" become the polarized possibilities, as does gender, categorized according to "feminine" and "masculine," and sexuality is labeled "homosexual" or "heterosexual." Yet in the early decades of the twentieth century, American literary and popular rhetoric was very much dependent on the binaries that governed sex, gender, and sexuality and that privileged heterosexuality. The very term *masculine woman* is a combination of two already existing social constructions employed in an attempt to create a new possibility. Sexologists were constricted by the same rhetoric; determining that male or female sexual inverts represented a new type, they could do no better than refer to these sexual inverts as a "third sex," linguistically built on the social assumption that two sexes already existed. Such a connection between historical fact and medical theories of "sexual inversion" rested in the very real seventy-two-year struggle for woman suffrage in the United States, which culminated with the ratification of the Nineteenth Amendment in 1920. It was a political flash point at which some independent-minded women first became "masculine women," and then, because of the sociomedical diagnoses that could only postulate that masculinity expressed its sexual desire toward femininity, these masculine women were assumed to be sexual inverts.

For literary models for the theoretical exposition in chapter 1, I rely on Gertrude Stein's early novel *Fernhurst* (1904) and Charlotte Perkins Gilman's short story "Turned" (1911), both of which alter the traditional sex-gender pairings of female-feminine and male-masculine. These texts present a masculine woman in a relationship with a feminine woman. Stein's text retells the allegations that befell Martha Carey Thomas, a Bryn Mawr dean, and Mary Gwinn, an English professor. In *Fernhurst,* the fictional Dean Thornton is portrayed as masculinely gendered, while Gwinn becomes the feminine Miss Bruce, suggesting that the initial step of imagining a female sexually inverted relationship is to assign each woman a different gender. Gilman's "Turned" takes Stein's possibility one dangerous step further by giving her female couple a child, thus suggesting that this relationship is procreative. Yet neither text accomplishes a radical revisioning of female same-sex relationships. Instead, both Stein and

Gilman trap their female protagonists in a still rigidly proscribed boundary of masculinity and femininity according to the heterosexual paradigm.

Chapter 2 grounds the theoretical in the historical moment that pushed the threat of the masculine woman to prominence, the U.S. woman suffrage movement. I explore the connection between the woman suffrage movement and the rise of theories in sexology and psychology that determined enfranchised women would assume the gender traditionally reserved for men and would become "masculine women," what sexologists referred to as "viragints." As the inevitability of the enfranchised woman began to permeate American society's collective psyche, so did the fearful images of masculine women and the "aggravated" figures of female inverts. Henry James's *Bostonians* takes as its subject a cell of the women's rights movement in Boston and clearly portrays Olive Chancellor and Verena Tarrant in a same-sex relationship. Chancellor's ultimate loss of the younger woman to Basil Ransom seals the indictment of the suggested female sexual inversion, as does the portrayal of Dr. Mary J. Prance, the defeminized physician who admits the frightening possibility of no difference between men and women. The metamorphosis of the suffragist to a masculine woman to an abnormal "pervert" and the enfranchised woman's threat to American society are even more vehemently articulated in Dr. William Lee Howard's aptly titled novel *The Perverts* (1901). Putting his medical experiences into fictional form, Howard constructs his masculine woman as Mizpra Newcomber, a woman whose increasing masculinity and feminism eventually lead to her violent death. In both of these works, masculine womanhood and female sexual inversion are directly linked to the woman suffrage movement.

During the first three decades of the twentieth century, the masculine woman and female sexual inversion are evident in the American literary arena. The masculine woman's inclusion in modern American literature, however, is contradictory and complex. Simply because she is allowed existence in American culture and is a viable character in fiction and illustration signals that her presence is acknowledged and that she enjoys some degree of social prominence. Just as clear, however, are the boundaries within which she must exist. Society retains ultimate control of the masculine woman, determines the proper agenda for social conversation and behavior, and effectively reaffirms the heterosexual and patriarchal status quo. Chapter 3 explores the first strategy authors used to disenfranchise the masculine woman, diagnosing her as organically aberrant and behaviorally criminal. Two newspaper accounts of female sexual inversion in the late nineteenth century form the basis for understanding the severe judgment society rendered. A third account examines the historical precedence of Mary E. Wilkins Freeman's murder-mystery story "The Long Arm" (1895). In this text, the supposition that masculine womanhood and same-sex intimacy lead to criminality is made manifest. Phoebe Dole's forty-year relationship with Maria Woods ends when Dole refuses to allow Woods to marry her longtime suitor by murdering him. Dole's guilt is quickly discovered, and her punishment is swift and unforgiving: imprisonment and death. The message is clear: such a gendering of politics leads to aberrant behavior, including female sexual inversion, and must be eradicated for the good of society.

With the increasing prominence of the woman suffrage movement in the United States, fears about masculinized women became even stronger and more widespread, and authors consequently used other strategies to dismiss the threat and engineer the fall of a politically and sexually independent woman. In chapter 4, I detail the use of the seduction plot to undermine or destroy the masculine woman. Popular press fiction, such as Carolyn Wells's "Beautiful House" (1912), Helen Hull's "Fire" (1917), and Richard Washburn Child's "Feminist" (1915), and Sherwood Anderson's novel *Poor White* (1920) portray women's genderings in same-sex relationships that were altered to fit the status quo. But female sexual inversion is not allowed to exist beyond the stories' endings. Domesticity and maternity were resurrected in the popular press and in characterizations of fictional women; ideal women discard any hints of masculinity and return to femininity. Moreover, contrary to Terry Castle's assertion that in "post-marital lesbian fiction [written after the 1950s] . . . male homosocial bonds are generally presented—from the outset—as debilitated to the point of unrecuperability" (85), one member of the initial same-sex relationship in these stories is seduced by a man—heterosexuality naturally prevails. Even in a failed seduction plot, as occurs in Floyd Dell's *Diana Stair* (1932) and Elizabeth Willis's aptly titled *Lesby* (1930), where the plot attempts a feminization of the masculine woman and a heterosexual rescue, it is clear that the masculine woman's gender and sexual deviancy make her unable to commit to marriage.

However, the psychological portrait of aberrant female sexual "perversion" and heterosexual seduction were unable to completely disenfranchise masculine women and female inverts. Two other strategies were employed to reduce masculine women and their sexual inversion to deviancy. Drawing particular attention to France, Lillian Faderman posits that even though "lesbianism was in high fashion among the literary and bohemian circles in the early twentieth century" (*Surpassing* 360), the masculine woman between 1920 and 1930 required eradication from heterosexual society. Perhaps because enfranchisement became a reality, and with it the possibility that antisuffragist fears would prove true, authors continued to disenfranchise the masculine woman, this time using parody and removal. These two techniques differed from seduction in that they allowed for the existence of masculine womanhood and female inversion; they were intent not on removing these possibilities but simply on removing her as a serious figure in society.

Chapter 5 examines the subversive nature of parody, mindful that a parodic rendering of an already subversive text only reinverts the subversion; that is, it ultimately reinforces the status quo against which the original text was working. *Vanity Fair*'s "When Helen Furr Got Gay with Harold Moos" (1923) appropriates the style and content of Gertrude Stein's short story "Miss Furr and Miss Skeene." But instead of supporting the same-sex possibility Stein proposed in her story, the magazine's parody only makes Helen Furr "less gay" by marrying her to Harold Moos. A little-known parody by Henry von Rhau entitled *The Hell of Loneliness* (1929) is, as the title indicates, a not-so-thinly-disguised absurdist portrait of Radclyffe Hall's *Well of Loneliness* (1928). Otto Kugelmann, the hero of von Rhau's satire, differs markedly from Stephen Gordon, the sympathetic character Hall proposed, yet by the end of the short parody Otto has been cuckolded by his wife's lover, the female Ivanova Feodronova-Kaskawisky, and as a result is a sympathetic character. This chapter concludes with special attention to the art that accompanied Djuna Barnes's wickedly satiric *Ladies Almanack* (1928). By appropriating images found in the French collection *L'imagerie populaire* (1925) to frame the satire of lesbian lives in literary Paris of the 1920s, Barnes challenges those traditional images and ideas of sex, gender, and sexuality. But her appropriation of visual and verbal genres dismisses literary and artistic history through parody, rendering *Ladies Almanack* a treatise on sterile reproduction, what I call the "inconceivability" of women's same-sex relationships.

In those instances when the masculine woman who exhibited sexual inversion was given serious fictional space, her acceptance was by no means guaranteed. Chapter 6 charts the removal of the masculinized female invert from twentieth-century American society. Whether given life only on specific holidays, as in Thomas Beer's short story "Hallowe'en" (1923), or as a result of sunstroke, as in Anthony Thorne's *Delay in the Sun* (1934), the masculinized woman and female same-sex relationship are clearly separated from accepted society. Beer's masculine woman appears only on Halloween, and by the time the holiday has ended, she and her partner are safely spirited away from small-town New England by a "lunatic wind." Thorne's *Delay in the Sun* uses a similar strategy by allowing same-sex sexuality only on a holiday and only when the two women leave the bustling center of commerce in a small Spanish village and venture across the river into a mystical garden. When the holiday ends and the women return to the center, their painful sunburn is all that is left of their short-lived relationship.

Two popular press authors, Mary Constance Dubois and Jeanette Lee, plot the removal of the masculine woman and her inverted sexuality from the fictional confines of all-girls' schools. Their masculinized females are safely tucked away behind the ivy-covered walls of their schools, an environment that gives them the opportunity to experiment with attraction but also proscribes the parameters in which their gender alteration and same-sex affection can occur. In the Dubois text, "The Lass of the Silver Sword" (1909), heterosexual attraction becomes the girls' only option once they leave their school. Although the girls in Lee's story, "The Cat and the King" (1919), are never seen by the reader outside the school's walls, the masculine endeavor of science is allowed in and transforms the same-sex relationship into a heterosexual one. In short, the girls lose interest in each other and transfer their passions to science. The same-sex sexual possibility barely exists in these stories and ultimately, because of its careful banishment, does not have even a remote chance of survival.

In the last chapter, I provide closure for the masculine woman of the early twentieth century and look ahead to other flash points in this century where she continued to be disenfranchised. My focus here is on the athletic female, once the purported embodiment of masculine womanhood and female sexual inversion but by the 1930s celebrated for her graceful curves and healthy outlook—in short, she, too, had been feminized. If she continues to act masculine, as the fictional golfer Anya Tenniel does in "Once a Lady Athlete, Always a Lady Athlete" (1933), a short story by the sportswriter Paul Gallico, she is deemed only a "lady athlete," not a woman. Gallico's fictional voice of wisdom explains: "Some of 'em look like women, dress like women, act like women—but they ain't. If they were, they wouldn't be athletes" (40).

After women's successful quest for political rights, many in society were asking, as Zephine Humphreys did in the *Woman Citizen*, if there was still such a thing as a woman, athlete or not. The other suffrage magazine, the *Woman's Journal*, provided a reassuring answer in the form of Helen Louise Walker's story "Kept Husbands" (1929). Lowell Medford's commitment to her career causes her husband to leave her and others to regard her childrearing abilities as suspect. But the ideal of a heterosexual relationship is restored when she is injured and wires her husband to return because she "needs him." The world that was turned upside down by the marching suffragists now, in the decade after ratification of the Nineteenth Amendment, became a *mundus reversus*, a world reinverted that reestablished the heterosexual status quo.

Each chapter of this volume begins by scanning the popular press for non-fictional and fictional accounts of the mixed message of sex and gender in portrayals of masculine women and female sexual inverts. Such a methodology begins to address the importance of interdisciplinary sources in examining literary tropes. In American literature, this approach begins to bridge the generic gap between "high" and "low" cultures, "popular" and "literary" texts, enhancing the literary critiques presented and securely grounding the criticism in the historical moment. Since the basis of my literary theoretical argument is the real event of the woman suffrage movement in the United States in the twentieth century—a movement that embodied the contradictions of sex and gender in the bodies of the "masculinized" suffragists—that theory must be derived from and complemented by the work of journalists, essayists, illustrators, and unacclaimed poets and fiction writers who filled the pages of the popular periodicals. Much of the criticism about the independent and masculinized woman appeared in the popular press in such magazines as the *Atlantic Monthly, Saturday Evening Post, Vanity Fair, Scribner's Monthly,* and *Ladies' Home Journal.*[3] These publications' interest in the masculine woman was, however, prurient. The intent of these authors and illustrators who seized upon the public's fancy of "masculine womanhood" and "female inversion" was not to present the masculine woman and her sexuality as a social or sexual equal to traditional sex-gender pairings and heterosexuality of mainstream American. Rather, the illustrative and fictional publicity unapologetically attempted to generate a disparaging social judgment of the masculine woman, proscribing the parameters of her character and existence and, the hope was, eradicating her. They, along with authors of what is canonically considered "literature," represent public and published reaction to the early-twentieth-century American disenfranchisement of the masculine woman and the viragent politics she practiced.

Notes

1. Even though this study's focus on the masculine woman implicitly suggests same-sex sexuality, what is now referred to as lesbianism, I have used the historically appropriate term *female sexual inversion.*

2. Numerous critics have researched the woman suffrage movement. See, for example, Kraditor; Wheeler; Camhi; and Jablonsky. Literary critiques of female homosexuality include Sheri Benstock's *Women of the Left Bank: Paris, 1900–1940;* Terry Cas-

tle's *The Apparitional Lesbian: Female Homosexuality and Modern Culture;* George Chauncey Jr.'s "From Sexual Inversion to Homosexuality: The Changing Medical Conceptualization of Female 'Deviance'"; Lillian Faderman's *Surpassing the Love of Men;* and Martha Vicinus's "'They Wonder to Which Sex I Belong': The Historical Roots of Modern Lesbian Identity."

3. The influence this mass marketing of ideas had on the American psyche cannot be understated since it was capable of reaching, and indeed did reach, a larger, more widespread audience than any single novel or well-publicized speech, as Ellen Gruber Garvey argues in *The Adman in the Parlor.*

1

Altered States

Envisioning the Masculine Woman

The re-sexing of their sex, even so far as to make it manly in habit
and action, they know to be impossible.
—Horace Bushnell, *Woman's Suffrage: The Reform against Nature,* 1869

In the December 26, 1925, *New Yorker,* Robert Benchley, a member of the
famed roundtable at the Algonquin Hotel, declared in a short piece called
"Sex Is Out" that "there is no such thing as absolute sex." If 60 percent of
your cells are masculine, he explained, then you "rate as male." Contrarily,
"if 60 percent are feminine, you sit with the girls. All combinations are
possible up to 99 and 1, but the 100 percenter in either sex is a myth." To
bolster the absurdity of such a claim, Benchley concocted a conversation
between a fictional Roger, intent on expressing his love through percentages, and Mary, his beloved, even though she is married to Fred. "Ever since
that night I met you at the dance, my male percentage has been increasing,"
Roger confesses to Mary. "I used to register 65 percent. Yesterday in Liggetts
I took a test and it was eighty-one." Mary credits Roger's increased masculinity to his heavier overcoat and attributes her rise in seven femininity
points to her diet. "I had cut down on my starches," she tells Roger. Her
inability (or unwillingness) to "understand what it all means" forces Roger to resort to a mean-spirited strategy—ridicule of Fred's declining masculine percentage (16).

According to Roger, when Fred was examined for life insurance last week, "his masculine cells totalled up to forty-seven and that included his American Legion button." A shocked Mary rejects the possibility of such a finding, but Roger assures her that "figures don't lie." The final blow to Fred's masculinity and Mary's beliefs is Roger's pronouncement that "the best Fred can ever be to you from now on is a sister," reiterating the infallibility of the percentages. As evidence of his masculine love for Mary, Roger breaks into song, singing "You and I Total Up to a Hundred." In it, Roger tells of "Alice who rated a cool sixty-two, / She wore knickers and called me her 'matey'"; Betty, who "on a clear day . . . registered eighty"; and Norma, "who gave seventeen, / As her quota of masculine units" (16). Benchley's humorous suggestion does raise the specter of rapidly changing ideas about the core identity of men and women. Imagine the possibilities he foresees. "Woman" and "man" are not absolutes but exist only as gradations on the same scale—at one end point lies "man" and at the other lies "woman." Although Benchley deliberately satirizes what causes an individual to slide along the scale—we certainly are not to believe that starches affect identity—the very notion that men and women can be something other than men and women is frighteningly provocative.

To be sure, Benchley's satiric portrait does confuse our contemporary sociological notions of the differences between sex and gender;[1] indeed, it proposes no difference between the two. A majority of masculine traits makes one a male; a majority of feminine characteristics, a female. Benchley's "absolute sex" is really "absolute gender," since in his formulations the combination of biological sex and gender presents only two options: a feminine female and a masculine male. Fred's loss of majority masculinity has, according to Roger, transformed him into Mary's "sister," a term used to describe a biological or social relationship. Moreover, gender identification seems to be determined by appearance. Mary's deflating comment about the heavy overcoat, Fred's American Legion button, and the reference in the song to Alice's knickers all signal that dress is an outward signifier of gender—predating late-twentieth-century critics who stress the draglike performance of gender—and can influence the gender-percentage reading. Despite his conflation of sex and gender and his reliance on traditional stereotypes in his role assignments, Benchley's *New Yorker* piece does clearly signal that sex and gender were not static categories but were remarkably fluid.

Feminist and gender theories in the late twentieth century made sure that the operational definitions of *girl* and *boy* and *woman* and *man* do not have the same shortcomings as Benchley's use of *sex* and *gender* as interchangeable terms. Critical approaches have centered on "gender relations," a category, Jane Flax explains, that is "meant to capture a complex set of social relations, to refer to a changing set of historically variable social processes" (628). Through "gender relations," two types of persons are created—man and woman—and both, according to Flax, are mutually exclusive categories. Simply put, "[O]ne can be only one gender and not the other or both" (628–29). Integral to gender relations is perhaps the more basic binary of biological sex: male and female, also mutually exclusive categories. "One important barrier to our comprehension of gender relations," Flax notes, "has been the difficulty of understanding the relationship between gender and sex" (632). Assigning one and only one particular gender to one and only one particular sex—and the relation of that gender to that sex—is therefore problematic. "We live in a world," Flax concludes, "in which gender is a constituting social relation and in which gender is also a relation of domination. Therefore, both men's and women's understanding of anatomy, biology, embodiedness, sexuality, and reproduction is partially rooted in, reflects, and must justify (or challenge) preexisting gender relations" (637).

Judith Butler concisely suggests that "gender is neither the causal result of sex nor as seemingly fixed as sex." "It does not follow," she asserts, "that the construction of 'men' will accrue exclusively to the bodies of males or that 'women' will interpret only female bodies" (*Gender* 6); gender is, as Butler makes explicit, an "act" (*Gender* 146), yet it cannot be "read" without the body to which it is attached (*Bodies* 237). This emphasis on the "cultural constructedness of 'gender' was an important move in feminism," Penelope Deutscher argues, "because it denaturalised stereotypes of masculine and feminine behaviour" (27)—female and male bodies could now be considered either feminine or masculine.

The inability to fasten a particular gender to a particular sex and, even further, to a particular sexuality drastically opens up possible identities. Judith Lorber, in *Paradoxes of Gender,* suggests these multiplicities:

> In Western societies we could say that, on the basis of *genitalia,* there are *five sexes:* unambiguously male, unambiguously female, hermaphrodite, transsexual female-to-male, and transsexual male-to-female; on the basis of *object choice,* there are *three sexual orientations:* heterosexual, homosexual, and bisexual (all with transvestic, sadomasochistic, and fetishistic variations); on the basis of *appearance,* there are *five gender displays:* feminine, masculine, ambiguous, cross-dressed as a man, and cross-dressed as a woman (or perhaps only three); on the basis of *emotional bonds,* there are *six types of relationships:* intimate friendship, nonerotic love (between parents and children, siblings and other kin, and long-time friends), eroticized love, passion, lust, and sexual violence; on the basis of *relevant group affiliation,* there are *ten self-identifications:* straight woman, straight

man, lesbian woman, gay man, bisexual woman, bisexual man, transvestite woman, transvestite man, transsexual woman, transsexual man (perhaps fourteen if
transvestites and transsexuals additionally identify as lesbian or gay). (59)

This list of possibilities makes clear that the rigid categories Western society
traditionally recognizes—heterosexual man, heterosexual woman, gay man,
and lesbian— are precisely that, classifications attempting to contain the explosive ambiguity of sex, gender, and sexuality.[2] What, after all, is society to
do with a hermaphroditic bisexual who appears feminine and engages in an
eroticized love relationship with a transsexual female-to-male who cross-
dresses as a woman yet refers to him/herself as a straight man?

It is important to recognize, however, that even this complicated question
is built on rigidly defined binaries, a criticism Judith Butler and other theorists level against such constructions. Instead of "working sexuality *against* . . .
gender" so that "the conceptual structures and cultural practices that define
and produce 'women' and 'men' are dismantled," Colleen Lamos argues (88),
such terms as *female* and *male* become even more codified. Yet it is not only
women and *men* that become the polarized possibilities. Gender, too, is categorized according to "feminine" and "masculine," and sexuality comes to be
labeled "homosexual" or "heterosexual." In short, homosexuality and heterosexuality seem to be "in the process of becoming normalized" (Lamos 88), a
critical assumption contained in both feminist theory and gay and lesbian
studies. Classifying female roles into "butch" and "femme" in sociological
theory today, posit Elizabeth Lapovsky Kennedy and Madeline Davis, "reso-
nates with the idea that masculine and feminine . . . traits transcend time and
culture, and are biologically based" (323).

There is, moreover, an implicit consideration to attend to when working with
such binaries. Instead of existing separately, these terms—*female/male, femi-
nine/masculine, homosexual/heterosexual*—work in conjunction with each other. Since females have traditionally been gendered as feminine and males as
masculine, the explicit binary in heterosexual couplings is female/male, and
the implicit binary is feminine/masculine. That is, heterosexuality has traditionally been defined not only by the different sexes but also by the different
genders. Kennedy and Davis suggest, "Gender was so identified with sexuality that it was not choice of a partner of the 'same sex' that indicated homosexuality, but the taking on of the role of the 'opposite sex' in the pursuit of
sexual relations with the 'same sex'" (325). This is evident in Benchley's piece.
Mary functions as Roger's heterosexual object of affection and becomes even
more desirable as her femininity points increase and, just as vitally, as his

masculinity quotient increases. That is, the more extreme representative of the feminine and masculine ideals they become, the more ingrained and practiced their heterosexuality.

The two problematic characters in Benchley's sex-gender-sexuality equation are Fred, whose masculinity points have so declined that he has ceased to be majority masculine, and Alice, whose "cool sixty-two" feminine points signal she is approaching a dangerous amount of masculinity, as her knickers would attest. In terms of sexuality, the results should be obvious. If traditionally gendered "opposites" no longer exist in a heterosexual relationship, heterosexuality is questioned and gives way to the suggestion of homosexuality. Despite marriage to Mary, Fred can now be only her "sister," erasing their heterosexual attraction and implying, perhaps, a metaphorical homosexual object choice. As for Alice, her inability to sustain a relationship with Roger suggests that her interest, since her masculinity and femininity points are dangerously close, is not in the masculine Roger or a heterosexual relationship but in someone else.

As Benchley's piece demonstrates, sexualities—both heterosexuality and homosexuality, or, to use the late-nineteenth- and early-twentieth-century term, *sexual inversion*—were implicitly and explicitly defined by gender. Female sexual inverts became visible because of their masculinely gendered behavior and appearance. Concretely, gender construction expressed itself in American society in a variety of manners that were both inwardly and outwardly signified. If women exhibited behavior that was thought to compromise their "natural" role as reproductive mothers, their femininity was questioned. Bodily, this manifested itself, as the sexologist Richard von Krafft-Ebing described in the early twentieth century, as "masculine features, deep voice, manly gait, without beard, small breasts, cropped hair." It suggested, he continued, "the impression of a man in women's clothes" (quoted in Smith-Rosenberg 272). Behaviorally, women who performed men's work and assumed their roles, often in men's clothing, also were not considered feminine. John D'Emilio and Estelle Freedman provide anecdotal stories about women who passed as men. "The account of 'Bill,' a Missouri laborer who became secretary of the International Brotherhood of Boilermakers, typified the successful passing woman, who lived as men did and loved other women: 'She drank . . . she swore, she courted girls, she worked hard as her fellows, she fished and camped, she even chewed tobacco'" (125).[3]

If, as the early-twentieth-century physician George Beard claimed, when "sex is perverted . . . men become women and women men, in their tastes, conduct, character, feelings, and behavior" (quoted in D'Emilio and Freedman 226), then the traditional categories of men and women, masculine and feminine, and heterosexual and homosexual assume a confusion that is only heightened when alternatives to traditional couplings are introduced. In the Progressive and modern eras, when the difference between *sex* and *gender* was not as carefully defined as it is now, a seemingly paradoxical figure developed. Labeled a woman because of her female sex, she also was considered masculine because she dared to take on some of the behaviors of men—wearing bloomers, smoking, drinking, and, as this study emphasizes, demanding political enfranchisement. The result was the oxymoronic, at least for the fin de siècle American society, "masculine woman."

Visually, this sex-gender anomaly is evident in a postcard produced in 1905. The cartoonist H. H. suggests how the masculine woman appears, complete with a verse that details her exterior gender markers:

She is mannish from shoes to her hat,
Coat, collars, stiff shirt and waist.
She'd wear pants in the street
To make her complete,
But she knows the law won't stand for that.

In another postcard, Bishop highlights both physical and psychological confusion when a woman assumes "mannish traits." Far beyond expressing masculinity through appearance only, what Katrina Rolley refers to as "the communication of identity through dress" (54), this "maid" exhibits psychological signifiers as well: the outer garments reflect her inner identity. Such cross-dressing presents "the heroine of misrule," a designation Susan Gubar assigns to women who sought "to transcend the dualism of sex-role polarities" (479).

Much of American society, however, would not have viewed the "masculine woman" as a transcendent figure. As Esther Newton makes clear, "From the last years of the [nineteenth] century, cross-dressing was increasingly associated with 'sexual inversion' by the medical profession" (558).[4] Fixing the date when homosexuality ceased to be defined by gender inversion and became classified by object choice is difficult. According to Kennedy and Davis, "[T]he idea that a homosexual was someone who was attracted to a person of the 'same sex' became slowly and unevenly incorporated into medicine, popular culture, and gay and lesbian culture" (325). Their research on a working-class lesbian community in Buffalo suggests that such a transition was occurring in the 1940s and 1950s (326). Yet earlier in the century, literary and popular rhetoric privileged heterosexuality because of its adherence to the binaries implicit in sex, gender, and sexuality. Conversely, a female homosexual relationship, constructed on the heterosexual model, required the pairing of a masculine woman with a feminine woman.

Two texts written by American women writers early in the twentieth century anticipate the presence of the masculine woman and the construction of a female same-sex relationship. The work of Gertrude Stein and Charlotte Perkins Gilman within the sexological milieu that swirled around them—particularly the notion that gender shaped an individual's sexuality and that masculinity was an integral part, perhaps even a cause, of female inversion—suggests not simply a relationship between women but a story deliberately complicated by gender that results in a complex sexuality, more commonly expressed in the decades following the appearance of Stein and Gilman.

Bonnie Zimmerman argues that "serious writers" of the 1920s and 1930s "relied upon codes and subterfuge to express lesbian desire, a strategy that protected them from censure." Employing such strategies as "suppressing pronouns, changing the gender of characters, inventing a cryptic language of sexuality, or hinting obliquely at relationships between women, these writers," she concludes, "could tell, but not quite tell, lesbian stories" (*Safe Sea* 16).[5] As evidence, she cites Virginia Woolf's *Mrs. Dalloway* (1925) and *Orlando* (1928), Gertrude Stein's "elaborate private code" in such texts as "Lifting Belly" (1915–17) and "A Sonatina Followed by Another" (1921), and texts by Willa Cather, Angelina Ward Grimké, and Amy Lowell (*Safe Sea* 7). Jan Hokenson concurs, suggesting that Stein's first novel, *Q.E.D.* (1903, published posthumously), was rewritten as "Melanctha" in *Three Lives* (1909). Instead of focusing on the lesbian coming of age, as she does in *Q.E.D.*, Stein, according to Hokenson, carefully transposes this early novel "to heterosexual terms among blacks in New York" in "Melanctha" (63). Terry Castle agrees, arguing that "the archetypal lesbian fiction decanonizes, so to speak, the canonical structure of desire itself. . . . It dismantles the real . . . in a search for the not-yet-real, something unpredicted and unpredictable" (90–91).

Yet the subterfuge proposed by Zimmerman and read by Castle—"tell, but not quite tell"—is prompted by the assumption that writers changed the gender of characters. Flax's theoretical musings, Zimmerman's more grounded literary analyses, and Butler's position of performance, however, fail to explain the complications that necessarily arise when traditional sex and gender pairings, female sex with feminine gender and male sex with masculine gender, are reversed. Zimmerman's position that characters' genders have been changed to avoid censorship is unclear if her changed "gender" means changed "sex," that is, if a woman is fictionally made male to have a relationship with a woman. The knowledgeable reader presumably knows when a "sex change" has occurred and then reads the male-female relationship as if it were two women. But this strategy necessitates an inordinate intuition and imagination on the part of the reader. A more practical suggestion is that it is not the sex that is changed to present a heterosexual relationship but that the gender is changed and the relationship remains homosexual. That is, these texts portray experimentations with gender identity rather than disguised homosexual relationships masked by conventional male and female roles.

Such a formulation, however, is not Stein's or Gilman's clever strategy of disguise but ultimately a plot of disenfranchisement. In working through the complexities of sex and gender, these authors offer the masculinely gendered woman as an amenable solution to conventional femininity. But it is not a satisfactory rendition of the masculine woman and her implicit sexual inversion. By presenting the homosexual woman as masculine and establishing her within masculine homosociality, Stein's and Gilman's writing of her is only a rewriting of masculine homosocial code and thus female sexual disenfranchisement.

Identity had been a lifelong struggle for Gertrude Stein; her unwillingness to accept her female sex and her reconciliation with her masculine "identity" are manifested most clearly in her relationship with Alice B. Toklas, who served as "wife," and in her repudiation of the feminist movement. Abandoned at the same time she left medical school, feminism (as expressed in the woman suffrage campaign) represented for Stein a misguided, shortsighted, and naive reform effort. "Had I been bred in the last generation full of hope and unattainable desires," the narrator of *Fernhurst* explains, echoing Stein's politics, "I too would have declared that men and women are born equal but being of this generation with the college and professions open to me and able to learn that the other man is really stronger I say I will have none of it" (7–8).

Stein's assumption of a masculinely gendered identity and her reluctance to embrace the larger feminist cause figure in her writings, particularly her early novel *Fernhurst* (1904, published posthumously). Marianne DeKoven posits that "internal evidence points to a shift in Stein's feeling toward femaleness" during the years she was a medical student at Johns Hopkins, 1900–1903. "Her sexual identity had been a terrible problem for her early in life," DeKoven notes, and Stein connected "self-hatred, insecurity, fearful dependency, passivity, and inertia, to her female gender" (134). This identity crisis was expressed in her early writings, where, as Catherine Stimpson argues, the prologue of *Fernhurst* marks Stein's separation of "herself from her sex in order to assail and herself enter a male world too strong for most women" (187).

Gertrude Stein's *Fernhurst* has received scant attention, often dismissed by

critics as an early, unsophisticated display of themes and styles far more deft-
ly handled in later works. Yet this short novel deserves critical attention precisely because it anticipates attitudes toward femaleness and sexual identity that
Stein explores in the complex relationships of her later works, such as *Three
Lives* or *The Autobiography of Alice B. Toklas. Fernhurst,* which she later incorporated into *The Making of Americans,* recounts the story of three academics
caught up in a romantic triangle. But instead of two men vying for the affection of a woman, one man and one woman seek to win the favors of Miss
Bruce, thereby distorting the traditional triangle of heterosexual desire and
homosociality. According to Leon Katz's introduction to *Fernhurst,* the novel
is the loosely veiled fictional account of the historical events at Bryn Mawr
College involving Alfred Hodder, a promising young philosophy professor;
Mary Gwinn, a professor of English; and Dean Martha Carey Thomas, known
as a brilliant lecturer who "set the tone of Bryn Mawr's intellectual life" (xxxiii).
Hodder taught with Gwinn for six years until, in 1898, he was forced to leave
after their affair became too much for the dean and institution to bear.

In Stein's novels, as Janice L. Doane notes, "rarely" are there "any male characters. But this does not mean that male positions are not represented." Rather, they "reveal all the ways women have of speaking and not speaking in a literary framework and culture that privilege the male voice and position" (Doane
xxv), as the fictional Dean Helen Thornton, who assumes a masculine position
in the novel, demonstrates. Yet Stein's insistence on a masculinely gendered
woman in *Fernhurst* entering into a relationship with a femininely gendered
woman, particularly in the early years of the twentieth century when the woman
suffrage movement was gaining momentum, provides a unique disenfranchisement of the masculine woman. By configuring the female-female relationships
in the gendered formation of feminine and masculine, she establishes a competition of two masculine characters for one feminine object, thereby grounding her work in the gendered structure of heterosexual society.

"There is a dean," the reader is told, "presiding over the college of Fernhurst
in the state of New Jersey who . . . believes totally in this essential sameness of
sex." This dean, the narrator continues, "is possessed of a strong purpose and
vast energy . . . is hard headed, practical, unmoral in the sense that all values
give place to expediency and she has a pure enthusiasm for the emancipation
of women and a sensitive and mystic feeling for beauty and letters" (5). Yet, in
accordance with "the male ideal," this women's college is governed by the students, who are "wholly centered in the dean who dominated by a passion for
absolute power administers an admirable system of espionage and influence.
. . . Honorably and manly are the ostensible ideals that govern the place" (5–

6). This description identifies the dean's masculine gender; indeed, Thornton's views of higher education for women and her aggressive business personality suggest the masculine ideal, as does her relationship with the "detached" and "transfigured" Miss Bruce.

As head of the English department, her reputation guaranteed by an article on the philosophy of English poetry, Miss Bruce "ideally fulfilled these demands of the Dean: that she would be permanent—who would have great parts and a scholarly mind and would have no influence to trouble hers" (18). Bruce came to Fernhurst "utterly unattached" because both of her parents had died just before she entered college. The contrast with Thornton's pedigree is striking, particularly since Thornton is one of "three remarkable women in three generations" (15–16). The matriarchy identifies the homosocial as well as familial bond between women; it also clearly defines her role in the romantic relationship. "It was impossible," the narrator recounts, "for her to be in relation with anything or anyone without controlling to the minutest detail" (17). The powerful and masculine matriarch of Fernhurst, who is in a suggestively intimate relationship with the quiet and feminine Miss Bruce, thus becomes the person against whom Philip Redfern, the newly hired philosophy professor, must compete.

As the novel approaches its confrontational conclusion, the competition does not disintegrate, even when the homosexual result becomes apparent. Redfern leaves at the end of the term; Miss Bruce returns to the confines of her relationship with Dean Thornton; and, after a period of time, "Fernhurst," the narrator relates, "was itself again and the two very interesting personalities in the place were the dean Miss Thornton with her friend Miss Bruce in their very same place" (49). Stein's portrayal of this erotic coupling thus invites a differently constructed eroticism—Bruce is both heterosexual object choice and homosexual object choice—but does not allow that difference to dominate. This portrayal also deviates from the historical conclusion of the college scandal. Alfred Hodder and Mary Gwinn eventually do marry, solidifying the heterosexual paradigm. Stein, writing Dean Thornton as a masculine woman involved in a relationship with the feminine Miss Bruce, allows for a homosexual relationship, but it is figured by the masculinized gender of one of its participants.

Less than a decade later, Charlotte Perkins Gilman took Stein's reformulation one step further by not only portraying a female couple but, even more socially frightening, allowing this couple parenthood.[6] As she does in so much of her other fiction, Gilman provides alternatives to the status quo in order to challenge it and, in many cases, to illuminate the absurdity of social mores. Her

1911 story "Turned" is, as the narrator bluntly explains, about "two women and a man. One woman was a wife: loving, trusting, affectionate. One was a servant: loving, trusting, affectionate—a young girl, an exile, a dependent; grateful for any kindness; untrained, uneducated, childish" (93). It is one of the many stories about marriage Gilman wrote to explore the inequalities between men and women. "The women have unequal status," writes Barbara A. White, "and the aggressor in the relationship is the one who plans, thinks, and earns the money—the teacher, the lawyer, the inheritor, the scientist. The characters in the 'female passive spaces'—wife, maid, and secretary—are recipients of the 'male' gaze and exhibit stereotypically female qualities" (quoted in Knight 205).

In "Turned," however, the "aggressor," although initially the husband, is in the end the wife, who is a college professor. The maid is certainly the "recipient of the 'male' gaze"—she is, after all, impregnated by the husband. By the end of Gilman's text, however, the husband's role has been usurped by his wife. Terry Castle theorizes that "it is the very failure of the heroine's marriage or heterosexual love affair that functions as the pretext for her conversion to homosexual desire" (85–86). Although there is no indication in "Turned" that Gilman is looking with horror upon the same-sex coupling—she actually turns it to the women's advantage and uses the outcome to express her disgust over the husband's "offense against womanhood"—this version of an altered gender construction would have been considered horrific and monstrous and would have embodied exactly what conservative social commentators, such as Horace Bushnell, who was anxious about "re-sexing," feared.

The descriptions of Mrs. Marroner and her servant, Gerta, establish that these two characters, no matter what socioeconomic differences separate them, are united by a bond stronger than money or social status, namely, womanhood. It also is clear that given their woman-affirming resolution of the tragic events that befall them, this bond cannot be broken by a man—husband or lover—but is as strong if not stronger than marriage. When the story opens, Mrs. Marroner and Gerta both lie sobbing on their beds—Mrs. Marroner in a "soft-carpeted, thick-curtained, richly furnished chamber" and Gerta in her "uncarpeted, thin-curtained, poorly furnished chamber on the top floor" (87)—because they have both received devastating news. Mrs. Marroner has just discovered her husband has impregnated Gerta, and Gerta has just been banished from the house because of her condition.

What precipitates this turn of events is Mr. Marroner's business trip that extends to longer than seven months, enough time for Gerta to begin showing the unmistakable signs of pregnancy. Unable to spirit her away before Mrs. Marroner suspects, Mr. Marroner sends an unsigned, type-written note to

Gerta promising to take care of her when he returns and a fifty-dollar bill in hopes that it will help in the meantime. Unfortunately, he mixes up the letters and envelopes and sends Gerta's letter to his wife and his wife's letter to Gerta. Once Mrs. Marroner overcomes her incredulity at the turn of events and figures out her husband's role in Gerta's pregnancy, she fires the poor servant.

Until this point in the story, there is nothing atypical about Mrs. Marroner's reactions, and although Greta's pregnancy is certainly tragic for her, it, too, even in 1911, is not an unheard of event. However, Gilman's placement of blame and final pronouncement on how to solve such a problem rely, as did Stein's *Fernhurst,* on an alternative sex-gender arrangement between women. Eventually, Mrs. Marroner takes pity on Greta and allows her to stay. White argues that a "strong erotic current pulses throughout" and that this is why what White calls a "woman-rescues-woman" story needs to be "read as a lesbian text" (quoted in Knight 201). Over the course of the story, and becoming more prominent as the plot progresses, is the suggestion that Mrs. Marroner, despite her marital status, is not a femininely gendered woman but instead assumes and increasingly expresses masculine characteristics, while Gerta becomes more dependent on her.

Economic relationships notwithstanding, the coupling of Mrs. Marroner and Gerta slowly begins to rival initially the relationship between a parent and a child but eventually a relationship between husband and wife, man and woman. The narrator offhandedly reveals that Mrs. Marroner has a Ph.D. and prior to her marriage held a faculty position at a college and that her taking care of the simpleminded Gerta "was like baby-tending." Moreover, the longer Mr. Marroner stays away on business, the better Mrs. Marroner is able to run the household, a feat he compliments in his letters. "If I should be eliminated from your scheme of things, by any of those 'acts of God' mentioned on the tickets," he writes her with an irony of which he would only too soon become painfully aware, "I do not feel that you would be an utter wreck. . . . Your life is so rich and wide that not one loss, even a great one, would wholly cripple you" (89).

Perhaps this is the germ of thought planted in Mrs. Marroner's mind that was needed to jar her out of her comfortable married, heterosexual, and submissive life, so that when confronted with her husband's unspeakable act, she is empowered. The longer Mrs. Marroner thinks about the event that has just turned her life upside down, the more impassioned anger she directs at her husband. "All that splendid, clean young beauty, the hope of a happy life, with marriage and motherhood," she thinks, "these were nothing to that man. For his own pleasure he had chosen to rob her of her life's best joys" (94). Not coincidentally, she comes to these thoughts as she reminisces over the "training of the twenty-eight years which had elapsed before her marriage; the life at college, both as student and teacher; the independent growth which she had made" (92).

Instead of blaming Gerta for the indiscretion, Mrs. Marroner squarely places blame on her husband, rejecting the socioeconomic and legal allegiance of husband and wife and instead falling to a more profound alliance, womanhood. "This is a sin of man against woman," she decides. "The offense is against womanhood. Against motherhood. Against—the child" (94). To counter the crime against womanhood and rid herself of the criminal man, Mrs. Marroner abandons the heterosexual homestead and moves, with Gerta and her child, to a college, where she resumes teaching. White, summarizing the outcome, says that "two women are 'turned' from heterosexuality by the behavior of a man" (quoted in Knight 202). When Mr. Marroner finally tracks his wife down, he is greeted by "Miss Wheeling," his wife who is now using her maiden name; Gerta, her "blue, adoring eyes fixed on her friend—not upon him"; and the baby. Instead of offering forgiveness, as Mr. Marroner expects, his "ex-wife" only quietly questions, "What have you to say to us?" (97).

Gilman's subscription to the adage that "turn about is fair play" is clearly evident in this remarkable story where the bonds of womanhood run deeper and stronger than those between a husband and wife. Certainly, Gilman's radical political idea that the man is complicit in unwanted pregnancies, particularly when unfairly using economic leverage, allows a feminist reading that invokes moral certitude. His crime is, according to the heroic Mrs. Marroner, "the sin of man against woman." Moreover, "Miss Wheeling's" willing entrance into a same-sex relationship can be surmised to be a "'euphoric' lesbian counterplotting," as Terry Castle describes such "utopic" scenes. "A new world is imagined," she writes, "in which male bonding has no place" (86).

With the genderings of the women and the signifiers attached to them, however, the story is more complicated than it initially appears. Gerta, the docile, obedient, childlike "victim" of "proud young womanhood," presents a stark contrast to Mrs. Marroner, who, with every passing week of her husband's absence, becomes less her married, feminine self and more a woman who has taken on the accouterments of masculinity. Her doctorate, her successful career before marriage, her late marriage at the age of twenty-eight, and her childlessness all contrast her to the clearly feminine and fecund Gerta. The "fault" of the Marroners' childlessness clearly rests with Mrs. Marroner, since her husband has proven his fertility. When at the end Mrs. Marroner decides to become "Miss Wheeling," return to her former life, and take Gerta and child along with her, she has effectively usurped the masculine role. She is now the economic support for the "family" and is the object of affection for the "blue, adoring eyes" of Gerta.

Mrs. Marroner's victory over the patriarchal oppression of women too poor or too docile to fight back must necessarily, then, be suspect, since her victory comes at the expense of her femininity. The argument that Gilman is challenging sex and gender roles rings hollow because she so stereotypically characterizes Gerta. What initially seems like a triumph for womanhood is actually a rewriting of the sex and gender roles that adheres to the heterosexual paradigm. In terms of gender and sex, the resolutions of *Fernhurst* and "Turned" are remarkably similar. The sexual relationship is established, eventually, between a masculine subject and a feminine object. Although traditional sex-gender assignments are not affirmed, traditional gender expectations are maintained, and the result is the expected and accepted coupling of masculine and feminine. This reaffirmation of masculinity allows the traditional coupling of a masculine subject and feminine object. The reliance on the masculine woman to right the wrong that has been committed against a feminine woman only reaffirms the power of masculinity. It does seem troubling that both Stein and Gilman, long heralded for their subversive constructions of womanhood, could not envision a female same-sex relationship that did not adhere to the heterosexual paradigm. Just how progressive were their portraits if, to show a triumphant woman, they were forced to construct her as masculinized?

Much criticism has rightly focused on the intersection of modern sexological theory and modern womanhood and the resultant sex-gender hybrids (such as the "masculine woman," "new woman, and "mannish lesbian") that were produced in the late nineteenth century and early twentieth. The creation of the nontraditional sex-gender combinations has its source in the nineteenth-century "feminist" movement, particularly, as Lillian Faderman argues, the "general homosociality of nineteenth-century society, which gave women of the middle class plentiful leisure to meet and share grievances" (*Surpassing* 180). Other reasons she suggests for the increasing feminism are the egalitarian ideals of the French Revolution, the rise of "humanitarian and betterment movements such as abolitionism, socialism, and various forms of utopianism" (*Surpassing* 178ff.), and the place women began to assume, indeed expect, in higher education.

Yet to move from the attributes of an independent-minded woman to the sex-gender monstrosity of the "masculine woman" and then its attribution in society as "deviant" required more than the emerging "feminist" movement. George Chauncey Jr. has argued that a number of developments in American fin de siècle culture were necessary to make this transition. The declining marriage and birth rate of the "native-born middle class," women's entrance into what traditionally had been men's spheres, and the shift from brute strength to mechanical means in the workplace all contributed to increasing turmoil and outright confusion about sex and gender roles. "Men who had lost power at the workplace may have needed to reassert power and to redefine their masculinity in their marriages and families," Chauncey avers, and "conservative medical pronouncements" only codified their fears (103–4). Masculine women, and for that matter feminine men, were considered sexual "inverts." Such prominent sexologists as Havelock Ellis and Richard von Krafft-Ebing thought women who engaged in same-sex intimacies that were tied directly to their gender were "sexually perverted" (Smith-Rosenberg 283). If a woman was masculine, then her sexual object also was masculine; hence, her libido was directed at a woman. This "'unnatural gender ape-ing,'" in the words of the sexologists, was a condemnation from which, Carroll Smith-Rosenberg asserts, they could not recover (283).

The threat of sexual inverts permeated society, even something as mundane as life insurance. Dr. William Lee Howard, addressing the American Association of Medical Examiners in 1906, warned that male "inverts" present special risks to corporations providing life insurance. Since the male invert's "whole psychic life" is "feminine, muscular exercise is repugnant to them, hence at about forty years of age we find them with fat, flabby bodies." As if this were not trouble enough, the invert "who does not meet with violent assaults or succumb to alcohol and other drugs develops some organic disease." As a result of the male invert's life, which Howard concludes is a "moral hazard," examiners should understand the "increased liability" and "appraise its value in his estimation of the risk." The female invert, however, presents no such increased risk, according to Howard, since "mentally and psychically we have a man with all the powerful desires of a man." Despite her female anatomy and sociality, her "masculine tendencies" insulate her from "personal assaults, and the alcohol she drinks seems to have a better physiological absorbing surface." Thus, unlike the femininely gendered male invert, the masculinely gendered female invert is, according to Howard, "a good risk" for life insurance ("Sexual Pervert" 207).

Howard's assessment, supported by his claim that he had "a large number of these unfortunate and misunderstood persons under personal care" ("Sexual Pervert" 206), is striking for its reliance on gender rather than sex as the predictor of human behavior. The feminine, not the female, is weak; the masculine tends to make the female invert immune from high risk behavior, but the anatomical male is powerless once feminized. Yet Howard's delicate separation of sex from gender is not the mark of precocious, theoretically novel thinking. He clearly uses *sex* and *gender* interchangeably: oxymoronically, the female invert, affected by her masculinity, is a "man." Howard does not, however, ascribe the same opposite physicality to the male invert, who remains biologically male, although compromised by femininity, and is never called a "woman." Such a careful distinction signals, in addition to an underlying fear of male homosexuality and emasculation, a scientific willingness to understand masculinity as solely the domain of the "man," even if exhibited by an "inverted" woman.

Another postcard published from 1908 to 1920 illustrates the final shift from physical to psychological to sexual and leaves no room for such ambivalence about a woman's masculinity and her sexual inversion. "Ps-s-s-t Nix Lady Nix! You're Not My Kind of Valentine," the caption declares about the short-haired, slim-hipped figure. Lacking the accouterments of femininity, this masculine woman does not receive romantic overtures from the male world that is interested only in feminine women. A second, more subtle reading also exists: the woman, although not a "Valentine" for the male heterosexual, is a "Valentine" for someone else, namely, the female sexual invert.

Critical analysis of the female sexual invert in early-twentieth-century American literature is scant and is founded on two major studies, Jeannette H. Foster's *Sex Variant Women in Literature* (1954)[7] and Lillian Faderman's *Surpassing the Love of Men* (1981).[8] Other critics, including Marilyn Farwell, Judith Butler, Terry Castle, Bonnie Zimmerman, Martha Vicinus, Diana Fuss, and Carroll Smith-Rosenberg, have approached the components of this large field, but none has attempted the comprehensiveness of Foster and Faderman. Both of these authors suggest that the first two decades of the twentieth century "might be called the age of innocence" (Foster 240) since, according to Foster, no published work referred to "overt lesbianism, variance was not a subject of dispute, and no particular school of psychological thought had come to the fore" (240). Faderman posits that "it took the phenomenal growth of female autonomy during and after World War I, and the American popularization of the most influential of the European sexologists, Sigmund Freud, to cast widespread suspicion on love between women" (298). Vicinus determines that "a host of competing sociobiological ideologies and disciplines grew at the end of the nineteenth century," such as social Darwinism, eugenics, criminology, and anthropology, which undoubtedly affected women's sexual relations (443).

Yet such readings fail to account for the monumental changes woman suffragists were proposing to the political and social status quo and the direct linking of suffragism with masculine womanhood and homosexual expression. If critics move beyond the early stages in which some lesbian historians have seemed, in Vicinus's words, "more concerned with finding heroines than with uncovering the often fragmentary and contradictory evidence which must make up the lesbian past" (435), the woman suffrage movement and its effects on sex and gender categories must join the list of cultural influences. The nineteenth-century social commentator Horace Bushnell, suggesting that the woman suffrage movement was a "reform against nature," declared that the political agitators were undergoing a "re-sexing of their sex, even so far as to make it manly in habit and action" (89). The rhetoric used during the woman suffrage campaign and the language that characterized the independent woman vitally influenced the characterizations of the masculine woman and female sexual invert in both the popular press and fiction. It is clear that such women did not enjoy a "last breath of innocence," as Faderman phrases it (297), prior to the 1920s. Nor did she enjoy a reprieve after ratification of the Nineteenth Amendment since her status as an enfranchised woman also made her subject to a backlash against independent women in the 1920s and early 1930s.

Relying on three autobiographical novels that fictionally chart the change in attitude toward female-to-female relationships—Canadian American Mary MacLane's *Story of Mary MacLane* (1902) and *I, Mary MacLane* (1917) and Wanda Fraiken Neff's *We Sing Diana* (1928)—Faderman contends a lesbian possibility existed before World War I, yet after World War I, specifically in 1920, "the atmosphere is entirely different," and "naiveté was no longer possible." By comparing MacLane's two autobiographical novels, Faderman determines that the "naiveté" of the narrator in the 1902 novel—"Are there many things in this cool-hearted world so utterly exquisite as the pure love of one woman for another"—was not possible in the 1917 sequel. According to Faderman, MacLane's reference to the love between women as "contraband" and "twisted," as well as her pronouncement that the "predilections" of lesbians "are warped," is evidence enough that monumental changes had occurred in the fifteen years between publications (*Surpassing* 300). Similarly, Faderman argues, when Neff's heroine was a student at a fictional women's college in 1913, "everyone engaged in romantic friendships, which was considered 'the great human experience'" (298–99). But by 1920, when that heroine returns to the same college to teach, "the atmosphere is entirely different. Now undergraduate speech is full of Freudian vocabulary. . . . And 'intimacies between two girls were watched with keen, distrustful eyes'" (299). By reading these novels as chronicles of the turning point in fictionalized women's same-sex relationships, from a pre-1920s "innocence" to a post-1920s "aberrance," Faderman concludes that prior to 1920 "it was not yet socially threatening if occasional independent women—those who, for example, could eke out a living as artists—chose to devote themselves to each other" (305).

Yet analysis of both the literature and popular press from the late nineteenth century to the early 1930s reveals that these allegedly "innocent" portrayals of sexually inverted masculine women were not nearly so naive as critics have postulated. According to Elizabeth Benson, a Barnard College student writing in *Vanity Fair* in 1917, a variety of forces contributed to the formation of the "outrageous" younger generation that was "riding high" the "wave of freedom." "The Nineteenth Amendment was passed while the present younger generation was just entering adolescence," she claims, "we cut our second teeth on 'Women's Rights' . . . and 'Birth control.' Margaret Sanger was one of our first memories. 'Sex,' which had been a word to whisper and blush at, was flung at us on banners carried by our crusading mothers" (68). Moreover, although World War I allowed and even required women to enter professional occupations in huge numbers and Freud's theories gained prominence during this same time, these changes cannot explain the derision and dismissal of masculine women and female sexual inverts during the first two decades of the twentieth century. Clearly, the perceptions about the woman suffragists stripped the innocence from woman-to-woman relationships and exacerbated the threat such masculine independence and same-sex intimacy manifested.

Literature and the popular press, in essays, fiction, and illustrations, admitted the existence of a masculine woman or her "most aggravated" type, the female invert. Independent women clearly espoused similar rhetoric and behavior that antisuffragists claimed the suffragists expressed. These independent women, moreover, assumed the accouterments of masculinity, either in behavior or thought, and often were thought to exhibit more than a hint of homosexual tendencies. Rhetorically and pictorially, the masculine woman and female sexual invert can be traced to the woman suffrage movement. American authors, responding to this threat to the heterosexual status quo, chose to portray independent women not as exhibiting a benign alternative sexuality but as a danger that required immediate dismissal. In doing so, they espoused the ideal woman with the "eternally feminine mind," as Henry C. McComas wrote in *Scribner's Magazine* in 1926, complete with "its tendernesses, devotions, affections, and its fascinating mutabilities" (433). The masculine woman was thus disenfranchised in literature and the popular press both before and after ratification of the Nineteenth Amendment. "Sex," as Robert Benchley concluded, was not "out" at all. Rather, those women who insisted on expressing the heretofore masculine characteristic of political enfranchisement became the menace of the era whose insistence on voting rights became the catalyst for social and literary disenfranchisement.

Notes

1. See Lorber for a thorough discussion of sociological studies about sex, gender, and sexuality and how all three complicatedly fit (or do not fit) together.

2. Gayle Rubin, in her essay "Of Catamites and Kings: Reflections on Butch, Gender, and Boundaries," attempts a similar complication by suggesting the difficulty in defining such terms as *butch* and *femme* and the freedom that ensues when such rigid classifications are loosened.

3. In a 1980 study that attempted to quantify homophobia, Mary Riege Laner and Roy H. Laner asked college students to respond to "Jane" according to three different gender types: hyperfeminine, feminine, and hypofeminine. The hyperfeminine Jane was described as a fashion design major whose primary pastime was gourmet cooking; she also preferred wearing jewelry, dresses, and makeup. At the other end of the scale was hypofeminine Jane, who was undecided about what to major in but did enjoy motorcycle riding in jeans, a leather jacket, and no makeup. The study concluded that "low homophobia among heterosexuals is related to the degree to which heterosexuals believe that homosexuals are conventional persons, at least in outward appearance" (352). I cite this study not for its direct bearing on the subject of the early-twentieth-century masculinized woman but for its confirmation of the persistence of gender in determining sexuality.

4. Esther Newton cautions against causality, suggesting instead that lesbians actively created a masculine identity so that they could better express their sexuality. Whether social constructions were dictated by such women is not as vital to this study as the confirmation that a homosexual relationship was perceived to be possible only if it contained a masculine-feminine pair. A masculine woman necessarily suggested sexual inversion, whereas a same-sex relationship between women often included a masculinely gendered woman.

5. In Bonnie Zimmerman's discussion, it is unclear whether she is employing *sex* and *gender* as interchangeable terms. Are, for example, authors changing one of their women characters into a male, or are they making her a masculine women? In the literature I discuss throughout this study, I argue that gender has been changed but that sex remains the same. Given Zimmerman's citing of *Orlando*, in particular, it appears that "changing the gender" could refer to both biological sex and culturally imposed gender. As a contrast, Zimmerman applauds the "unambiguous inscriptions of lesbian sexuality and identity" by Renee Vivien (*Safe Sea* 6).

6. Charlotte Perkins Gilman, interested in generally portraying how the rights of women had been stripped, was active in a more particular cause, woman suffrage. In

January 1896, she addressed the Twenty-eighth Annual Women's Suffrage Convention in Washington, D.C., and the House Judiciary Committee on the subject of "The Ballot as an Improver of Motherhood" (Scharnhorst 45).

7. According to Bonnie Zimmerman, Foster's 1956 classic "surveys dozens of other novels, plays, and stories by male and heterosexual female writers that depict lesbians at length or in passing. Most of these, however, were strongly laced with the homophobic stereotypes of predatory, masculine, infantile, or hopelessly unhappy lesbians that were the legacy of early twentieth-century writing" (*Safe Sea* 8).

8. Martha Vicinus remarks that "lesbian history is still in its initial stages, inhibited" not only by the "suspect nature of the subject" but also by a lack of scholars willing or able to pursue "half-forgotten, half-destroyed, or half-neglected sources" (433). Even history as recent as the early twentieth century is often ignored for the more easily accessible culture after the 1950s, when lesbian literature experienced a publishing explosion.

2

Unsightly Evidence

"Female Inversion" and the U.S. Woman Suffrage Movement

Yours it is to determine whether the beautiful order of society . . .
shall continue as it has been [or] whether society shall break up
and become a chaos of disjointed and unsightly elements.
—The Reverend Jonathan Stearns, "Female Influence and the True
Christian Mode of Its Exercise," 1837

In an early-twentieth-century cartoon by H. C. Greening that brazenly announced its politics in its title, "Giving the Freaks a Treat," a dime museum manager shouts to his charges "tuh hustle out an' blow dereselves tuh a look!" (see figure 1). From the placards posted around the entrance boasting of the freakish "Octopus Man" and the "Pigheaded Boy," it would seem the carnival barker should be shouting to the passersby on the street, enticing them with promises of the "Human Toad" and other freaks of human and animal nature. Instead, the museum manager calls to his "freaks" to come outside and see creatures more freakish than they, suffragists, holding placards of their own that declare "Votes for Women" and "We Demand Our Rights"—sentiments and possibilities even more outrageous than the "Octopus Man" with four legs and four arms. The suffrage procession causes the inversion of the normal order of events—the freak show exhibits are called to look at the people on the street rather than the people enticed to look at the museum's living collections. Greening's cartoon clearly asserted that women advocating their enfranchisement were organic

GIVING THE FREAKS A TREAT.

Manager dime museum (as suffragette procession passes) —'' Hey, Chimmie ! Chimmie ! tell d' bunch tuh hustle out an' blow dereselves tuh a look !''

Figure 1. Cartoon by H. C. Greening, n.d., in *Caricature, Wit, and Humor of a Nation in Picture, Song and Story*, 8th ed. (New York: Leslie-Judge, 1911), n.p.

oddities. The root cause of what had now become a congenital inversion, the viewer can easily infer, was the political novelty of enfranchised women, whose campaign also encompassed some degree (more perceived than real) of economic autonomy and personal independence.

The critic Richard Le Gallienne, in his 1924 *Vanity Fair* article "The Modern Girl—and Why She Is Painted," wondered if "woman herself is losing the feminine virtues" as a result of her new independence. "In short," he queried, "is she becoming more of a man, or less of a woman?" Le Gallienne answered his own question: "No, not less of a woman, I think. She is too shrewd for that. But more of a man, perhaps. . . . It may be that she is thus evolving toward a more complete human being than either man or woman has ever been before. A new sex!" His discovery was not simply androgyny but an altogether new sex, which suggested that the two sexes, male and female, no longer could contain the changes in gender that have occurred. For Le Gallienne, two types of women in particular embodied this confusion of traditional sex and gender pairings: the suffragist and the flapper, both of whom Le Gallienne characterized as the "awful feminine example" and the "menace of the hour" (27).

Although Le Gallienne certainly did not go so far as to label his "new sex" a "third sex," as some sexologists termed homosexuals in those days,[1] his more-than-androgynous conflation of the modern woman with maleness, of her becoming "more of a man," is important, as is the linking of the suffragist with the flapper, who is identified with sexual promiscuity and appropriation of male behaviors—for example, smoking, drinking, driving. Le Gallienne envisioned an entirely new construction since neither the suffragist nor flapper fit comfortably, if at all, into the traditional pairings of sex and gender: female-feminine and male-masculine. In essence, Le Gallienne argued for the creation of a third sex-gender combination, defined by marriage custom and political rights, that was both female and masculine. Le Gallienne's "new sex" was what other writers termed the "masculine woman." A fashion advertisement from *Vanity Fair* in 1914 visually suggested that the female and male gender assignments of feminine and masculine were not absolute, unchangeable pairs but could result in a woman's possessing "the ways of a maid with the modes of a man" (see figure 2).

Le Gallienne was not the first to suggest the fluidity of gender. Richard Barry, a journalist writing in *Pearson's Magazine* in March 1910, proposed sex-gender fluidity specifically in relation to the U.S. woman suffrage movement as he attempted to answer "why women oppose woman suffrage" (n.p.). In the present civilization, Barry wrote, a man who is all masculine and a woman who is all feminine do not exist. What is usually called the "normal" man has about 85 percent masculine traits and 15 percent feminine ones; the woman has about 85 percent feminine and 15 percent masculine. Thus, Barry concluded, the "perfect marriages" are formed when the 85 percent men marry the 85 percent women, and "havoc comes when an 85 percent man marries a 60 percent woman, or vice versa." As an unabashedly antisuffrage polemicist, Barry's proposed his gender theory to trap the suffragists by their own words and illustrate their "perversity" in order to "discredit the movement as a whole" (Camhi 26). Barry reported that when he asked National American Woman Suffrage Association president Anna Howard Shaw about his theory,[2] she allegedly replied, "I think the ideal person would be 50 percent masculine and 50 percent feminine." Barry concluded from Shaw's remark that she "unconsciously made an estimate of her own mentality and her own personality." Since Shaw was one of the leading suffragists, Barry pointed out, her comment was "an exceedingly significant sidelight." For Barry, it proved that the suffrage movement caused an increase in masculinity and a decrease in femininity in women and, thus, was a hindrance to the formulation of a "perfect marriage" because two clearly defined opposites (masculine and feminine) were no longer so secure.

For a summer forenoon a
blouse of colored handkerchief
linen, such as this, is charming

A gentle feminine relative of the
masculine waistcoat is this buttoned-
up blouse of white crêpe with turned-
over collar, and cuffs of a new type

A hat purloined from the sterner
sex crowns a trim outfit consist-
ing of a sheer, colored linen blouse
with white linen collar and cuffs
and a shirt of heavy white golfine, which are particularly smart
for country wear

A slim maid tops her skirt of
heavy white crêpe with a very
mannish looking linen shirt
topped by a "sure-enough" man's
collar, and supplements the whole
with a walking stick. Models
from Maison Blanc

Comfortable tennis shoes, just
like a man's except for size

A boon in the country are rub-
ber-soled buckskin boots

Against the green of
the lawn or the blue of
the sea a top-coat of
bright golfine stands
out boldly

THE WAYS OF A MAID
WITH THE MODES OF A MAN

Figure 2. Advertisement in *Vanity Fair*, May 1914, n.p.

The woman suffrage movement, however, did not so much suggest alternatives to women's gender and sexual behavior as it offered men and women afraid of perceived changes a tangible movement on which to blame their fears.[3] That is, the suffragists themselves did not propose alterations in woman's femininity or appearance, nor did they predict such changes should emancipation be realized. They were ardent defenders of the roles and behaviors traditionally assigned to males and females, as evidenced by Elizabeth Cady Stanton, who more than fifteen years before the ratification of the Nineteenth Amendment, validated women in their domestic and feminine roles. Writing in *Collier's Weekly* in April 1902, Stanton argued that without the vote, a "woman has no voice as to the education of her children or the environments of the unhappy wards of the State." Stanton's argument, reliant on "the love and sympathy of the mother-soul" (9), was consistent with domestic rhetoric, particularly since women were traditionally understood to be the educators of young children. A literate voting population was vital, she explained, to make well-informed decisions about family life, orphans, and charitable organizations—all areas that women were expected to oversee and legislate and where they were presumed to have more expertise than men. The Reverend Anna Garlin Spencer was even more succinct in her reasoning about why women should be given the vote: "The instant . . . the State took upon itself any form of educative, charitable, or personally helpful work, it entered the area of distinctive feminine training and power, and therefore became in need of the service of women" (quoted in Evans 154).

The rhetoric of other suffragists also asserted not the rejection but the validation of femininity if women were to achieve the vote. In 1917, the Federal Suffrage Association published a memorial sketch of Clara Bewick Colby called *Democratic Ideals.* Its purpose, as Olympia Brown, the president of the Federal Suffrage Association, stated in the introduction, was to advance Colby as a hero of the woman suffrage movement, holding her up as a godmother, of sorts, because "[n]o woman was ever more loyal to the cause of woman's suffrage and none ever made greater sacrifices for it" (xi–xii). The glowing tribute honored Colby by assigning her the characteristics of an ideal woman with impeccable motivations: "Even in her advocacy of Woman's Suffrage her chief thought was not so much the practical advantage of the vote to women, as the maintaining of the integrity of our republic, the fulfillment of the promise made by the Founders of our Government" (xi).

Brown asserted that Colby's pedigree also took on typically feminine ideals: "Unassisted and from humble beginnings she became a well known and honored advocate of Woman's Suffrage, a devoted reformer in many lines, a

consecrated church worker, a writer of marked ability, and interpreter of poets and philosophers." Then, as unassailable evidence of character and a clear
defense against those who feared enfranchised women would lose their femininity, Brown noted that Colby was "amid all an exceptionally fine housekeep-
er and excellent cook. She was a loyal friend, and always a faithful worker in
whatever engaged her attention" (xi). Elizabeth Cady Stanton received similar accolades from Lizzie Boynton Harbert in an essay included with her novel *Out of Her Sphere* (1871). Stanton, she wrote, "reigns a queenly mother of
seven children. Twenty years of her life she devoted to her children, and when
they had outgrown her care, she devoted her maturer years to loving, maternal care for society, for humanity" (180).

Carrie Chapman Catt, the leader of the National Woman Suffrage Association, also addressed many concerns of the antisuffragists in her introduction
to *The Woman Citizen: A General Handbook of Civic Duties, with Special Consideration of Women's Citizenship* (1918). Using the rhetoric of militarism pop-
ularized by World War I, Catt clearly articulated that a woman was first and
foremost "the mother, the wife," even before she was a "loyal American," an
order solidly fixed since her "real desire is to protect the interests of [her] sons
and husbands." Her "burning patriotism" was summoned not so that she
could voice her opinions on "principles of government," war, defense strategy, or even educational policy. Rather, a woman should be involved politically in the same areas she oversaw in the home. "The housewife's own knowledge must enter into food conservation," Catt wrote, and "the nurse's own
experience must obtain to make the Red Cross do its effective best" (8–9).
Woman's domestic talents were useful "to keep the camp zone clean," and her
maternity, her "mother's voice," was "above all the one which will be wanted
for deliberation about an increased birth rate to make up for war's ravages"
(9). This philosophy was rendered pictorially by the National Woman Suffrage
Association's journal, the *Woman Citizen,* on July 28, 1917 (see figure 3). As
"Mrs. Voteless Citizen" looks up to the legislative mountain top and sees wres-
tling male politicians, she notices (as does the viewer) that the "food problem"
hangs precariously in the balance. Her political expertise is couched in the
language of "responsible" housekeeping by the illustrator Lou Rogers. Manip-
ulating the domestic agenda requires the talents of those best suited for such
tasks, a married woman who clutches canning jars in her left arm as evidence
of her competence. As this rhetoric of the women suffragists exemplifies, enfranchisement promised to retain woman's traditional feminine formulations
and maintain her not only in the domestic sphere but as the feminine and
heterosexual object of her successful husband.

Figure 3. Cartoon by Lou Rogers for the cover of the *Woman Citizen*, July 28, 1917.

If it was not the suffragists who proposed radical revolutions in the conceptions of sex, gender, and sexuality, who was responsible? Certainly, the notion of women assuming the masculine prerogative to vote, sanctioned by a constitutional amendment, was novel. Yet unlike the late-twentieth-century women's rights movement in which women's same-sex relationships were proposed as a step toward female independence, the U.S. woman suffragist movement was not campaigning for tolerated sexual "inversion." Susan E. Marshall reports that antisuffragists charged that suffragists were "not seriously interested in political reform" but instead were exercising "selfish ambition, political intrigue, and noisy notoriety"; "in the words of one male opponent," Marshall notes, women were drawn to politics by "monomania" (105). The concern was that women, once enfranchised, would run for public office, leave the home to vote and campaign, and, as a result, neglect the domestic duties to which they had been assigned by virtue of their sex. Even more specific was the worry that woman suffrage would destroy domestic bliss, pictorially rendered by the severe-looking suffragist who aims to kick down the "HOME" a young girl has constructed (see figure 4). "The awards of women's office, which interfered with maternal duties, would put a premium on singleness and childlessness," Aileen S. Kraditor explains. "Women who thus invaded the masculine sphere would forfeit their right of chivalry, that mode of male behavior which enabled society" (23).

THE HOUSE THAT JILL BUILT

Figure 4. Cartoon in *Life,* February 27, 1913, 424.

Antisuffragists, according to the historian Jane Jerome Camhi, attempted to prevent women's enfranchisement by employing two rhetorical strategies. First, their arguments were "almost all proscriptive—intimating, if not explicitly detailing, the evil consequences that would ensue if woman suffrage were enacted." Second, they were "imputative," presented so that the "suffrage question emerged as a mere symbol of what was assumed to be the real issue, the threat of the spread of feminist ideas" (6). This attempt to confuse suffragism with the wider-ranging "feminism" relied on the suffragists' call for equality. Antisuffragists sought to preserve a "separate, but equal" policy, allowing women to retain their uniqueness from men and, indeed, applauding that distinctiveness. "Far from apologizing for the differences between the sexes," Camhi argues, "the Antis looked upon them as not only divinely inspired, but also as the crowning step in an evolutionary process," culminating in the "masculine man" and the "feminine woman" (922). In her "talk to women on the suffrage question," Emily P. Bissell, an active opponent of woman suffrage, succinctly illustrated the Antis' position in 1909: "Biology teaches her the tremendous value of sex. All the way from the one-celled amoeba up to man, the greater differentiation of sex is the mark of higher development. Man and woman are not alike and are not meant to be alike. They become more different the more they perfect their own development, and the development of the race" (n.p.).

These antisuffrage arguments rang hollow against the practical reality of suffrage parades, where suffragists went to great lengths to demonstrate their virtues. As Linda Lumsden details, "A wagon full of babies joined a small torchlight parade on New York's First Avenue in 1915 to show that suffragists were devoted mothers." Not only did these suffragists' babies establish the women were feminine and maternal, but more deeply it showed them as heterosexual and procreative, addressing two fears central to the rhetoric of female inversion. Because their femininity was questioned, "individual marchers also took pains to appear feminine," Lumsden continues. "One Grecian herald in the 1912 parade cooked dinner for her mother before marching to prove that she could be both feminine and a suffragist. The press dependably latched onto parades' 'distinctly feminine points,' such as the pretty girls who tossed a crowd candy wrapped in suffrage messages" (87).

Antisuffragists, however, had an even greater fear than a woman's neglect of her domestic duties and her emphasis on her unique characteristics of her sex.[4] Antisuffragists cautioned against physiological changes, claiming that a woman's physical beauty would be compromised—she would become, using Greening's term, a "freak." In short, the suffragist would become, in the words of Robert Afton Holland, "large-handed, big-footed, flat-chested, and thin-lipped." A California newspaper reporting on a suffrage parade, noted, however, "Judging from the delegation, the square-jawed, short-haired suffragist is a mere creature of a comic weekly, while the real thing is a vision of loveliness" (quoted in Lumsden 87).

Such "loveliness" had its drawbacks, though. If antisuffragists could not criticize suffragists for being less feminine, they could criticize them, as Linda J. Lumsden notes, for "flaunting their sex" (88). In a statement released by the National Association Opposed to Woman Suffrage (NAOWS), the "sex appeal" expressed by suffragists in a 1913 march was "flagrant and the dominant note in the parade" (88). Josephine Dodge, president of NAOWS, contended that the uneasy balance of femininity in the suffrage movement proved that at its heart was a "sex disturbance" (quoted in Lumsden 89). It is, perhaps, not surprising that the Miss America Pageant held in Atlantic City, New Jersey, was started in 1921, only a year after woman suffrage became a reality and that the winner embodied, according to Samuel Gompers of the American Federation of Labor, "the type of womanhood America needs—strong, red-blooded, able to shoulder the responsibilities of home-making and motherhood. It is in her type that the hope of the country resides" (quoted in Banner 269).

Edward Allsworth Ross, writing in his *Changing America: Studies in Contemporary Society* in 1912, sketched the following picture of the social harm an independent woman could cause: "Society can have the kind of woman it wants. Take the women of eastern Prussia, for instance. These peasant women bear a child in the morning; in the afternoon they are out in the field. . . . I have seen them, and what a type they are, squat, splay-footed, wide-backed, flat-breasted, broad-faced, short-necked—a type that lacks every grace that we associate with woman" (74–75). Speaking of women who work in the city, Ross continued:

> Now, there will be a disappearance of the race, if we extend no hand to help these working girls. What will happen will be that the girls of a distinctly feminine type, the girls who have the qualities of finesse, grace and charm will prove too fragile to meet the conditions. They will collapse and go to the bad, they will lose their health, or if they endure until they are married and become mothers, they will not be able to be mothers of full families, of sons and daughters that will endure to the end.
>
> But some there be who would stand the condition. And of what type would they be? They would be of this other type—the type that appears in those peasant women. In three or four generations we would have in this country all through the lower stratum that coarse type replacing the high-strung, high-bred, feminine

type which is our pride and which extends up and down through layers of society in this country. (75)

The fear Ross expressed drew on a history of sex role expectations explained by Drs. Jordan and Davieson in a series of lectures delivered at the Museum of Anatomy in Philadelphia in 1871. As a woman becomes sexually mature, they contended, "the bust develops, the eyes sparkle with vividness and expression, indicative of soul and feeling: the periodical indisposition peculiar to her sex commences, girlish playfulness is exchanged for that graceful bashfulness [*sic*] and retiring modesty which are so pleasing in girls of this age, her mind is occupied with ideas pure, but strange and absorbing; in a word, she is a woman, 'fairest of creation, last and best of all God's works'" (80). If a woman were allowed to work, not only would she fail to achieve this expected physical ideal, "last and best of all God's works," Ross argued, but her maternal ability would be affected.

Fifty years later, Avrom Barnett, in his 1921 *Foundations of Feminism: (A Critique)*, continued the argument of Jordan, Davieson, and Ross. Claiming that a "critical appreciation of biological limitations will help the student as nothing else can to an intelligent reading of Feministic literature, throughout which a most surprising ignorance of the modern biological situation is everywhere" (47), Barnett undertook a critical reading of both biological sex differences and sociological expectations. "The ironical Feminist reading this," Barnett claimed, "will regard [Ross's conclusion] as an illustration of the universal masculine self-assumed prerogative of dictating what women shall do and how they must look. . . . Feminists very likely will even laud this 'splay-footed, flat-breasted, broad-faced, short-necked' type" (87–88). "Feminists," he later concluded, "do not seem to be alive to the fact that the working woman who practices self-flagellation by going to work, like the mediaeval monk, attains an ideal but ruins her health" (93).

In June 1907, the *Woman's Tribune,* the "official organ of the International Council" for the National Woman Suffrage Association, reprinted the following verbal caricature of British suffragists, originally published in the British humor magazine *Punch,* called "A Bit of Fun":

> The context at Hexham appears to have produced some fresh varieties of suffragettes, alias suffragists, namely, "Suffragines," and "Suffragelles." Suffragines, according to the Daily Mail Special Correspondent, are widely differentiated and readily distinguished from the true Suffragettes. Whereas the Suffragette's eye gleams with the light of battle, the Suffragine wears a gloomy look of discontent. The former on political grounds attacks the Government; the latter bears a grudge

against the male sex in general. The Suffragelles, again, are a corps of lady suffragists enrolled to skirmish on the Liberal side against the attacks of Miss Fras-
er's Border Suffragettes. We do not wish to appear in any way to indulge in suf-
frajibing or suffrajeering. But one is tempted to ask with some apprehension,
whether any further liberties on these lines are going to be taken with the English
language. Is a harangue, for instance, of the now familiar kind to be described as
"a suffrajaw?" Are the militant suffraJills to entangle their suffraJacks in adventure which are calculated to end in suffragaol? The possible upspringing of all these
verbal monstrosities is an excessively painful subject with which we dare not further suffrajoke. (44)

That the editors of the *Woman's Tribune* chose to reprint the satiric "bit of fun"
may have been an act of appropriating the oppressor's language to defuse its
power. It may also have been a show of solidarity with British women, who
were struggling to gain their political autonomy at the same time. Of more
importance, however, is what the piece revealed about the opposition's fears
of women in the suffrage movement.

Suffragists, according to the piece, were divided into distinct groups: the
"suffragettes" and "suffragists," and their varieties, the "suffragines" and the
"suffragelles." The "suffragettes" were recognized by their militant eyes agleam
at the political battle to be waged and their impending attack on the government. The other group, the "Suffragines," was discontentedly gloomy and bore
a grudge against males in general. This dichotomy was further strengthened
by the implication that the "militant suffraJills" would, presumably by aggressive sexuality, "entangle their suffraJacks in adventures which are calculated
to end in suffragaol." The agency ascribed to the militant suffragists was remarkable in its ability to manipulate sexually "calculated" adventures designed
to "entangle" the male suffragists.

Punch's characterization of the British suffragists clearly signaled a move
toward the construction of a masculine woman, derived particularly from
woman suffragists. Men were supposed to initiate sex, often cleverly entangling
their female prey. In this satirical account, it was the militant "SuffraJills" who
were on the sexual offensive, and men were the passive recipients of sexual
aggression. Masculinity, at least in terms of sexual prowess, had been trans-
ferred from the male to the female. This picture was countered by the grudge-
bearing "Suffragines," who were gloomy, presumably, because they were unhappy with their place in life and man's existence in the world. It was easy to
infer that these "suffragines," since they begrudged men, had no use for men
as either platonic or sexual partners. "Suffragettes," as the *Punch* piece declared,
were of two types: militant and sexually aggressive "suffragelles" and man-

hating "suffragines." Both types, and thus all women who support their right to vote, at the very best, abandoned their femininity since they had abandoned men. At the very worst, they appropriated masculine characteristics, assumed the role of sexual subject and pursuer, reduced men to objects, even emasculated them, and became masculine themselves.

The writer J. George Frederick, however, dismissed this as merely hypothetical. "Woman is now attempting very daring arrangements of her destiny," he warned in the *Woman Citizen,* and man "hardly realized that the athletic ideal for woman necessarily implied certain psychic changes of deep significance—one of them, the unmistakable introduction of virility into female character" (8). James M. Buckley, writing in *The Wrong and Peril of Woman Suffrage* (1909), confessed, "*I believe* that there are two objects in nature alike obnoxious—a mannish woman and a womanish man" (86). Both of Buckley's "objects" were created by the fluidity of sex and gender combinations and the attachments of nontraditional sex-gender pairings. Yet the "womanish man," while certainly an "obnoxious" development, was not nearly as intriguing or inflammatory as the sex-gender opposite, a "mannish woman," whom Buckley traced directly to the woman suffrage movement.[5] An even more pointed critique was Dr. H. W. Frink's remark in *Morbid Fears and Compulsions:* "A certain proportion of at least the most militant suffragists are neurotics who in some instances are compensating for masochistic trends, in others are more or less successfully subliminating sadistic and homosexual ones (which usually are unconscious)" (quoted in Macy 134). "B. V. Moodus," the "first U.S. Suffragette Senator" depicted by the cartoonist Thelma Grosvenor Cudlipp in *Vanity Fair* in 1920, visually epitomized these anxieties: her masculine appearance was directly attributable to her politics (see figure 5). In short, the changes in the political status of women would cause aberrant, disruptive psychological and physiological changes.

The antisuffragist crusader Horace Bushnell made the link explicitly organic. Suffrage for women is "radical enough," he wrote, "when time enough is added, to alter even the type of womanhood itself. At first, or for a short time, the effect will not be so remarkable, but in five years, and still more impressively in twenty-five, it will be showing what kind of power is in it." After one hundred years of voting, the changes in women would become "a fact organic" and would become a trait of the race. The physical characteristics Bushnell attributed to political enfranchisement were many: "The look will be sharp, the voice will be wiry and shrill, the action will be angular and abrupt, wiliness, self-asserting boldness, eagerness for place and power will get into the expression more and more distinctly, and become inbred in the native habit"

Figure 5. Cartoon by Thelma Grosvenor
Cudlipp in *Vanity Fair*, August 1920, 34.

(135). Even more ominous, the "race" of these "forward, selfish, politician-women" would be characterized by "thin, hungry-looking, cream-tartar faces" that would be "touched with blight and fallen out of luster" (136).

The middle-class women who were active in the suffrage movement, according to John D'Emilio and Estelle Freedman, formed same-sex ties "in an age when their society still validated female bonding," but "they also lived in an era when same-sex relationships came under sharper scrutiny" (193). Physicians, reflecting the cultural prejudices of their society, were explicit in making the link between the suffrage movement and female inversion. By the end of the nineteenth century, European writers such as Richard von Krafft-Ebing "were describing same-sex relationships in medical terms, as signs of mental and physical degeneration" (D'Emilio and Freedman 193) and were linking "women's rejection of traditional gender roles and their demand for social and economic equality to cross-dressing, sexual perversion, and borderline hermaphroditism" (Smith-Rosenberg 272). Havelock Ellis, even though he subscribed to a congenital theory of inversion, declared in *Sexual Inversion,* "Having been taught independence of men and disdain for the old theory which placed women in the moated grange of the home to sigh for a man who never comes, a tendency develops for women to carry this independence still farther and to find love where they find work" (262). Their insistence on remaining unmarried, establishing themselves in a career, gaining the franchise, and entering into a relationship with another woman "emerged within Ellis' model as 'unnatural' and selfish" (Smith-Rosenberg 278). The female invert "denied the boundaries that separated the genders and 'unnaturally' inverted traditional femininity both sexually and socially," Smith-Rosenberg concludes (278). One physician succinctly commented, "The driving force in many agitators and militant women who are always after their rights is often an unsatisfied sex impulse, with a homosexual aim" (quoted in D'Emilio and Freedman 193).

In an attempt to explain why "sexual inversion in women" was increasing, that is to say, why women were acting more like men, Ellis connected homosexuality in women to "influences in our civilization to-day which encourage such manifestations." In particular, he cited "the modern movement of emancipation—the movement to obtain the same rights and duties, the same freedom and responsibility, the same education and the same work"—as responsible for the increase in observed "inversion." Although Ellis noted that the movement was "on the whole a wholesome and inevitable movement," he emphasized that it carried with it certain disadvantages, including an increase in women's criminality and insanity ("Sexual Inversion in Women" 155). Since these two "disadvantages" had been increasing, Ellis's explanation continued, so had homosexuality, "always . . . regarded as belonging to an allied, if not the same, group of phenomena" to which criminality and insanity belong. As a disclaimer, Ellis admitted that these "modern movements" could not be understood to cause sexual inversion directly, but he still assigned them indirect blame, noting that they "promote hereditary neurosis." "They develop the germs of it," Ellis concluded. These "modern movements" like women's emancipation, "probably cause a spurious imitation," Ellis explained, "due to the fact that the congenital anomaly occurs with special frequency in women of high intelligence who, voluntarily or involuntarily, influence others" ("Sexual Inversion in Women" 156). In 1908, Iwan Bloch made an even more exact connection: "There is no doubt that in the 'women's movement'—that is, in the movement directed towards the acquirement by women of all the attainments of masculine culture—homosexual women have played a notable part" (511).

The physician James B. Weir Jr. argued that the suffrage movement would lead to a demand for a "matriarchy"—reasoning that "the right to vote carries with it the right to hold office, and, if women are granted the privilege of suffrage, they must be given the right to govern" (817). Weir pronounced that this would be a regression for human society, "distinctly, and emphatically, and essentially retrograde in every particular" (818). In his article "The Effect of Female Suffrage on Posterity," published in the *American Naturalist* in September 1895, Weir explored "this atavistic desire [matriarchy] in the physical and psychical histories of its foremost advocates" (815).

"I think," he confidently reasoned, "that I am perfectly safe in asserting that every woman who has been at all prominent in advancing the cause of equal rights in its entirety, has either given evidences of masculo-femininity (viraginity), or has shown, conclusively, that she was the victim of psycho-sexual aberrancy." He followed with examples of "every viragint of note in the history of the world, [who] were either physically or psychically degenerate, or both," and provided Joan of Arc, Catherine the Great, and Messalina, "the depraved wife of Claudius," as historical precedent. Weir added that Messalina was so much a woman of "masculine type, whose very form embodied and shadowed forth the regnant idea of her mind," that her "gross carnality" and "lecherous conduct shocked even the depraved courtiers of her lewd and salacious court" (819).

Not all women in favor of female suffrage, however, belonged to Weir's class of viragints. Some women were motivated by a single, feminine purpose, such as universal temperance or "the elevation of social morals," and thus were not comparable to those women who desired a share in the government, the initial step, Weir reasoned, in the establishment of a "matriarchate." "Woman is," Weir continued, "a creature of the emotions, of impulses, of sentiment, and of feeling" (821). If a duty like suffrage were to be added, he reasoned, a woman's environment would "very materially change" and "would entail new and additional desires and emotions which would be other and most exhausting draughts on her nervous organism" (823). Even greater than the effects of suffrage on the individual woman, however, would be its influence on society. Although Weir admitted that the right to vote carried with it "no immediate danger," he asserted that the "final effect of female suffrage on posterity would be exceedingly harmful." "Probably many years" after suffrage, Weir surmised, the worst effects would be realized, when woman, "owing to her increased degeneration, gives free rein to her atavistic tendencies and hurries ever backward toward the savage state of her barbarian ancestors . . . toward that abyss of immoral horrors so repugnant to our cultivated ethical tastes— the matriarchate" (825).

Clearly, those suffragists to whom Weir attributed matriarchal desires, those women suffering from "viraginity" or "psycho-sexual aberrancy," were most threatening. "The pronounced advocates and chief promoters of equal rights are probably viragints," Weir concluded, "individuals who plainly show that they are psychically abnormal" and whose abnormality is "occasioned by degeneration, either acquired or inherent, in the individual." Weir, however, pushed his discussion of viraginity further, knowingly detailing the "many phases" of the physical and psychological aberrances. The "mild form," Weir wrote, was the tomboy "who abandons her dolls and female companions for the marbles and masculine sports of her boy acquaintances." The "loud-talking, long-stepping, slang-using young woman" was another form, as was "the square-shouldered, stolid, cold, unemotional, unfeminine android (for she has the normal human form, without the normal human *psychos*)." But "the most aggravated form of viraginity," he claimed, was "homo-sexuality" (822). What Weir accomplished by linking suffrage to viraginity and viraginity to homosexuality was to imply that homosexuality was responsible for the woman suffrage movement (later, after 1920, the quest for more expansive women's rights) and that woman suffragists were homosexuals.

Fictionally, these organic changes were most apparent in two texts: Henry James's *Bostonians* (1886) and William Lee Howard's *Perverts* (1901), texts that focus on a variety of women activists who embody, in varying degrees, the sharp looks, eagerness for power, and lusterless complexions that suffragists and feminists were thought to manifest. Both novels provide the crucial fictional link between the woman suffrage movement and the reconstruction of the women in the movement, physically, psychologically, and sexually. Most specifically, the portrayal of the relationship between Olive Chancellor and Verena Tarrant in *The Bostonians* has attracted significant attention as critics have argued over its implied homosexuality. Earlier readings, as Terry Castle relates, dismissed the same-sex attraction (150–51). Hugh Stevens notes that other critics "engage in full character assassination of Olive Chancellor, who emerges as 'unnatural' as opposed to the healthy, life-affirming Basil Ransom" (92). In the face of such duplicitous reaction, Castle wonders how "can James's novel not be a 'a study of lesbianism,' if its central character . . . is in fact a 'horrid' lesbian? What else besides such a character . . . would one need?" (151).

Expanding this debate about sexuality to more than the figure and motivations of Olive Chancellor, to include other female characters in the text, clarifies the vital connection between politics and physiology. Ruth Evelyn Quebe argues the connection between fiction and suffrage history, suggesting that the disagreements among James's reformers reflected the split between the National Woman Suffrage Association and the American Woman Suffrage Association (95).[6] Reading these women activists according to their varying levels of commitment to the cause permits us to see just how women's activity in politics influenced their physical and psychological character—at least according to these authors. Early in the novel, after Basil Ransom has arrived from the South, he attends a meeting with his cousin, Olive Chancellor, where the women's reform orator, Mrs. Farrinder, will speak. Interestingly, it is Mrs. Farrinder who exemplifies the rhetoric of the woman suffragists themselves and whose appearance demonstrates that the activists still embodied femininity, domesticity, and maternity. According to the narrator, Farrinder "was held to have a very fine manner, and to embody the domestic virtues and the graces of the drawingroom; to be a shining proof, in short, that the forum, for ladies, is not necessarily hostile to the fireside." As the final pronouncement of her adherence to womanly characteristics and most specifically to her heterosexuality, the narrator adds, "She had a husband and his name was Amariah" (39). This example of a true, independent-minded female reformer in a clearly feminine body, however, does not assume prominence in the novel.

Rather, the most egregious example of the woman reformer is Dr. Mary J. Prance, the physician who, "[e]xcept for her intelligent eye . . . had no features to speak of" and "looked like a boy, and not even like a good boy" (47). An even more frightful figure than Miss Birdseye, who belongs to the "Short-Skirts League" (36), Prance exemplifies precisely the qualities that antisuffragists had predicted.[7] Physically, she has lost all semblance of femininity—she was even "bored with being reminded . . . that she was a woman" (53)—evidenced by her lack of feminine curves and bobbed hair. "She was a plain, spare young woman, with short hair and an eye-glass" (39). Politically, she embodies an even more radical notion. Although she has little sympathy for the woman suffrage cause, only attending the meeting because she is curious about what is occurring in the apartment above her own, Prance clearly has the most radical views about the social place of women since she remarks that there is no difference between men and women. They "'are all the same to me! . . . I don't see any difference. There is room for improvement in both sexes. Neither of them is up to the standard'" (48). With these words, Prance distances herself from the reformers who, like Mrs. Farrinder, still espoused the domestic and maternal role for women. Instead, she adopts a rhetoric that demands not simply equal enfranchisement and opportunity but no differentiation between the sexes and their social status. Prance does seem to excuse these views by declaring that the women reformers have "'a capacity for making people waste time. All I know is that I don't want any one to tell *me* what a lady can do!'" (53), but she is the manifestation of antisuffrage predictions come alive still decades before the ratification of the Nineteenth Amendment and a warning of what would occur if feminism were expressed in its extreme. Valerie Fulton succinctly declares that Prance is "the best ally in the novel against the woman's suffrage movement" (246). As Ransom witheringly remarks about her, "It was certain that whatever might become of the movement at large, Doctor Prance's own little revolution was a success" (53).

Having established the two extremes of women's reform in Mrs. Farrinder, who espouses suffrage rhetoric but still embodies femininity, maternity, and domesticity, and Dr. Prance, who exemplifies everything the antisuffragists had predicted, the novel then turns to reform-minded Olive Chancellor, whose "union" with Verena Tarrant does not simply dismiss heterosexuality but for a time affirms a same-sex relationship. Ransom, who cynically opposes the reforms women are advocating, delights in the evening because it confirms what he has long believed about political women's disastrous effect on society. Olive Chancellor embodies Ransom's thoughts, as the narrator notes. "What Basil Ransom actually perceived was that Miss Chancellor was a signal old maid. That was her quality, her destiny; nothing could be more distinctly written. There are women who are unmarried by accident, and others who are unmarried by option; but Olive Chancellor was unmarried by every implication of her being. She was a spinster" (29). It is, of course, Chancellor who, immediately upon seeing the young Verena Tarrant, falls in love with her and her speaking talents. Never able to publicly express her own views on women's reform, Chancellor prefers to work behind the scenes, using her social and economic connections to advance the cause. Comfortably affluent on Charles Street, although perhaps a trifle embarrassed by her wealth, Chancellor is a dangerous embodiment of women's independence. Self-supporting (and financially supportive of the movement) and believing in the right of suffrage and equality, she utterly shuns marriage and, for much of the novel, removes the beautiful Verena Tarrant from heterosexual practice.

Verena herself, despite her involvement in reform efforts, does not pose the risk of a woman like Olive Chancellor. A "delicate, pretty girl," according to the narrator, Tarrant warrants the physical accouterments that the other women in the novel are not accorded. "She was strong and supple, there was colour in her lips and eyes, and her tresses, gathered into a complicated coil, seemed to glow with the brightness of her nature. She had curious, radiant, liquid eyes (their smile was a sort of reflection, like the glisten of a gem), and though she was not tall, she appeared to spring up, and carried her head as if it reached rather high" (61–62). Her conventional appearance befits a woman; she is, according to Alfred Habegger, "constituted by the familiar feminine traits, and the commenting author insists that this vulnerable femininity is her greatest triumph" (338). Her young age excuses her from her reliance on her parents, most notably Selah Tarrant, the mesmerist who prepares her to speak by "the mysterious process of calming her down" (62).

At various times throughout this text, Verena Tarrant does serve as the mouthpiece for women's reform, which seems to suggest she is committed to the cause. Yet her feminine appearance and behavior contradict such a reading. Verena Tarrant is no women's rights advocate; she simply speaks its rhetoric. As she prepares for her first speech, after Mrs. Farrinder refuses to address the group, she is "stroked and smoothed" by her father, who glories in the theatrics. Indeed, according to the narrator, Verena is readied for a "performance" (62). When she finally does begin to speak, the narrator remarks of Ransom, "It was not what she said; he didn't care for that, he scarcely understood it." Ransom is not so much impressed with Verena's claims of the "goodness of women" and "universal sisterhood" as he is enthralled by her delivery; he was "delighted to observe that such matters as these didn't spoil" the performance (63). It was, at last, "simply an intensely personal exhibition," and "the argument, the doctrine, has absolutely nothing to do with it" (64).

Selah Tarrant gives way to Olive Chancellor, who now becomes Verena's handler, preparing speeches for her and arranging her public engagements. It is the political world that has united Olive and Verena since that first oration. "'Are they very much united?'" Basil Ransom asks Miss Birdseye. "'You would say so if you were to see Miss Chancellor when Verena rises to eloquence,'" she answers. "'It's as if the chords were strung across her own heart; she seems to vibrate, to echo with every word. It's a very close and very beautiful tie, and we think everything of it here. They will work together for a great good!'" (192). From this description, it is seemingly Olive who is most enamored of Verena, specifically her rhetorical abilities. It is also apparent that their relationship is sanctioned, even cheered, by the other reformers, who look to the union as amenable to the cause.

The two women's relationship, though forged out of the movement, is not based on a shared political viewpoint, however. During their trip to Europe, Verena confesses to Ransom that Olive Chancellor makes her speeches for her, "'or the best part of them.'" "'She tells me what to say—the real things, the strong things. It's Miss Chancellor as much as me!'" she exclaims, apparently oblivious to the strings by which she is controlled (195). Although she holds her own when feminist views are playfully challenged by Ransom, Tarrant obviously does not have an original and independent thought. It should be no surprise, then, that the novel concludes with Verena's forsaking Olive Chancellor and choosing Basil Ransom, acquiescing again to the stronger power, in this case heterosexuality. Chancellor resumes the status she had at the start of the text, that of "spinster" or "old maid," her same-sex "union" with Tarrant thwarted and ultimately destroyed by the man.[8]

The melee that occurs backstage, as Ransom attempts to remove Verena physically from the auditorium and psychologically from the feminist cause, brings the novel and Olive Chancellor to a swift and unforgiving conclusion. Powerless to act in the face of Ransom and the heterosexuality he represents, Chancellor can do nothing but watch as Verena Tarrant's mask of political interest dissolves to reveal her true ambivalence about women's rights. Even though she calls out for Olive as she is violently whisked out of the theater by Ransom and even sheds tears, the indictment is clear. Olive Chancellor's power over the impressionable young woman is no match for the heterosexual status quo; to return the society to its heterosexual norm, the same-sex relationship is not allowed to persist. "The reason he manages to win Verena," Habegger posits, "is that he has nature on his side" (337).

Moreover, as Mrs. Farrinder makes clear when she comes backstage to ascertain why Verena has failed to deliver her address, the blame rests with Olive. "'Well, Miss Chancellor,' [Mrs. Farrinder] said . . . with considerable asperity, 'if this is the way you're going to reinstate our sex!'" (382). Since Mrs. Farrinder is seemingly unaware of the drama surrounding Verena and her choice of love, her denouncement of Olive carries a dual meaning. Her husband, Amariah, remarks on "a want of organisation" (383), clearly the area where Olive has been most successful for the movement. But this criticism also emanates from the heterosexual and married Mrs. Farrinder and can be read as a condemnation of Olive's "union" with Verena. The way to "reinstate" the female sex into society, in other words, is through the heterosexual status quo, not through same-sex unions and feminist rhetoric.

This fictional rendition of women reformers did not escape their real-life counterparts, who challenged some of the conclusions James's novel offered. Writing a review of *The Bostonians* in the *Woman's Journal,* a magazine devoted to covering the activities of the National Woman Suffrage Association, Lucia True Ames decided that the novel was "evidently intended as a tremendous satire on the whole 'woman question'" since Olive's "bitter, unnatural antipathy towards marriage and men" was decidedly atypical, as the glowing tributes to Stanton and Colby illustrated (82–83). Nevertheless, James's fiction of the women's movement does provide a valuable glimpse into the rhetoric and public perception of those politics that plagued the quest for woman suffrage. Olive Chancellor may ultimately elicit pity for having to face an impatient Boston audience at the end of the novel; Castle regards her as "English and

American literature's first lesbian tragic heroine" (171). Yet pity does not extend to her brief expression of same-sex sexuality. That move, from "old maid" to "lesbian," when coupled with Dr. Prance's "revolution" into gender indeterminacy, signaled that the fear of woman suffrage and political independence had come to pass.

The physician William Lee Howard's 1901 novel *The Perverts* presents an even more frightening possibility than James's Olive Chancellor and Dr. Mary J. Prance. Howard's familiarity with the latest scientific theories regarding heredity and mental health were two subjects that he entwined in his medical work and his writing. In a *New York Medical Journal* article in 1900, he wrote, "The female possessed of masculine ideas of independence, the virago who would sit in the public highways and lift up her pseudo-virile voice, proclaiming her sole right to decide questions of war or religion, or the value of celibacy and the curse of woman's impurity, and that disgusting antisocial being, the female sexual pervert, are simply different images of the same class—degenerates" ("Effeminate Men and Masculine Women" 687).

Howard's novel fictionalizes his medical conclusions by focusing on two fighting siblings with nervous disorders inherited from their parents, who, according to the narrator, were too old to produce mentally healthy children. According to Leigh Newcomber, hero psychologist of the novel, his nervous disorder—"dipsomania," which is successfully controlled through "scientific methods" (35)—was "inherited." He was given, the narrator explains, the "exhausted nervous organism of his immediate progenitors, and all the instability, infirmness, swaying and distorted characteristics belonging to a decaying family." So, too, were his three sisters. Zora, the eldest, shows "no intellectual force, no moral perversion, no mental activity." Marcia, however, is an egotistic, "typical hysteric, whose uncontrollable impulses have been fostered on account of the objective symptoms of her hereditary psychopathic soil." In short, according to Leigh, "this unfortunate woman is so desirous of mating that she is continually on the man hunt" (38). Mizpra is the youngest and "most unfortunate of the family." "Her condition," Leigh writes in his notebook, "appears to be a constant perversion of all the normal womanly attributes." Even "her mind . . . is not the ordinary female kind" since it is, according to Leigh, "a strange mixture of deceit and cunning. She is deep, sinister, and forbidding" (39).

As the novel progresses, traditional sex-gender assignments become even more pronounced. Leigh, who early in *The Perverts* allows his dipsomania to reduce him to a drunken philanderer consorting with prostitutes, slowly regains control of his nerves and becomes not only a faithful husband and father but also a strong, morally superior protector of society from the mentally ill. Mizpra, however, attempts to gain total control of her widowed mother's assets and becomes even more masculine. When Leigh receives a letter from Mizpra, he notices that although her handwriting is familiar, it is "somewhat changed in its character. It was masculine; a masculinity that would have done credit to Catherine de Medici." Furthermore, her "large jaws were now prominent, her muscled neck, small hips, uncomely waist, her black hair and large hands, all make a bold frame from her hard and coarse features." When she tells Leigh that he "'need not attempt to see [his] mother,'" her voice comes from what the narrator characterizes as a "masculine larynx" (49). The physiological effects of Mizpra's "nervous disease" and transgressions are clear: the more evil she becomes, the more masculine. Even more important is the converse: the more masculine she becomes, that is, the more she adopts the nontraditional, unaccepted gender to her female sex, the more evil, or to use Howard's term, the more "perverted," she becomes.

To lend validity to such notions, Howard allows Leigh Newcomber ample opportunities to lend scientific support to Mizpra's dangerous behavior, termed "her latent criminal instincts." Although Leigh does exonerate Mizpra's actions because she lacks the "force or power" to control herself as a result of her unfortunate heredity, even positing that "she had no knowledge of her abnormal condition, of her moral epilepsy" (50), the indictment of Mizpra's criminality and assumption of masculinity is obvious. "What we look for most in the female is femininity," Leigh recalls one of his teachers remarking. "And when we find the opposite in her we must look for some atavistic anomaly, which is generally of a criminal type" (50–51). In Mizpra's case, the anomaly makes her "an enemy to every living thing" (65).

Mizpra's "perversion," however, extends beyond her appropriation of a "masculine" voice and physique. In a conversation with her mother, Mizpra remarks that both of her sisters have married, which prompts Mrs. Newcomber to declare that Mizpra, unless she is careful, will become an "'old maid.'" Mizpra's vehemence at her mother's comment, declaring that marriage is "'disgusting,'" illustrates her even further fall into "perversion" and loss of femininity. "'What poor, weak, helpless creatures women are!'" Mizpra fumes, emphasizing that marriage is "'such a disgusting, vile, humiliating acceptance of the loss of personal freedom'" (87). Still, Mizpra does marry, although she never consummates the relationship. Her husband, Burke Wood, is a weak man; according to the narrator, he "was one of those unfortunate bipeds whom men despise, women hate, and the females of perversive instincts employ as useful adjuncts to their much-scorned skirts" (193). The marriage is strictly one of convenience; Mizpra needs a secretary. Neither does Mizpra accept the female's role of maternity, declaring that there are "'too many babies now,'" or the female's reliance on femininity, pronouncing that with her weak husband, she will use her "'intellect, my power over him,'" not the traditional "'feminine baubles of Eve'" (204).

The scientific issue of genetic inheritance is, at least in terms of Mizpra, displaced by the delineation of psychic and physiological changes caused by her perversion. Mizpra's and Mrs. Newcomber's move to Colorado Springs, presumably to enjoy the benefits of a "Western lung resort," prompts Mizpra to establish a "select young ladies' school." She considers herself to be "an emancipator of female slaves" by teaching the town's young girls to "give up their lives to the slavery of the hearth and home" since "it was beneath the dignity and rights of their sex" (90). Moreover, Mizpra continues her scientific experiments, as she tells her mother, to "prove in the future, without dissent, the strength, the force, and reasoning power of the female mind" (85).

But Mizpra's teaching methods are suspect, as Burke Wood informs her. "'I have heard that you have been instilling some of your brilliant ideas into your pupils' minds,'" Burke tells Mizpra. When Mizpra discovers the daughter of town's physician, Dr. Camp, wears corsets, she makes her take them off before the whole school. "'Then it is said,'" Burke recounts, "'you stood her on the platform and with your hands on her flesh, marked out the creases formed by the corsets. She told her father your hands were so cold and rough, the treatment so humiliating, that she fainted.'" Dr. Camp, he adds, "'tells everyone that his daughter had a severe nervous shock in consequence of your treatment, and that you ought to be driven out of town'" (92). Mizpra is nonplussed by this account and excuses her actions by saying that Dr. Camp's daughter "'is suffering from the feminine folly of imitating the male in all animal life on the globe—that is, the garnishing of the body to attract the opposite sex. In the animal kingdom such folly is the sole prerogative of the male'" (93).

The psychology and physical manifestations of "perversion" are certainly the focus of Howard's novel. But his characterization of Mizpra, whose actions dismiss femininity and maternity, as "evil" contrasts sharply with his treatment of the male sibling and his "perversions." Leigh, despite initial failings, is able to control his nervous disease and at the end of the novel force Mizpra to her death, thereby saving not only himself but, the worried reader can infer, all of society as well. Yet it is virtually impossible to determine causality in Mizpra's psyche. Is she evil because she has masculine characteristics? Or does her inherited perversion manifest itself physically in masculinity, signaling that a perverse psyche causes a perversity in sex-gender assignment? Leigh's inheritance is of no help in determining blame, since he, despite the narrator's insistence on the irrepressible power of heredity, is able to overcome his dipsomania by scientific method, which, at least for Leigh, is stronger than genetic disposition.

But Mizpra's perversion, more particularly her physical and psychical expression, clearly is meant to be the most important aspect of her being. Even if her "perversion" can be forgiven because it was inherited, the manifestations of such perversion cannot; Mizpra's ultimate "perversion" is located in her denial of marriage and maternity. Even more explicit than the physical same-sex attraction suggested in Mizpra's handling of Dr. Camp's daughter is the passing reference to a "mild sort of fellow-feeling—not womanly—"she experienced with a female physician who was, the narrator knowingly suggests, "one of the big-footed, short-haired kind" (286). Despite Howard's claim that the entire Newcomber family is afflicted with hereditary "perversion," clearly some perversions, those that confuse traditional sex-gender assignments and allow for the possibility of sexual inversion, are more "perverse" than others.

Yet it is not simply that there are varying degrees of perversions. Hereditary sources, too, are ascribed different values of perversion in the Newcomber family. Although initial speculation offers both the father and mother as causes, blame finally rests on maternal heredity. Mrs. Newcomber married late, at the age of thirty-six; by this time, the narrator explains, "her maternal and reproductive instincts had been starved and enfeebled by a life of wrong training and misdirected study, augmented by the unphysiologic life of the disappointed *femme sole.*" The narrator attributes Mrs. Newcomber's "wrong training" and "misdirected study," which result in her reproductive enfeeblement, and hence Mizpra's evil perversion, to "the false and unhealthy ideas of New England woman suffragists" (205). Mizpra, last-born child of the mistrained mother, "only needed a strong character, a decided maternal and womanly guide and adviser" to give "proper stimulation" to foster the "normal development of the sexual cells in the cortex of the brain" (206–7). But Mrs. Newcomber, the reader is told, because her "physical and mental activities [had] been in channels far removed from anticipation and thoughts of married life," lacks the maternal factors necessary for Mizpra to develop properly. More specifically, Mrs. Newcomber's belief and involvement in the woman suffrage campaign are transformed into a genetic anomaly and become the cause of Mizpra's perversion, her "abnormal pleasures and passions" (206).

Echoing Howard's 1900 article in the *New York Medical Journal,* his scientifically minded narrator elucidates the effects woman suffrage ideas supposedly had on women. "The female possessed of masculine ideas of independence, the viragint who would sit in the public highways and lift up her pseudo-virile voice, proclaiming her sole right to decide questions of war or religion, or the value of celibacy and the curse of woman's impurity" is, the narrator posits, a "degenerate," whose inheritance does not excuse her behavior, even though she is a "victim of poor mating" (207). There is, however, a far worse type of degeneracy. "That disgusting anti-social being, the female sexual pervert," is simply a "different degree of the same class" of "degenerates" to which Mizpra and her mother undoubtedly belong:

> When a woman neglects her maternal instincts, when her sentiment and dainty feminine characteristics are boldly and ostentatiously kept submerged, we can see an anti-social creature more amusing than dangerous. . . . [But] should this female be unfortunate enough to become a mother, she ceases to be merely amusing, and is an anti-social being. She is then a menace to civilizations, a producer of non-entities, the mother of mental and physical monstrosities who exist as a class of true degenerates until disgusted Nature, no longer tolerant of the woman who would be a man . . . allows [her] to shrink unto death. (207–8)

The vitriolic explanations of "perversions" continue, although now the narrator expands the definitions far beyond Mizpra and Mrs. Newcomber to include fictional and nonfictional society:

> The female who prefers the laboratory to the nursery; the mother quick with child who spends her mornings at the club, discussing "Social Statics," visiting the saloons and tenements in the afternoon, distributing, with an innocence in strange contrast to her assumptions, political tracts asking the denizens to vote her ticket, is a sad form of degeneracy. Such females are true degenerates, because they are unphysiologic in their physical incompleteness. The progeny of such human misfits are perverts, moral or psychic. Their prenatal life has been influenced by the very antithesis of what the real woman would surround her expected child with. The child born of the "new woman" is to be pitied. . . . (208)

Finally, the narrator makes the most pointed references to the degenerate "new woman," particularly the challenges she poses to the medical establishment:

> It is this class that clamors for "higher education" for the woman; that crowd the public halls shouting for the freedom of women and demanding all the prerogatives of the men. It is these female androids who are insulted in the dark umbrage of ignorance and delusion regarding their negative nature; who are fadists, 'ismites, and mental roamers. Ideally mobile, they go from the laboratory to the convent, even restless, continuously discontented, morbidly majestic at periods, hysterically forcible at times. They demonstrate their early perverted mental growth by their present lack of reasoning powers. . . . They claim to know more about the

science of medicine without study than the men who have devoted their lives to that science. (209)

Howard sought to instill hereditary causes of perversions to bolster his claim in the preface that people suffering from such "nervous diseases" should be confined to a hospital so that their mental illness can be controlled. The literary case exemplifies the medico-scientific theories of the day positing inheritance as a definite influence. Dr. Charles L. Dana, a nineteenth-century neurophysiologist, speculated that "if women achieve the feministic ideal and live as men do, they would incur the risk of 25 per cent more insanity than they have now" (n.p.). Dana excuses his projections by noting that "I am not saying that woman suffrage will make women crazy," but Howard, by locating the source of Mizpra's perversion in her suffragist mother's independent activities and delayed interest in maternity, certainly suggests that perversion is caused by woman's emancipation. If the empirically knowledgeable narrator is to be believed, the politically active woman en route to enfranchisement is the source and cause of "perversion." Or, as Dana explained: "woman suffrage would throw into the electorate a mass of voters of delicate nervous stability . . . [and] add to our voting and administrative forces the biological element of an unstable preciosity which might do injury without promoting the community's good" (n.p.).

This connection of masculinized women to woman suffrage to female inversion persisted through the early decades of the twentieth century, particularly as the woman suffrage movement progressed to its decisive constitutional victory in 1920. Havelock Ellis, Smith-Rosenberg reports, insisted that "the numbers of lesbians had steadily increased since the expansion of women's roles and institutions." According to Smith-Rosenberg, "Feminism, lesbianism, equality for women, all emerge in Ellis's writings as problematic phenomena. All were unnatural, related in disturbing and unclear ways to increased female criminality, insanity, and 'hereditary neurosis'" (279). The marriage reformer J. W. Meagher was explicit in linking women's rights activists to abnormal sexuality: "The driving force in many agitators and militant women who are always after their rights is often an unsatisfied sex impulse, with a homosexual aim. Married women with a completely satisfied libido rarely take an active interest in militant movements" (quoted in Smith-Rosenberg 283). Sigmund Freud also strengthened the connection between masculine gender and inversion in his *Three Essays*. As George Chauncey Jr. points out, "Freud, like Ellis and the whole of turn-of-the-century sexology, continued to assert that 'character inversion' was a regular feature of *female* inversion, although no longer maintaining that this was true of male inversion" (94). After World War I had decimated the number of eligible men, Christine Bolt observes, fears of a declining middle-class birthrate intensified. "Under these circumstances," she concludes, "'deviant' sexual behavior by women, of whatever kind, remained unacceptable on both sides of the Atlantic" (270).

This inversion of enfranchised women, accomplished through scientific theory, popular press illustrations, and fictional predictions of impending sociobiological disaster, was succinctly echoed by Professor Lionel J. Tayler, a nineteenth-century London University lecturer in biology, who was experiencing firsthand the sex-gender confusion of marching suffragists. "It is for the good of all concerned," he wrote, "that the unlikeness between man and woman exists, and . . . any effort to change woman's nature to the end that she may become a female man will and should fail" (quoted in "Woman and Man" 175). Although the success of the woman suffrage movement contradicted Tayler's forecast of failure, the fear of sex-gender confusion embodied in the suffragists remained solidly affixed in the public's mind, clearly articulated by the organic discontent of Greening's "freaks." As a desperate counter to such perverted possibilities, literature and popular press accounts attempted to disenfranchise this masculine woman and the perverted politics she was thought to practice. Authors relied on more subtle means to eradicate the masculine woman and her "freakish sexuality" from the acceptable status quo. A woman who acted contrary to the feminine gender, as the suffragists were thought to have done, needed to be labeled aberrant, seduced, parodied, or removed to maintain social order, strategies that the following chapters trace.

Notes

1. The sexologist Edward Carpenter attached this term to male and female inverts as an attempt at more fully defining and understanding just what this nontraditional sex-gender combination was.

2. In the early twentieth century, two groups dominated the suffrage movement. The National American Woman Suffrage Association was the largest, with two million members by 1917. Dr. Anna Howard Shaw presided from 1905 to 1915, when Carrie Chapman Catt took over. After 1920, it became the League of Women Voters. The National Woman's Party, headed by Alice Paul, employed more militant tactics, such as picketing the Wilson White House in 1917. For detailed studies of these groups, as well as the entire woman suffrage history, see Kraditor; Lumsden; Marshall; Camhi; and Jablonsky.

3. Linda Lumsden suggests that the members of the National Woman's Party (NWP), who introduced more radical strategies than the conservative National American

Woman Suffrage Association (NAWSA), in many ways embodied this fearful perception that suffragists were masculine. In the picketing of the Wilson White House, Lumsden claims that "[t]he pickets came directly to the paramount symbol of American male power. They not only did not care if they were perceived as unwomanly but also hoped to offend and provoke the male establishment" (118). The militancy of the NWP only exacerbated the perceptual conclusions about the women suffragists; the members of both the NAWSA and the NWP provoked the same fearful response—they were acting contrary to their sex.

4. Susan E. Marshall has categorized rhetoric from 214 antisuffrage writings according to gender and political issues. Breaking the movement into three periods—1867 to 1899, 1900 to 1912, and 1913 to 1921—she claims that "male attacks on suffragists' personality," jibes directed at their changing gender roles, "escalated over time" (105). See table 4.2 (101) in her study.

5. Buckley's connection of these nontraditional sex-gender combinations to the woman suffrage movement did not only explain the "mannish woman"; according to Marshall, male antisuffragists "attacked male supporters of women's rights as 'feminine men and mollycoddles,' a 'deplorable spectacle of human weakness'" (105).

6. The National Woman Suffrage Association supported a broad platform of women's causes, whereas the American Woman Suffrage Association sought the franchise within each state. Quebe places Olive and Verena "on the more radical side of the schism" (95).

7. Frederick Wegener reads Dr. Prance as a wholly positive figure who "personifies the ideology of unassisted self-making re-sanctioned so piously in Gilded-Age America" (170). Her placement within the woman's rights movement in relation to the reformers does, however, force a narrower reading of her. The self-made woman was, and still is, a problematic figure.

8. Sara DeSaussure Davis reads this fictional love triangle as based on historical fact. "James was personally acquainted" with various people involved in the suffrage movement, Davis writes, including Anna Dickinson, Susan B. Anthony, and Whitelaw Reid (571). He used Dickinson as the model for Verena Tarrant, while Anthony and Reid became fashioned as Olive Chancellor and Basil Ransom, respectively. "The striking similarity between the triangle of Anthony-Dickinson-Reid and of Olive-Verena-Basil is easily recognizable," although James did alter several important aspects of the historical model. Most notably, according to Davis, James "goes beyond what was known or publicly realized about Anthony and Dickinson. . . . in all likelihood [James] drew additionally from his observations of the friendship between Kate Loring and Alice James" (580).

3

Aberrant Assumptions

Disenfranchising the "Most Aggravated Type"

> We, the jury, find the defendant, Alice Mitchell, insane and believe
> it would endanger the safety of the community to see her at liberty.
> —M. C. Gallaway, jury foreman, 1892

In 1913, the popular press illustrator A. B. Walker, contributed two cartoons
to *Life* magazine. The first, published February 20, 1913, showed a slightly
built husband who asks his plump wife, Jane, whether he has lost weight
or mistakenly put on his wife's pants (see figure 6). He clearly looks confused; Jane now wears the same clothes he does. The husband's confusion
is surpassed only by the contemporary viewer's nervousness at seeing such
a disregard for gender roles. As a result, Jane becomes the absurd figure because she has opted out of her dress, the outward marker of femininity, and
into the masculine signifier, trousers.

Walker's April 17, 1913, cartoon proposed an even more threatening possibility than Jane's decision to wear pants. Here, clothing styles are completely reversed: the woman wears the man's tuxedo and the man appears
in the woman's fancy long gown, replete with jewelry and stylish hat (see
figure 7). Even more apparent, however, is the man's effeminate pose—left
hand on hip, left foot prominently displayed from beneath the gown, right
pinkie finger delicately extended—that is more threatening than the cross-
dressing because it signals, like Greening's freaks, an organic change visible in behavior. To retain some semblance of masculinity about the man,

"AM I LOSING WEIGHT, OR ARE THESE
YOUR TROUSERS, JANE?"

A. B. WALKER.

Figure 6. Cartoon by A. B. Walker in *Life*, February 20, 1913, 368.

Walker gives him a mustache and beard, as if without facial hair, the man would cease to be recognizable as a man. As for the woman, she retains her curves, only now encased in the man's suit. The cartoon humorously suggested what things would be like if the styles were reversed, yet whatever nervousness it provoked, the cartoon's hypothesis remained in the realm of possibility.

The illustrator Rodney Thomson was reflecting perceived reality in his *Life* magazine cartoon, published March 27, 1913 (see figure 8). Entitled "Militants," Thomson portrays "militant" woman suffragists who wear ribbons on their lapels proclaiming "Votes for Women." Drawing them as dour, angry, and unattractive women in the top row, whom Thomson has labeled "As They Are," does not fully capture their politically influenced physiology. Mocking their self-perception in the second row, "As They Think They Are," the same women appear as saints, angels, and mythical goddesses. The third row pictures these suffragists "As They Appear to the Police and Shopkeepers." Here, their facial features are virtually identical to the top row of drawings, but they have even more severe grimaces, and, most notably, horns have been added. They are, in short, demonized; their politics have not only removed from them

IF
THE STYLES WERE REVERSED

Figure 7. Cartoon by A. B. Walker in *Life,* April 17, 1913, 778.

all vestiges of attractive femininity but have put them in league with evil as well. Together, these three cartoons in *Life* presented a striking portrait of anxiety in an age of suffragists and suggested that even the assumption of such an aberrant possibility had to be quickly dismissed.

The final blow to the woman suffragists' character, even worse than the "immense moral transformation that is going to be wrought in their personal temperament and character," the antisuffrage crusader Horace Bushnell cautioned (137), was the suspicion of what occurred to their sexuality as a result of these other masculinizing changes. Psychologists, physicians, and sexologists were finding sexual expression increasingly interesting. Magnus Hirschfeld, Karl Westphal, Richard von Krafft-Ebing, Hans Ulrichs, Edward Carpenter, and Havelock Ellis were the most prominent clinicians at the turn of the century who undertook to explain sexuality, including homosexuality. As Carroll Smith-Rosenberg briefly outlines, "With the 1890s male physicians and social critics initiated a new wave of attacks upon the New Woman. The second debate commenced as male asylum directors, doctors, academics, psychiatrists, and psychologists (all members of new bourgeois professions and bureaucracies) shifted the definition of female deviance from the New Woman's rejec-

Figure 8. Cartoon by Rodney Thomson in *Life*, March 27, 1913, 616.

tion of motherhood to their rejection of men" (265). Using case studies of patients who exhibited such pathological behavior, Havelock Ellis acquired the interpretive license to suggest that "sexual inversion" was a congenital condition and that laws criminalizing homosexual behavior were therefore unjust. Despite Ellis's attempt to repeal such laws, his approach to male and female sexual differences, as John D'Emilio and Estelle Freedman point out, "did claim distinctive sexual modes for each gender. Men were characteristically active, aggressive, sexually insistent, and easily excited, while women, if not quite passive, needed the attention and stimulus of the male to be aroused" (224).

Once these differences were established, it was natural to recognize men and women who acted contrary to these sex differences, the sexologists' version of social Darwinism.[1] As D'Emilio and Freedman explain, in the 1880s there was little agreement as to what caused "homosexuality." Initially, theory posited that it was degenerative, a type of insanity. By the early twentieth century, "opinion had shifted toward a congenital model, and a rough consensus developed that sexual 'inverts' were born that way. Not until the 1920s, when Freudianism swept competitors from the field, would the pendulum swing back to the position that homosexuality was an acquired condition" (226). Christina Simmons posits that in the 1920s, although theories of "congenital abnormality still appeared," homosexuality was increasingly thought to be caused by "environmental explanations." "The ascendancy of psychodynamic explanations focused attention on the process whereby young people 'acquired' homosexuality and strengthened efforts to control it by changing their predisposing environmental factors," Simmons writes. "Both lay and medical writers loosely included factors from social as well as from family life among possible sources" ("Companionate Marriage" 56).

Since gender was seen as an implicit part of sexuality, early ideas tended to define same-sex sexuality not as homosexuality but as "sexual inversion," a complete exchange of gender identity, of which erotic behavior was but one part. George Beard, an eminent American physician, wrote in 1884 that when "sex is perverted, they hate the opposite sex and love their own; men become women and women men, in their tastes, conduct, character, feelings, and behavior" (quoted in D'Emilio and Freedman 226). Such an emphasis on a person's behavior became the marker of a person's true identity. Women who acted like men became "men." Their sexual object choice also assumed the prerogative of the male, and the fear of "female inversion"—of same-sex sexual relationships among women—was the result.

Writing in the medical journal *Alienist and Neurologist* in 1895, Havelock Ellis presented not only theories but case studies of "sexual inversion in women."

Although "homosexuality has been observed in women from very early times," Ellis asserted, "comparatively little" is known about it, for several sociological reasons (141). Men's indifference to women's homosexuality may be one reason, as may the fact that "it is less easy to detect [homosexuality] in women" because society is accustomed to "a much greater familiarity and intimacy between women" (141, 142). The same society, Ellis continued, is "less apt to suspect the existence of any abnormal passion," perhaps because "we have also to bear in mind the extreme ignorance and the extreme reticence of women regarding any abnormal or even normal manifestation of their sexual life" (142).

Nevertheless, "sexual inversion" did occur in women and, according to Ellis, in a variety of forms, including a distinction between the passive and "active" inverts. The first type was immediately identifiable because they were "not repelled or disgusted by lover-like advances from persons of their own sex" (147). What Ellis called the "actively inverted woman" differed from the passive woman because the active woman had "a more or less distinct trace of masculinity." She was, however, not necessarily a "mannish" woman who might "imitate men on grounds of taste and habit unconnected with sexual perversion." Unlike the passive woman who might possess only a "preference for women over men," the active woman as a rule "feels absolute indifference towards men, and not seldom repulsion" (148). In addition to "masculine elements," inverted women also exhibited, according to Ellis's case study of twenty-six-year-old "Miss B," a fondness for exercise and smoking, an affinity for artistic tastes, and an indifference to dress (148–49).

Ellis made the connection between "inversion" and masculinity even more explicit as he detailed the case of "Miss X," an unmarried, thirty-year-old woman whose paternal family had a history of "eccentricity" and "nervous disease." Beginning at age four, "Miss X" exhibited clear signs of her physical attraction to females, while her "first rudimentary sex feelings," associated with dreams of whipping and being whipped, appeared at the age of eight or nine (149). In her later years, the woman "occasionally had erotic dreams about women," particularly "womanly women," a distinction Ellis made as he characterized these women as "sincere, reserved, pure, but courageous in character" (151). Although he hesitated to label "Miss X" a "masculine woman," he sharply contrasted her with the women to whom she is attracted, the "womanly women." Ellis was prompted to reiterate that in the "inverted" population, "the chief characteristic of the sexually inverted woman is a certain degree of masculinity" (152). Even when such women retain feminine dress, which, according to Ellis, is often the case, other masculine traits, "all sorts of instinctive gestures and habits," suggest to female acquaintances that such a person "ought to have been a man." "Brusque energetic movements," "direct speech," the "masculine straightforwardness and sense of honor," and "especially the attitude towards men, free from any suggestion either of shyness or audacity" (153) signaled to Ellis, and hence society, that the woman's masculinity identified her as a "sexually inverted woman."

The woman with masculine characteristics and possibly inverted sexuality did not remain confined to the pages of medical treatises. Although American literature has been populated with same-sex relationships, they once were characterized as benign. The popularity of Mary E. Wilkins Freeman and Sarah Orne Jewett attested to the peaceful coexistence of "female friendships" with American society. Yet by 1896, with the increasing fervor of the woman suffrage rhetoric and the rise in sexological theories of inversion, it was clear that female same-sex relationships and masculinized women were unnatural expressions. Such unconventional behavior was not tolerated. Masculine women, determined to hold true to their gender and inverted sexuality, ultimately were labeled "aberrant" and their actions criminalized.

In the late nineteenth century, two newspapers, one in Colorado and the other in Indiana, provided accounts that detailed not only gender inversion and female same-sex sexuality but also social reaction that deemed such relationships perverse. Under a headline of "Mad Infatuation," the *Aspen Times* in May of 1889 recounted "one of the most peculiar cases that has ever engaged the attention of a court in any part of the world. Assigning the two women the fictitious names of "Belle" and "Blanche," the *Aspen Times* reported that Blanche declared she wanted to marry Belle.[2] Arguing that "'I am in full possession of my reasoning faculties and never was more sincere in my life,'" Blanche confessed to Belle's father, "'I love your daughter as she never was loved and never will be loved again.'" Acknowledging that such love was "'out of the usual order of things,'" Blanche nevertheless admitted that her passion was "'my being's destiny'" (4).

To socially sanction her love, Blanche proposed that she and Belle ride to Aspen to get married. Blanche, since she was "somewhat masculine in appearance and figure," would dress as a man so that the conventional genderings of a heterosexual couple in love can be replicated. There was some discrepancy regarding Belle's feelings for Blanche, however. The Aspen newspaper quoted Belle as telling her father that Blanche "'hugs and kisses and squeezes me nearly to death. She won't let me out of her arms after we go to bed and presses me so close to her I can hardly breathe. She says if I don't marry her she will kill me . . . Papa, she is killing me by inches'" (4). Yet the *Denver Times* reported two months later in an article entitled "Lovelorn Girls" that their elopement had occurred. Despite a search of Denver for the women, reporters were unable to find any trace of them. "If they are in any of the hotels in the city," the report surmised, "they are under assumed names" (6).

The case of Delia Perkins and Ida Preston in Indianapolis had a similar scenario. The two women, Dr. Charles H. Hughes recounted, had run away from home together; Delia had even cut off her hair to sell it so that she might finance their trip. They were caught, and Delia was returned home, but only after "imprinting burning kisses upon the cheek and lips of the paramour of her own sex on parting," Hughes noted. When her mother demanded that she not run away again with Ida, Delia replied, "'Then I will kill myself and you will be responsible . . . Ida is the only one I ever loved and I will continue to love her until I die.'" If they were not allowed to run away together again, "'*I will kill myself and her, too,*'" she declared (558–59). As with the Colorado "Mad Infatuation," the two women were not, apparently, equally complicit. Ida Preston admitted that she did not want to leave home. "'I like the girl, but don't believe I care as much for her as she does for me,'" she said, purportedly agreeing to go with her only because she feared for her life (559).

In both accounts, the behavior was determined to be a result of unnatural passion, linked to criminal behavior and insanity. The *Denver Times* declared, "Society in this section of the country has been rent from center to circumference during the past six weeks over the sensational love affair" (6). Although afflicted with physical ailments, such as "nervous prostration," Blanche and Belle were defined almost solely by their mental status. Blanche deemed it necessary to posit that she was "in full possession of [her] reasoning faculties," while a neighbor defended her as "clear headed, clever, and undemonstrative," although "not strong minded." Other judgments were not so mild. The *Aspen Times* declared the relationship an "apparently insane infatuation." Belle's father labeled the elopement plans "nonsense" and "trash" and told Blanche, "'You will really persuade me soon that you are becoming insane.'" Even the neighbor who initially seemed so understanding ultimately suggested that the relationship was composed of "morbid sentimentality" and "monstrous, unnatural affection." One woman, the neighbor commented, "suggested a dose of cowhide as the most practical method of curing such thoughts in Miss Blanche" (4). In Indianapolis, Delia Perkins's perverted sexuality manifested itself not only in illness and criminality—she was arrested by the chief of police for running away with Ida Perkins—but also in suicidal and homicidal behavior.

The popular press was not the only medium providing evidence of the public's reaction to masculine womanhood and sexual inversion as aberrancy. Even

Mary E. Wilkins Freeman, best known for her portrayals of the quiet small-town New England life, was complicit in her story "The Long Arm," first published in 1895, which presented the masculine woman in a same-sex relationship as a threat to the heterosexual social order. Two real-life murder mysteries in 1892 supposedly were models for "The Long Arm": the Lizzie Borden and Alice Mitchell cases.[3] According to J. Bradley Shaw, it was Freeman's friend J. Edgar Chamberlin who suggested "that they 'solve' the Fall River ax-murders" with an "inventive revision of the Borden mystery" (213). Accounts of the sensational case alleged that daughter Lizzie bludgeoned her stepmother and father in the Borden home in Fall River, Massachusetts. The defense established that no ax head was found on the Borden property, Lizzie did not have any bloodstained clothing in her room, and a search of the house, barn, and garden failed to produce suspicious garments or any other direct evidence that would link her to the crime. Lizzie was acquitted and remained in Fall River until her death in 1927, and no one was ever convicted of the brutal murders. In Freeman's and Chamberlin's story, the fictional Sarah Fairbanks is initially suspected of the murder of her father and, like Lizzie Borden, is acquitted of the crime because of lack of evidence. However, in "The Long Arm," the murderer is eventually brought to justice.

Elements in Freeman's "Long Arm" also seem to have their source in a sensational Tennessee murder case in 1892, which the January 26, 1892, front page of the *New York Times* headlined as "A Most Shocking Crime; A Memphis Society Girl Cuts a Former Friend's Throat" (1). It was a crime that attracted nationwide attention not only because it was so violent but also, as Lisa Duggan suggests, because it embodied the emergence of the subjective lesbian body. "Contests over the meanings of stories of lesbian identity expressed profound social anxiety over the boundary of masculine/feminine itself," Duggan avers (794). She quotes the *New York World*'s attempt at understanding the sexual dynamics of the crime: "a sober American community and an unimaginative American court must deal in matter-of-fact fashion with matters which have been discussed hitherto by French writers of fiction only. . . . Judge DuBose, of Tennessee, will have cited to him, as bearing on the case of an American girl, the creations of French writers whom he and all his associates have looked upon as perverted creatures, dealing with matters outside of real life, or at least outside of American life" (795).

The subheading of the article in the *New York Times* read, "Alice Mitchell, Daughter of a Wealthy Retired Merchant, Jumps from a Carriage, Seizes Freda Ward, and Kills Her." According to the newspaper account, both Alice Mitchell, age nineteen, and Freda Ward, age seventeen, were familiar figures in society, Ward's father having made his fortune as a "planter and wealthy merchant" in Gold Dust, Arkansas. "A few minutes before 4 o'clock," the article read, "a buggy containing Miss Alice Mitchell and Lizzie Johnson drove up to the broad sidewalk around the Custom House block leading to the levee. . . . Suddenly from out the carriage came Miss Mitchell. Grasping Miss Ward by the neck, she drew a bright razor from out the folds of her dress and without a word drew it across the throat of her victim. Miss Ward sank to the pavement in an instant, the blood pouring in torrents from the severed jugular" (1).

Once the crime was committed, Mitchell reportedly jumped back into the buggy her accomplice Lizzie Johnson had kept readied, and with the exclamation "Drive on, I've done it!" seized the whip, and together the two "were soon around the corner into Madison Street and away from the scene of the tragedy." Later in the evening, Mitchell was arrested by police at her home. The motive for the crime remained speculative at best, since initially Mitchell refused to speak to anyone about the murder. The *New York Times,* however, did suggest that "on former trips to Memphis, Freda Ward had been a 'guest' of Mitchell's." "Lately," however, "she refused to partake of the hospitality of the Mitchell household and refused, also, to recognize Miss Mitchell on the street. It is alleged that Miss Ward had made remarks of an uncomplimentary nature regarding Miss Mitchell, and this is supposed to have been the cause of the tragedy." The newspaper account continued, "Tonight the murderess made a singular statement . . . that she loved Freda desperately, better than any one in the world; that she could not live without her, and that long ago they made a compact that if they should ever be separated they should kill each other." Mitchell had been "forbidden" to speak with Ward and "knew nothing else to do but to kill her." As a result, the story concluded, Mitchell "is regarded as demented" (1).

Three days later, the *New York Times* followed up with a story entitled "Jealousy the Motive," which outlined the motivation behind the murder and her attorneys' plan for defending her. Mitchell's lawyers pleaded "insanity," stressing that her mother had a history of being "mentally unbalanced," particularly "prior [to] the birth of her oldest child, and again immediately before the birth of Alice." Supporting Mitchell's insanity plea was her claim to her defense attorneys that "'I killed Freda because I loved her, and she refused to marry me. I asked her three times to marry me, and at last she consented. We were to marry here and go to St. Louis to live. I sent her an engagement ring and she wore it for a time. When she returned it I resolved to kill her. I would rather she were dead than separated from me living.'" Freda Ward appeared to have "willingly consented" to the marriage proposal, according to letters that had been discovered, and "the time was fixed." "It is certain," the *Times* suggested, "that Miss Mitchell still thinks she did the proper thing in killing her fiancee." In the very next sentence, however, the *Times* discredited Mitchell and Ward's "proposed marriage" by noting, "On other subjects she is entirely rational" (1).

Both Mitchell and Johnson were indicted for murder. Testimony showed that Johnson had assisted not only in Mitchell's escape but also in planning the crime. "Miss Mitchell and Miss Johnson," the story related in detail that proved the sexologists' theories about female inverts, "dressed themselves in men's clothes and went aboard the steamer Ora Lee on the Monday preceding the murder, when it was reported that the Misses Ward would take passage on the boat for home" ("Alice Mitchell Insane" 1). This evidence of cross-dressing was used as additional support of the murderers' "mental unbalance" as well as premeditation. According to Duggan, their "gender-crossing and elopement plans were a red flag signaling that these young women had gone too far and that their relationship had to be viewed as dangerous and possibly sexual rather than as foolishly but harmlessly romantic" (799).

On July 31, the *New York Times* reported the verdict of the case, a decision that took the jury only twenty minutes of deliberation: "'We, the jury, find the defendant, Alice Mitchell, insane and believe it would endanger the safety of the community to see her at liberty,'" wrote the foreman, M. C. Gallaway. The jury had decided that Mitchell was insane; if ever released from the asylum as sane she could then be tried for murder since only her present mental unsoundness had been at issue. When the verdict was read, the *Times* noted, "a faint smile spread over the defendant's features, as if she had been confident of the jury's verdict," and she left the courtroom for jail "gaily chatting as she went" ("Alice Mitchell Insane" 1).

Medical journal accounts of this case provided even more specific information about the alleged sexual character of the two women than did the popular press. On July 23, 1892, before the verdict, the New York *Medical Record* headlined a brief report of the case entitled "Lesbian Love and Murder." The "lesbian relations" and "perverted sexuality" of the pair were discussed, and although "victims of sexual perversion" might be "insane," the writer doubted the law would find Alice Mitchell "irresponsible" (n.p.). In the *New York Medical Standard* on August 13, 1892, Dr. Shrady challenged the "insanity" of Alice Mitchell while betraying his allegiances to the medical biases of the time: "If this alleged lunatic had been treated for worms, leukorrhea (vaginal discharge), constipation, or some other of the frequent mechanical excitements of unhealthy sexual desire, or if she had been taken in hand early by those in authority and received a course of bread and water and, perhaps, some strong corporeal applications, she would not have become a Lesbian lover or a murderess" (quoted in J. Katz 556).

The language in the case studies and medical opinions about Alice Mitchell certainly conformed to turn-of-the-century accounts of "female inversion" in general. Such mental unbalance was not a sudden occurrence, the medical wisdom suggested, but had been part of their psyche for years and perhaps had even been inherited. Johnson's claim that her health was being impaired by imprisonment allowed the *New York Times* to suggest, "It appears from the proof taken that the defendant [Johnson] has been in precarious health since a mere child that she suffers continuously with headache, and often with nervous prostration" ("Mitchell Murder Case" 9).[4] According to Dr. T. Griswold Comstock of St. Louis, writing in the *New York Medical Times,* Alice Mitchell's "sexual perversion," or "urning," had been caused by her mother's deep mental disturbances more than thirty years earlier, a case he knew well because he had attended Mitchell's mother. The facts about Alice Mitchell, Comstock wrote, "will long be treasured in medical works on insanity, and mental and moral perversion." It was of great importance, Comstock declared, that such a case be "thoroughly analyzed by the medical profession," especially by the most "reliable medical experts." There must be, Comstock claimed, "something radically abnormal in the mental and physical development of such a murderess." The Alice Mitchell case, he concluded, "must cast its dark shadows far and wide" (n.p.).

If, indeed, Freeman based her "Long Arm" on the scintillating Borden and Mitchell murders, clearly these cases cast their shadows at least as far as Freeman's fictional New England. The similarities of the three murder mysteries are striking, particularly the evidence of "female inversion." J. Bradley Shaw quotes Edith Coolidge Hart, a Fall River resident, who wondered, "Did Lizzie Borden have a friend before and after the murder trial? It is safe to say that in that era there were very few, if any, laissez-faire friendships. There were certain 'crushes' that caused a great deal of talk but in good society parents kept a close watch and restricted intimacies. It is difficult to picture the restraints of that era unless you have lived through it. . . . I never heard the words homosexual or lesbian until after my college days" (230). Despite the lack of established words for "female inversion," it is clear, as Carroll Smith-Rosenberg notes in *Disorderly Conduct,* that notions of female sexuality were changing rapidly during the late nineteenth century and that female friendships no longer had the benign understanding they had once enjoyed (245ff.). In the Mitchell case, although the object of the murder was a woman, "female inversion" was explicitly suggested, and the motivation for the killing—maintenance of the same-sex relationship—was echoed by Freeman's murderer, who, like Alice Mitchell, was eventually caught and brought to justice.[5]

Artistic license and creative imagination most certainly account for some of Freeman's deviations from the real-life plots. Yet the combination of particular elements also suggests a careful attempt by an experienced writer to present a small slice of New England life that was rarely seen, even in her own extensive portrayals. The two women at the center of "The Long Arm" do not conform to the great majority of Freeman's fictional women, who, Mary Reichardt contends, "form an intricate social network with each other on which they depend for emotional interaction," especially since they are "often estranged emotionally or physically from fathers, husbands or lovers" (*Web* 103). Frequently, the younger woman in the relationship receives a marriage proposal; intensely jealous, the stronger woman forbids her to marry. "Eventually," Reichardt explains, "the weaker woman rebels, and the stronger woman, made to 'see' her error, is humbled and (usually) relents." "In general," Reichardt continues, "this theme emerges as a pattern in Freeman's depiction of women in mutual relationships" (*Web* 106). "The Long Arm," however, presents an altogether different conclusion: the jealous, domineering woman steadfastly refuses to allow the other woman to marry her longtime love.

Freeman's story also markedly deviates from her usual generic form. "The Long Arm" is a detective story, replete with initial police ineptitude, an outside investigator, and eventual justice for the murderer. That Freeman was interested in the emerging genre of detective fiction should not be surprising. By 1891, Freeman enjoyed remarkable success as a short story writer; her reputation and income were firmly established. Reichardt suggests that after 1891 "she felt more at liberty . . . to experiment with her work . . . she was artistically ambitious and sought to try her hand at other genres as well" (*Reader* xiii). What Reichardt calls "her interest in the human psyche" led Freeman to write of "the psychology of those so 'set' in one track they are unable to deviate from it" (*Reader* xi), a character flaw that spans more than forty years in "The Long Arm." Moreover, at this time detective fiction—by 1895 more than forty years old[6]—was witnessing the birth of its most well-known ratiocinative mind, Sherlock Holmes.[7]

Certainly, the Bacheller Newspaper Syndicate's contest soliciting the year's best detective story and the accompanying $2,000 prize may have persuaded Freeman to write in the genre.[8] She also may have been motivated by her belief that "every New England village hides a mysterious secret or a hidden crime," as Edward Foster related from J. Edgar Chamberlin himself (135). What is most intriguing, however, is not that Freeman wrote a detective story but that she chose to frame the content of this story in that form. As a "transgressive act," Heta Pyrhönen comments, "crime brings into play, as if automatically, moral considerations, for it is, by definition, a breach of the boundary of what is socially and morally permitted" (51, 50). The solution to the fictional crime story provides social reassurance; "those who tried to disturb the established social order were always discovered and punished" (Symons 11).

Martin Fairbanks, "The Long Arm" relates, is a widowed, middle-aged man who is found murdered one morning in the house he and his daughter, Sarah, shared. Sarah is immediately suspected and arrested as his murderer because all the doors and windows to the Fairbanks' house are locked from the inside. She apparently has motivation enough also, since her father forbade her, under threat of disinheritance, from marrying Henry Ellis, the man to whom she has been engaged for five long years. The town's law enforcement, however, is unable to find any evidence to tie Sarah to the murder—no witnesses, no bloody clothes, no murder weapon—and she is acquitted, which leaves her free to dedicate herself to discovering her father's killer. The police are unable to convict anyone, even though Martin Fairbanks was cruel enough to have supplied a motive to numerous people. Finding clues the unobservant police have missed and assisted by an intuitive male detective from Boston, Sarah discovers the true murderer. Moreover, the motivation for the crime comes to light—a complicated hidden love triangle between Phoebe Dole and Maria Woods, who have lived together for more than forty years, and Martin Fairbanks, Maria's longtime secret lover; Martin and Maria had at last planned to marry. Unlike Freeman's other relationships between women that eventually end with the dominant woman's relinquishing her hold on the passive one, Phoebe never does permit Maria to marry Martin. Instead, she murders him because, as Phoebe confesses, "[t]here are other ties as strong as the marriage one, that are just as sacred. What right had he to take her away from me and break up my home?" (402).

When the socioscientific context in which this story was written is expanded to include not only the emphasis on logic, reason, and scientific infallibility but also the increasingly important field of "sexology" and its fin de siècle rhetoric about the "female invert," Freeman's "Long Arm" cannot be described simply as a "lesbian story" (Koppelman 43) or "a work of no great originality" (E. Foster 135). On the contrary, Freeman's presentation of a jealous and murdering "female invert" under the guise of a detective story ultimately indicts lesbian sexuality by offering scientific evidence for the unnaturalness of

Phoebe's attraction. The generic form (atypical for Freeman) becomes then a means of defining the same-sex attraction as an unnatural phenomenon worthy of scientific study and eventually of infallible condemnation.

During their well-hidden relationship, Maria Woods has lived with Phoebe Dole, a woman who, the narrator notes, "always does things her own way. All the women in the village are in a manner under Phoebe Dole's thumb." Even though Maria "sews well . . . Phoebe does all the planning," and all the townswomen's "garments are visible proof of her force of will" (385). This relationship between Phoebe Dole and Maria Woods is described by the narrator, Sarah Fairbanks, as one clearly operating according to a masculine-feminine power hierarchy: "Maria Woods has always been considered a sweet, weakly, dependent woman, and Phoebe Dole is undoubtedly very fond of her. The two have lived together since they were young girls. Phoebe is tall, and very pale and thin; but she never had a day's illness. She is plain, yet there is a kind of severe goodness and faithfulness about her colourless face, with the smooth bands of white hair over her ears" (386). Freeman's descriptions of these two women, one femininely gendered and the other masculinely gendered, and her hints of the "female friendship" existing between them adhere to the pattern she established with numerous other woman-to-woman relationships in her fiction. Not surprisingly, these pairs mirror the heterosexual status quo of a masculine man and a feminine woman and reflect Ellis's description of active and passive female inverts.

Phoebe Dole, however, is not the only woman who appears to act contrary to her sex. Sarah Fairbanks's role as detective suggests more masculine reason than feminine intuition. Her discovery of numerous clues attests to not only the poor job of investigation by the police but also her remarkable acuity in discovering these clues. Once she is acquitted of her father's murder, Sarah vows:

> My father's murderer I will find. Tomorrow I begin my search. I shall first make an exhaustive examination of the house. . . . Every room I propose to divide into square yards, by line and measure, and every one of these square yards I will study as if it were a problem in algebra.
>
> I have a theory that it is impossible for any human being to enter any house, and commit in it a deed of this kind, and not leave behind traces which are the known quantities in an algebraic equation to those who can use them. (390)

Her reliance on mathematical language and reason follows the pattern of other detectives, namely, Edgar Allan Poe's C. Auguste Dupin, who is described as both "poet" and "mathematician," and Sir Arthur Conan Doyle's Sherlock Holmes, who prides himself on his method of deduction. The purposeful division of each room—"I took a chalk line and a yardstick, and divided the floor into square yards, and every one of these squares I examined on my hands and knees" (391)—provides the geometric structure of Sarah's investigation.

The portrayal of a mathematically methodical detective by a woman writer certainly was not without precedent; Anna K. Green is considered to have written the first detective novel, *The Leavenworth Case,* in 1878. Sarah's rational focus and reliance on algebraic and geometric principles clearly take precedence over any expected feminine intuition. Yet despite Sarah's use of the orthodox detecting strategies of reason and logic, she is unable to understand the significance of the objects she finds. On her first day of investigation, she admits she has found "literally nothing," even though she has noticed three inches of blue sewing silk and "five inches of brown woollen thread—evidently a ravelling of some dress material" that will play a vital role in solving the mystery. Unable to extrapolate their meaning, Sarah dismisses them as "only possible clues . . . and they are hardly possible" (391).

Sarah's extraordinarily well-reasoned and successful search continues; she uncovers "two bloody footprints on the carpet which no one had noticed before" (391), blood stains on the door, a "black enamelled metal trousers-button" (392) from a pair of men's pants, and the secret hiding place of a never-worn wedding ring with two dates, one in August forty years ago and the other in August of the present year (394). She is, however, unable to do anything with these clues except collect them in "a white pasteboard box," which she labels "clues" (392). Nor is Sarah able to imagine what sort of follow-up to do. When she realizes the wedding ring could not have been her mother's because it had been buried with her, Sarah wonders, "'What does it mean?'" but then she stops her inquiry and decides, "'This can hardly be a clue; this can hardly lead to the discovery of a motive, but I will put it in the box with the rest'" (394).

Given Sarah's decidedly limited knowledge and imagination, solving the mystery requires the use of another detective, one who is able to look at Sarah's box of "clues," what J. Bradley Shaw aptly concludes is "domestic" evidence (226), and piece together a coherent and correct narrative. Like the more famous fictional detectives that preceded him, he is necessarily a city dweller and a sleuth of upper-class origins so that he will be recognized as intellectually superior to his country "cousins." In "The Long Arm," his name is Francis Dix from Boston, a first cousin of Henry Ellis. Dix has been "remarkably successful in several cases," Sarah remarks, but his masculine vitality is suspect: "his health is not good" because "the work is a severe strain upon his nerves" (390). He is "thin and cleanly shaved, with a clerical air" and comes not only to help Sarah but also to sell a *Biblical Cyclopaedia* (394).

Dix's remarkable acuity in discerning the importance of colored threads and making sense out of Sarah's box of clues is surpassed only by his total lack of overt masculinity. His weak nerves and stature suggest effeminacy, and he hunts for no more clues, relying instead on those Sarah has already found. But his outsider status and his secondary goal of selling *Biblical Cyclopaedias* exonerate his gender transgression. Dix's status as outsider, an inhabitant of the large city of Boston, suggests that he is operating according to a different set of masculine ideals. Moreover, he will return to Boston once the mystery is solved, thereby not permanently altering the rigidly traditional structures that govern the town. He is not a physical laborer like the farmers of Sarah's town; instead, he relies on his intellect. His serious attention to religious matters suggests that he focuses less on the flesh and more on otherworldly interests, which would allow his nontraditional sex-gender pairing to carry less importance than the more earthly Phoebe Dole's. Finally, Dix's ability to escape censure for his feminine side may simply be a societal bias that Freeman's text reflected—masculine women were far more threatening than feminized men.

Together, these two detectives appear to form a perfect match—physical and mental, concrete and abstract, logical and intuitive—thereby maintaining the genre's tradition of "doubling." Moreover, the reversal of roles would seem to suggest that Freeman is boldly envisioning a less rigidly traditional sex-gender system, particularly since up until this point in the story, the relationship between Phoebe Dole and Maria Woods has implications of only inequality, not abnormality. Dix examines Sarah's clues and then puts them in their larger context; the enamelled button, for example, causes him to examine Martin Fairbanks's wardrobe. When Dix finds no buttons missing from Fairbanks's clothes, he prods for information about what Fairbanks wore to protect his good shirt and trousers. It is only at this question that Sarah remembers the overalls that he wore and cannot now be found. Dix, seemingly guided by an extraordinary sense of direction, walks to the dry and boarded-up well and retrieves the overalls that Phoebe had used to cover herself during the murder—a temporary, although complete masking of Phoebe's female sex with masculine accoutrements. He is even able to discern "how the murderer went in and out and yet keep the doors locked" (397) when he notices a cat door that leads from the outside into the kitchen. He gives Sarah two tasks: first "'Find all your father's old letters, and read them,'" and second, "'Find a man or woman in this town whose arm is six inches longer than yours'" (398).

Sarah does discover the remarkable, yet heretofore unnoticed fact that "Phoebe Dole's arm is fully seven inches longer than mine." This disproportionately long arm, according to Dix's explanation, allowed Phoebe to reach her hand from the outside through the cat door and into the kitchen and re-fasten the door lock as she made her escape after committing the murder, thereby completing the closed-room mystery. In fact, Sarah relates, "'I never noticed it before, but she has an almost abnormally long arm'" (399). It is only a matter of a few more pieces of evidence before Francis Dix is convinced the murder was committed by Phoebe Dole, although Sarah considers his suggestion "'an absurd possibility'" (400). Curiously, her reasons for disbelieving Dix challenge traditional notions of sex and gender behavior. After Dix suggests the murderer is Phoebe, Sarah replies, "'It is impossible!'" When pressed to explain her reason, she says because "'she is a woman'" (401), and even though Dix remarks that "'crime has no sex,'" Sarah remains not wholly convinced until Phoebe, "advancing with rapid strides like a man" (402)—it already has been determined that the two bloody footprints left on the carpet were "widely spread," even to the point of being "wider than [Sarah's] father's shoes" (391)—walks into Sarah's house and confesses. Interestingly, the *New York Times* made a similar pronouncement when it decided that Alice Mitchell's murder of Freda Ward was "the most shocking and malignant ever perpetrated by a woman" ("Mitchell Murder Case" 9), suggesting, as does the fictional Sarah Fairbanks, the incongruency of women and murder. "'I did it!'" Phoebe cries out to Sarah. "'I am found out, and I have made up my mind to confess. She was going to marry your father—I found it out. I stopped it once before. This time I knew I couldn't unless I killed him. She's lived with me in that house for over forty years. There are other ties as strong as the marriage one, that are just as sacred. What right had he to take her away from me and break up my home?'" (402)

The fictional murder of Martin Fairbanks takes on significance far different from the real-life murder of Freda Ward by Alice Mitchell. In the Tennessee murder case, there was no suggestion of a male love interest for Freda Ward—Alice killed Freda because she had been forbidden to see her anymore. Freeman's story takes this conclusion one step further. As Maria Woods sobbingly explains "the story of her long subordination to Phoebe Dole," she confesses that she had, before Martin Fairbanks's original marriage proposal forty years ago, "promised Phoebe she would not marry; and it was Phoebe who, by representing to her that she was bound by this solemn promise, had led her to write a letter to [Martin] declining his offer, and sending back the ring" (401). Unlike the Mitchell case, however, where the woman who broke her vow to Alice Mitchell became the murder victim, "The Long Arm" provides a different ending. Martin Fairbanks is murdered to remove the heterosexual love interest from the story, a move that seemingly signals Freeman's desire to maintain the same-sex suggestion. Perhaps she also intended to criticize the patriarchal heterosexual system that refused to value the integrity of these women's emotions and to hint at the validity of a same-sex relationship whose "tie" is just as "strong as the marriage one."

Yet this reading would sympathize with Phoebe Dole; clearly the story suggests that she is a monstrous character who did not conform to the ideals of femininity, including heterosexuality. That the suggestion of sexual abnormality in this story, written in 1895, came during strong scientific and social reaction against the masculine woman and her supposed "inversion" is seemingly more than coincidental; to be a masculine woman in 1895 clearly was not desirable. When Freeman's suggested benign female friendships are read within the sexological context in which they existed, the so-called dominant woman, Phoebe Dole, rivals one of Ellis's "active inverts," while the childlike Maria Woods suggests one of Ellis's "passive inverts," whose sexual soul is still salvageable since she, in the words of Ellis, only "preferred" her own sex to men. In Maria's case, there is even the possibility of mental and physical confinement in the same-sex coupling. It is Maria Woods, finally, who holds the key to the solution of the mystery. "'What was Phoebe Dole doing in your back-yard'" the night Martin Fairbanks was murdered, she asks Sarah. "'I saw Phoebe come out of your back shed-door at one o'clock that very night. She had a bundle in her arms. She went along the path about as far as the old well, then she stooped down, and seemed to be working at something. When she got up she didn't have the bundle'" (402). Not only is Maria's testimony the final piece of evidence needed to convince Dix and Sarah of Phoebe's guilt, but also it dismantles the women's suggested relationship from within, inversion turned against itself.

J. Bradley Shaw dismisses "Sarah's detective abilities, its happy resolution, and promise of marriage" (234) as "simply reactionary and conservative insofar as it clears the name of a 'normal' heterosexual young woman and finds the true culprit emerging from the dark side of female friendship." Shaw instead focuses on how "the story empowers its women through its creation of feminine terror" (231), a deliberate invocation of the gothic that "allows a woman writer to overleap gender prescriptions without losing her feminine innocence" (236). Yet he also admits that the relationship between Phoebe and Maria, when "viewed through the lens of the gothic," appears "aberrational and Phoebe's domination over the 'sweet child-like' Maria seems morbid" (229). Freeman's deliberate emphasis on the masculine qualities of Phoebe Dole, as well as her presentation of Phoebe as a "masculine woman," clearly conforms to and confirms the sexological theories of the day that attributed active "inversion" to masculinely gendered women, inside or outside a gothic framework. Sarah Fairbanks is unable to speculate beyond rationally meticulous analysis and is therefore ultimately unable to solve her father's murder. The condemnation of her masculine method—an inability to exercise feminine intuition and reliance on logical investigation—when coupled with Phoebe Dole's clear expression of masculinity becomes strikingly apparent. Clearly women who display masculine attributes are not successful, either in crime solving or love, until, as is the case with Sarah, she abandons her masculine pursuits and returns to her role as grieving daughter and fiancée. This resolution also challenges the notion that masculinely gendered women are women at all, proving Sarah Fairbanks's assertion that since such a crime could not have been committed by a woman, Phoebe Dole must certainly be something other than a woman. Even Maria Woods, Phoebe's companion of forty years, remarks that she is now afraid of Phoebe: "'She's been dreadful strange lately'" (402). Finally, Phoebe's abnormally long arm reflects her psycho-sexual abnormality, making it clear that she is indicted because she is "abnormal."[9] By endowing the murderous lover with a long arm, Freeman synechdochally insinuates the unnaturalness of her attraction.

Success for a detective often depends on the ability to "see" through the accepted conventions and expectations to the truth that lies below. Freeman allows her detective the same ability, yet Francis Dix's vision not only reveals the real murderer of Martin Fairbanks but also offers a stern indictment of female inversion. What other characters have simply accepted at face value in the story—the forty-year relationship between Phoebe and Maria—and have understood to be a "female friendship" is, as the story progresses, discovered to be an unequal power struggle between the dominant and the dominated. It is as if the conventions of the normality of female friendships become at this time "abnormal," the truth the detective finally uncovers. Since detectives are able to "see" through the accepted conventions of "female friendships" and uncover the perversions that really do exist, no wonder Francis Dix, the self-proclaimed detective in the story, is the one to discover the terrible act Phoebe has committed and the terrible reason, the "sacred" tie between "female inverts," that motivated her. As a final indictment, the condemnation of "female inversion" is replaced by the triumph of the established social order, heterosexual love. Sarah's fiancé, Henry Ellis, returns to claim her, and she "'suppose[s] we shall be happy after all'" (404), particularly since her father had a much larger estate than she had realized. One month later, the story concludes with a report that Phoebe Dole has died in prison—the actively inverted element has been not just discovered, contained, and convicted but also completely eradicated.

Freeman's initial publication of this story in the popular press supports Duggan's contention about the portrayal of women's same-sex relationships in newspaper stories of the 1890s. "When successful partnerships between women were mentioned in the news columns, they almost always appeared in desexualized forms only. The suggestion of sexuality, however subtle or implicit, was generally paired with bloodletting" (808). That Freeman should choose to depart from her own plot structure and the real-life Alice Mitchell sensation and to encapsulate these changes in the popular genre of detective fiction suggests that "The Long Arm" is more sinister than a generic deviation.

By positioning "The Long Arm" at the intersection of detective fiction, the popular press, and sexological theory about female inversion, Freeman employs scientific evidence to prove the unnaturalness of Phoebe's attraction. Physically and sexually, Phoebe is "abnormal," a premise supported by unimpeachable scientific rationalism. This critical verdict—that Phoebe Dole's masculine behavior and sexual feelings were transgressive acts and that the relationship she shared with Maria Woods was dangerously impossible—documents same-sex sexuality as aberrant and detectives, like sexologists, as rationally able to recognize socially unacceptable and criminal behavior.

The popularizing of aberrant sexual behavior lent its own momentum to the disenfranchisement of the masculine woman and her sexual inversion. With newspaper accounts of Blanche and Belle, Delia Perkins and Ida Preston, Alice Mitchell and Freda Ward, the practice of same-sex sexuality was confirmed; the graphic detail of their love and verbatim transcription of their professed commitment certainly provided salacious opportunity for newspapers to attract readers. Yet these accounts also functioned as a kind of public service announcement about the perverseness of such women. To promote the community's good, both journalistic and fictional social commentary rendered independent women as masculine and dangerous criminals and enacted a solution to their gender and sexual inversion. Declaring them aberrant proved to be the salvation of the public, and condemning them to a life of criminality and insanity, and in Phoebe Dole's case, a swift and unforgiving death, utterly dismissed this "sad form of degeneracy" from a viable position in American society.

Notes

A portion of this chapter previously appeared in "Detecting Deviation in Mary E. Wilkins Freeman's 'The Long Arm,'" *American Literary Realism* 31 (Fall 1998): 75–91.

1. The push at the end of the nineteenth century to classify, categorize, taxonomize, and, in short, precisely order—in ascending evolutionary order—virtually everything in the world can be seen in the sexologists' careful delineation of sexual behaviors. "Now specific sexual acts, fantasies, fetishes, sensations, became the subject of taxonomical scrutiny," Smith-Rosenberg observes, with the aim of asserting order in a changing world (267). Mike Hawkins, in *Social Darwinism in European and American Thought, 1860–1945,* offers a detailed overview on the interaction between Darwinism and the sexual difference between men and women. He then argues that three women, Eliza Burt Gamble, Charlotte Perkins Gilman, and Ellen Key, appropriated the tenets of social Darwinism to support their feminist agenda.

2. On July 6, 1889, the *Denver Times,* in an article entitled "Lovelorn Girls," identified the two women as Miss Clara Dietrich, a postmistress and general storekeeper at Emma, and Miss Ora Chatfield, both nieces of the Honorable I. W. Chatfield (6).

3. For more in-depth studies of the Lizzie Borden case, see Porter; and Rappaport. For an examination of the press reports of the Alice Mitchell case and similar same-sex murder cases, see Duggan.

4. The *New York Times* never did provide an account of the criminal proceedings against Lizzie Johnson, if indeed she ever did stand trial for the murder.

5. Shaw reads "The Long Arm" entirely within the context of the Lizzie Borden story and the gothic ethos he surmises it reflected. My emphasis on "female inversion," however, ties Freeman's text more closely to the Alice Mitchell murder case, where same-sex attraction was the salacious focus and ultimately the damnable offense.

6. Most critics begin the chronology of detective fiction with Edgar Allan Poe's publication of "The Murders in the Rue Morgue" in 1841.

7. Arthur Conan Doyle introduced Sherlock Holmes to the world with the publication of *A Study in Scarlet* in 1887.

8. "The Long Arm" was written in uncharacteristic collaboration with the *Boston Evening Transcript* columnist J. Edgar Chamberlin. J. Bradley Shaw reports that "Chamberlin modestly recalled that his revisions to [Freeman's] draft consisted only of the 'technical work of fitting it for the Bacheller Syndicate requirement.'" Even though the $2,000 prize was split equally, Shaw concludes that Chamberlin's "exact contributions to the story's final text are not recoverable, and his name has never appeared as coauthor in any of the story's publications" (213–14). Because of the paucity of evidence suggesting a detailed collaboration, I refer to "The Long Arm" as Freeman's text, with a caveat that further scholarship may reveal that Chamberlin's influence on the story is greater than currently known.

9. Phoebe Dole's abnormally long arm also conjures up images of Poe's accidentally murderous orangutan in "The Murders in the Rue Morgue" and perhaps also suggests Darwinian evolutionary rhetoric that posited humans were more civilized than their beastly and less advanced ancestors.

4

Enticing Acts

The Sexuality of Seduction

> There was something back of her desire for a man. She wanted
> something more than caresses. There was a creative impulse in her
> that could not function until she had been made love to by a man.
> —Sherwood Anderson, *Poor White*, 1920

In the years surrounding the ratification of the Nineteenth Amendment, the perceived threat independent women embodied drew fearful social criticism that simultaneously venerated the feminine ideal of the nineteenth century and reduced the image of the masculine woman to a dangerous entity. Authors, both male and female, recognized this masculinization of modern woman and the potential damage to the male homosocial, heterosexual society. In numerous fictional accounts, the rapidly changing woman was no longer submissive to domesticity and male authority; she supported herself financially, often working in occupations traditionally considered masculine. Authors spoke of women who were not only ignoring feminine virtues and traditional domestic duties but also losing femininity completely and becoming what some writers referred to as "odd women," "spinsters," or "unsexed Amazons." It is precisely these women who acted masculine, who expressed independence both economically and emotionally, and who socially and fictionally elicited nervous concern. Ultimately, they received the most strenuous literary efforts to return them to femininity and heterosexuality.

Increasingly, the popular press rhetoric reflected and constructed the ideal woman, strongly emphasizing her "core feminine identity" and vehemently praising her similarities to a "womanly woman." Those women who failed to achieve traditional femininity and, more specifically, those women who clearly showed signs of masculine womanhood and sexual inversion were subjected to a fate that removed the stigma of their gender and sexuality anomalies by first demasculinizing them and then seducing them with heterosexuality. This feminization and seduction removed the threat of the masculine woman from the fictional space and returned her femininity and heterosexuality that was thought to have been abandoned by suffragist women, whose desire for political autonomy was read not only as a desire for independence from men but also as an abandonment of heterosexual union. The cartoonist Lester's April 1913 *Life* magazine cartoon, "Past, Present, and Future," visually exemplifies this philosophy (see figure 9). Spanning the rather narrow range from Eve to an angel, these images of woman are not masculinized but epitomize the "true woman." That *Life*, in 1913, felt the need to reemphasize the ideal qualities of womanhood is further indication that certain women's feminine identity was suspect. Given the close connection between gender and sexuality that sexologists posited, rewriting this "core of feminine identity" was necessarily an attempt by authors to make the masculine woman not only feminine but also heterosexual, to right her sexual inversion by writing her into a heterosexual seduction plot.

In the popular press, poetry, in particular, seemed to be the literary form of

PAST, PRESENT AND FUTURE

Figure 9. Cartoon by Lester in *Life*, April 17, 1913, 771.

choice to articulate criticism of American society. Many of these poets' plaints reflected the complexity of the times, which included a focus on the young modern woman as subject. Some cut deep with sarcasm and wit; others longed for a simpler time when a woman did not present the difficulty of definition that she did in the early twentieth century. In this poetry, the absence of the masculine woman as subject is strikingly apparent because so much of the poetry is bound by constructions of heterosexual love or of sharply delineated subject matters for men and women.

The content of this popularly published poetry in the early twentieth century reflects the conservatism that gripped society as the woman suffrage movement gained momentum and obtained the Nineteenth Amendment. What occurred was a backlash of sorts, intended to mitigate some of the perceived threats that the woman suffrage movement produced; it was a deliberate action calculated to keep men from totally rejecting independent women. More to the point was a move toward the ideal woman that began in the nineteenth century and progressed through the early decades of the twentieth century to counter a fear of rejection, a lack of focus, or, a view expressed by many older feminists, the bad name younger women, in their scanty dress and bobbed hair, were giving to all women.

The contemporary woman was, according to "The Girl of To-Day," a *Harper's Magazine* poem of April 1922 written by the humorist Carolyn Wells, neither a "lady" nor a "woman" but merely a "girl" or, worse, a "maid of impertinent manners" and a "Damsel of insolent mien." Her qualities, "full of astounding vagaries," were seen solely in the appearance she had adopted. Her apparel, with "nothing much of a bodice" and "less of a skirt," barely conceals and "half discloses" her body. Her hair, "bobbed off like a Fiji," is covered by a hat that "entirely eclip[ses] one eye" and completely negates her ears. The "crudest vermilion" colors her lips, while her "cheeks have a cochineal tint" that is "more Indianlike than civilian." Finally, her "nose is a powdered marshmallow," and her chin is "like a round lump of tallow." Ceasing even to be an entire body, the "girl of today" is simply a collection of decorated and absurd-sounding parts, disembodied and dismembered, and unrecognizable as human (685–86).

But lest the reader think the narrator is, as she says, a "rabid exhorter," the final stanza suggests the narrator's maternal interest in the girl's reputation should such costume become even more extreme:

I hate to contemplate, my dear,
If your skirts *should* get very much shorter—

Or your stockings a trifle more sheer;
If you paint your face any more thickly,
Or don a more scanty array—
I pray that reform may come quickly,
Oh, Girl of To-day! (686)

But the narrator's exact fear is never disclosed should her worst scenario come to pass. What specifically is she worried about—a complete exposition of a naked female body in public? The decline in morality that would, presumably, follow should skirts shorten even more? A total loss of the feminine ideal that would implicate all women, not just the "girl of to-day"? Simply the mere possibility that femininity is not absolute?

Wells's narrator is, of course, a "rabid exhorter," no matter how carefully and lovingly she renders her criticisms. Moreover, this was not Wells's only narrative exhortation to women about how they should behave. Considered the chief woman humorist of the first two decades of the twentieth century, Wells wrote anthologies of humorous verse that were best-sellers. Her light contributions to popular periodicals were numerous, provoking her to boast in her autobiography: "If the magazines I have written for in the course of my writing career could be hung on a rack they would rival any corner newsstand of today" (quoted in Dresner 556). Prior to 1911, she published a short poem entitled "The Last Straw," as much a critique of feminism as femininity:

I don't denounce all suffragists—
Some few of them are rather nice;
But one of them declared last week
That they are "not afraid of mice"!

Shades of eternal feminine!
This is the last and hardest blow!
But let us hope there's some mistake,
Perhaps it isn't really so.

We have forgiven many things—
From night-keys to divided skirts.
They've lost their clinging-vine effects;
But this new message really hurts.

Oh, woman, if it's come to this,
That you, unmoved, a mouse may see,
Nor scream and climb up on a chair,
You've lost your femininity! (84)

Ridiculing notions that femininity could be reduced to behavior as simple as a fearful reaction to mice, Wells clearly considered such shallow definitions of *femininity* worthy social structures to be dismantled by her ironic wit. Yet to prove her point, she specifically pronounced that it was the "suffragists" who were to blame because they exhibited this unfeminine behavior. Moreover, it was not just the suffragists' actions in the presence of mice that caused Wells to question their femininity. Even though "we have forgiven many things," the mere mention of "night-keys," "divided skirts," and independence signaled that these behaviors contributed to the suffragists' questionable femininity. Although Wells did not satirically suggest the suffragists were "masculine," she clearly used her parodic poem to denounce the confusion of traditional sex and gender roles.

Wells was not alone in her "rabid" interest in women's roles. In 1926, *Vanity Fair* published the comments of well-known men who were asked to list the attributes of "The Ideal Woman." Excluding the humorist Ring Lardner, whose ideal woman had everything from lockjaw to hereditary obesity and fallen arches, the men replied fairly uniformly, highlighting beauty, modesty, submissiveness, and charm—in short, the very virtues that the nineteenth-century "cult of true womanhood" espoused. Rudolph Valentino listed "fidelity" and "beauty" among his ten attributes; Florenz Ziegfeld offered ideal physical proportions—5 feet, 5 1/2 inches tall, 117 pounds, and a size 5 foot—as well as the requirements of "femininity, an overworked term," he admitted, "but indicative of loveliness, grace and imagination" ("Ideal Woman" 53). Cartoonist Rube Goldberg's irony could not cover the decidedly antisuffragist sentiment that "the perfect woman cannot be a leader. If a woman is strong she will want to inaugurate some movement or other—a movement, for example, to make hens lay square eggs" ("Ideal Woman" 90).

Fiction published in the popular press in the 1910s also portrayed women who illustrated the cultural inseparability of gendered appearance and sexual behavior. Yet it is not Valentino's and Ziegfeld's ideal woman but the masculinized woman who appears in the short stories of the popular press. These women are not reproductive but are economically independent from men and therefore threats to the comfortable world of feminine womanhood and heterosexual society. Having staked a claim in the masculine worlds of business or education and having renounced a dependent heterosexual existence or, in some cases, embraced sexual inversion, these fictionalized masculine women drew as much fear and ire as the real-life suffragists did. This connection between a woman's masculine appearance and sexual inversion, then, was clear and required an equally decisive fictional strategy to disenfranchise her. What resulted was the seduction plot, enacted to dismiss masculine sexual expression and to affirm heterosexuality, what Terry Castle terms "fictional and ideological convention" (74). "The Beautiful House," by Catherine Wells, appearing in *Harper's Monthly Magazine* in March 1912, recounted the story of a thinly veiled same-sex relationship severed permanently by a handsome man. "The Fire," by Helen R. Hull, published in the *Century Magazine* in November 1917, suggested an attraction between a spinster artist and her younger pupil. Richard Washburn Child's story "The Feminist" was arguably the strangest of the three. Published in February 1915 in *Cosmopolitan,* the tale followed the wild-animal trainer, circus owner, and self-professed feminist Hester Golden and her "feminist" pet Diana, a thirty-two-foot-long python, into the clutches of heterosexual love (for both woman and snake) and eventual domestic bliss.

The seemingly flawless love that befalls Mary Hastings in Catherine Wells's "The Beautiful House" is as lovingly constructed and violently destructed as the country cottage that serves as a metaphor for the relationship. Mary Hastings enjoys a quiet and comfortable existence as a landscape-painter. "Spinsterhood," the narrator relates, "suited her temperament and had not faded her vitality in the slightest degree; indeed, her independence and the passage of time had marked her only with a finer gravity of bearing." Yet when she meets the younger Sylvia Brunton, the narrator relates, Mary "fell in love" with Sylvia, and "with a few meetings their mutual liking flamed to intimacy." "Between them," the narrator judges, "there was that sense of rapport, that effect of rapid mutual understanding, which finds some of the happiest exemplars among women." Finally, as the capstone to this already seemingly idyllic relationship, Mary and Sylvia discover the beautiful house of the title, "which gathered together the threads of their love, and held it as a body should its soul" (503).

Despite the focus on the women's erotically charged relationship, their love is foreordained by the house itself to be short-lived. Asked why the owner calls the house by the extraordinary name of "Love o' Women," the butler replies, "'He says it won't last long, miss'" (505). That the owner may be referring to the love of a woman for a man is really not borne out since the only expressed intimacy in the story at this time is the love between Mary and Sylvia. Thus, even though the love of the two women is apparently perfect, the authorizing male figure who literally owns the house and figuratively possesses the women's relationship declares that it will not be permitted to exist indefinitely. Like the house that will be irretrievably lost in fire, the love between women will be destroyed.

The physical cause of the disruption between the women is the handsome Evan Hardie, Sylvia's distant relative with whom she had spent time. Sylvia's incessant and ebullient talk of Evan makes Mary jealous; when Sylvia announces that Evan will come to the house, Mary "had a sudden spasm of astonishment at the idea of showing it to anyone" (507). Once Evan is introduced, the relationship between Mary and Sylvia begins to disintegrate, and female homosocial and homosexual bonds are displaced by the socially acceptable heterosocial and heterosexual bonds. In fact, Evan assumes the position that Sylvia had reserved for Mary and their relationship; the metaphor of the "beautiful" house is replaced by the reality of Evan, whom Sylvia calls a "beautiful, beautiful thing," full of "'all light and color and movement'" (509).

Hearing this pronouncement, Mary understands that "something far stronger than she had claimed her beloved for its own." That night, Mary has a dream indicting Evan as the "little elfish creature" that is tearing the house apart brick by brick. In her dream, Mary "saw one impish form low down on the wall stripping off the ivy with peculiar zest; one after another the long, wavering strands fell back limply with their pale, flattened rootlets stretching out like helpless human things in pain. She ran forward and seized the little wretch by the arm. He turned his face toward her, and it was Evan Hardie's face, twisted into an expression of diabolical malice. He clawed viciously at the hand that held him, and stung by the pain of it she saw a long scarlet scratch start out upon her wrist" (509). That Evan should be destroying the house so beloved by both women renders the verdict on same-sex relationships, particularly when confronted with the socially accepted heterosexual coupling. The house is easily dismantled; the ivy, and by association the naive love of the women, cannot defend its weak "rootlets" against the force of heterosexuality. Initially, the "Love o' Women" can be enjoyed for only a small sum. Now, the love between two women fulfills that economic predictor. The house is easy to dismantle, because, despite its beauty, it is poorly constructed. Its beauty is only superficial, easily spurned and destroyed by the more appropriate male and heterosexual hands doing the destruction.

The house, fictionally and metaphorically, is completely and inevitably consumed by fire shortly after Evan's introduction. Mary watches the blaze from her bedroom window, awakened by her horrible dream. Their trek to the ruins that day, at Sylvia's insistence, provides closure but an even sterner indictment than Mary had anticipated. With Sylvia's announcement that she is going to marry soon and that "'we shouldn't have come here again so very much'" anyway, the words "fell between her and Mary's heart-aching with the steely separation of a guillotine." But the end of the relationship, manifested by the total destruction of the house, is not the only affirmation of the success of the heterosexual seduction. Up in the glade, watching the women as he sits astride a chestnut horse, is Evan Hardie, "conquerent, triumphant," who "looked to be a robuster, pagan Saint George, whose coat of mail was all of woven sunshine" (511).

Evan serves the same purpose that Saint George did when he slew the dragon and saved England. He overcomes the dangerous creature who threatened social order, and in so doing, he reaffirms heterosexual society. Catherine Wells's story utterly indicts the woman who dared to express masculine object choice and same-sex intimacy. The spinster Mary's love for the younger and passive Sylvia ultimately is replaced by a love that is most importantly heterosexual. Even Mary, spinster guardian of the "beautiful" possibility of same-sex relations, is forced to admit through tears, as she stares at Sylvia and Evan and the burned-down house, "how glad she was, how very glad" (511).

Helen R. Hull's fictional Miss Egert in "The Fire" exhibits a reaction similar to Mary's when her younger love is heterosexually seduced, a scene familiar to Hull, perhaps, since she may have been privy to any number of same-sex "crushes" during her long career as an English professor. "The Fire" is one of sixty stories (in addition to twenty-two novels) Hull published while she fulfilled her academic duties, first at Wellesley and Barnard and then at Columbia, from 1917 to 1958.[1] Hull's primary fictional interest was to explore marriage and family life in America, which included serious studies of "female friendships," such as are detailed in her novels *Quest* (1922) and *Labyrinth* (1923).

Miss Egert, like Mary Hastings in "The Beautiful House," is characterized as a "spinster" or "old maid," terms Christine Bolt explains as "sexualized." Sexologists, Bolt notes, "were sympathetic to male homosexuality as a 'congenital inversion,'" but "the female variety was frequently regarded as a 'pseudo,' 'artificial or substitute' inversion, resulting from the repression of sexuality enjoined particularly upon women. The consequences of such reasoning . . . was the sexualisation of spinsterhood and the stigmatising of lesbianism" (230–31). The younger Cynthia, like Sylvia, is passive and not marked by the label of "spinster." Havelock Ellis, a contemporary of both Wells and Hull, might have posited that several of the conventional traits of the female invert as seducer—an older woman seduces a more inexperienced or naive younger woman, who may be disappointed in love or living alone—are present (Seidel 211). For Ellis, the older woman "would seem to be ripe for inversion," according to Kathryn Lee Seidel (211). But more than spinsterhood signals such "female inversion" in Mary Hastings and Miss Egert.

In an article exploring the lesbian possibility in Kate Chopin's fin de siècle text, *The Awakening*, Seidel posits that critics "have noted Mademoiselle [Reisz's] close relationship with Edna [Pontellier]" and "commented on her appearance," "her role as an artist," and her "attraction to Edna." But, Seidel notes, these same critics "have stopped short of considering the source of that attraction" (199). Mademoiselle Reisz is "not only an eccentric spinster" and "not merely an isolated artist"; she embodies "the traits of the female artist as lesbian" (Seidel 200), a connection Havelock Ellis suggested in his case study of "Miss B."[2] Chopin's ability to portray Reisz as a lesbian and to suggest lesbian overtones in the relationship between Mademoiselle Reisz and Edna Pontellier is a result of the late-nineteenth-century understanding that homosexuality was a curiosity associated with artistic creativity (Seidel 202), evidenced by the infamous trial of Oscar Wilde that permitted public exposure to Wilde's unique views about art. According to Richard Ellmann, Wilde believed that art was by its nature the destroyer of convention and that the life of the artist need not include such categories as moral or immoral (322). This late-nineteenth-century association of homosexuality with the artistic profession is apparent in the spinster painters Mary Hastings and Miss Egert of 1910s popular press fiction.

In "The Fire," Cynthia's mother has forbidden Cynthia to visit Miss Egert. Faced with the realization that she cannot visit Miss Egert again, "could never go hurrying down to the cluttered room they called the studio for more of those strange hours of eagerness and pain when she bent over the drawing-board, struggling with the mysteries of color" (106), Cynthia retrieves her paintings from the workroom and tells Miss Egert that she cannot come anymore. In so doing, Cynthia manages to "tell, but not quite tell," the real reason for her mother's stern warning:

> "Mother thinks"—She fell into silence. She couldn't say what her mother thought—dreadful things. If she could only swallow the hot pressure in her throat!
> "Oh. I hadn't understood." Miss Egert's fingers paused for a swift touch on Cynthia's arm, and then reached for the candle. "You can go on working by yourself."
> "It isn't that—" Cynthia struggled an instant, and dropped into silence again. She couldn't say out loud any of the things she was feeling. There were too many walls between feeling and speech: loyalty to her mother, embarrassment that feelings should come so near words, a fear of hurting Miss Egert. (109)

Miss Egert seems to understand completely the unspoken reasons and makes no effort to repudiate the charges that have been silently leveled against her. The ability of both women to know the precise act to which Cynthia's mother was referring is not only a ploy Hull uses to introduce same-sex intimacy without directly articulating it but also a careful attempt to deny its identity.

As a result, their relationship is, in Castle's words, "oblique" and "not-yet real" (90–91), yet another way of characterizing "the love that dare not speak its name." Instead, Miss Egert invites Cynthia to her garden bonfire, which not only serves the similar destructive function fire did in "The Beautiful House" but also seems to be a beacon for Cynthia's mother, who finds the two painters holding hands and watching the shadows cast on the garden's wall.

As Cynthia watches the blaze, "excitement tingled through her; she felt the red and yellow flames seizing her, burning out the heavy rebellion, the choking weight." For Cynthia, the destructive element of fire also cleanses, not only ridding her of the thick veils of confusion but also inspiring her to actively seek what she yearned to know. But for Miss Egert, the fire can only illuminate what she cannot possess. Cynthia demands that Miss Egert paint the dancing apple tree, but the woman cannot. "'It's too late. . . . I must be content to see it,'" Miss Egert wistfully admits, adding, "'Perhaps some day you'll paint it—or write it'" (110). With the mother's decree, time literally has run out for painting lessons and metaphorically for the intimate relationship the two artists enjoyed. Moreover, Miss Egert's age leaves her little time to acquire another. It is left to Cynthia not only to capture the apple tree but also to sustain the greater idea of intimate relationships between women.

Despite being forced away from the garden by her angry mother, Cynthia is poised at the end of the story to do precisely that. Her rebellion returns as a "swift, tearing current" that "swept away her unhappiness, her confused misery." She saw, "with a fierce, young finality that she was pledged to a conflict as well as to a search. As she knelt by the window and pressed her cheek on the cool glass, she felt the house about her, with its pressure of useful, homely things, as a very prison. No more journeyings down to Miss Egert's for glimpses of escape. She must find her own ways. Keep searching! At the phrase, excitement again glowed within her; she saw the last red wink of the fire in the garden" (114). When the story ends, Cynthia is trapped by her mother in the house, the sphere reserved for women, reduced only to plotting her escape and imagining freedom while still confined in her domestic prison. Even more important, the same-sex intimacy she once enjoyed has been severed, its obliqueness obliterated by the more forceful voice of a threatened heterosexuality.

Mrs. Bates returns Cynthia to the hierarchy of the heterosexual status quo. Cynthia's zeal for the ideas of Miss Egert may be similarly short-lived, for her excitement glows just as she sees the bonfire she had shared with Miss Egert extinguish itself with "the last red wink of the fire in the garden." The story's conclusion may signal that Cynthia's searching, radical self can exist even in the feminine domesticity to which she is returned. However, it also challenges the notion that her commitment can exist beyond the moment, now that the source of her excitement, symbolized by the bonfire, has been extinguished. All that is left at the end of Hull's story is a pile of ashes that had once been same-sex intimacy; Cynthia, hidden in the heterosexual prison, is unable to rekindle the fire. Although she resolves to "keep searching" for her own happiness, the energy for such a task is consumed by the ebbing flames, and the reintroduction of her "awkwardness" and her "self-consciousness" is a very real possibility, particularly given her self-professed inability to see beauty without Miss Egert and especially the domestic heterosexual confinement in which she now must exist.

So it is with Mary Hastings in Catherine Wells's story, once the beautiful house and Sylvia are lost. She presumably returns to her artist's cottage and spinster's prisonlike existence, painting her landscapes and living on memories. The message is clear: women who express masculine prerogatives, including attraction to a female, are exhibiting only a finite and flawed phase of development. For a while, such alternative sexuality is allowed to exist, and women are even permitted to act on their feelings for another woman. But when inevitably confronted with the overpowering and socially sanctioned heterosexuality, their relationships cannot endure. Even more telling, in these stories, it is the younger woman, whom Havelock Ellis would have termed "heterosexual" because of her passive receptivity to an aggressive "female invert," who has been seduced by heterosexuality. The spinsters, Mary and Miss Egert, Ellis's "homosexuals," are left unloved and deeply hurt, unwanted and perhaps even unavailable to heterosexual society. The seduction is complete: masculine womanhood and female inversion have been overwhelmed by femininity and heterosexuality.

The seductions in the first two stories are tame compared with those in Richard Washburn Child's "Feminist." In this third story, written before the ratification of the Nineteenth Amendment and the only one of the three written by a man, feminism and implied inversion are forcibly dismantled and the woman stripped of independence. Hester Golden, a self-professed feminist, and her "feminist" snake, Diana, both ultimately endure the same fate, namely, true love with a male mate and subsequent submission to the heterosexual status quo. Billed as an "unusual story" with that "rare quality of being 'different,'" Child's "Feminist" appeared in *Cosmopolitan* in February 1915.[3] The editor's prologue offered the reader an interpretive challenge:

You will ask yourself whether Hester Golden is not going a little too far in her conception of feminism, or whether, quite deceived as to the real character of her ophidian friend, she is not entirely on the wrong track. A woman stand alone, indeed! Can she attain the highest freedom by rejecting all dependence on, or cooperation with, the opposite sex? Certainly, Man has never made any such assertion about "masculinism." And do you think the conduct of Diana really changed Hester's convictions about womankind? No matter what conclusion you come to, you are going to be mightily entertained throughout the whole of this absorbing narrative. (227)

But entertainment was surely not the sole purpose of "The Feminist," nor was it to be "no matter what conclusion" the reader reached. Child's message for women who considered themselves feminists and thereby challenged their preordained feminine role and the heterosexual tradition was explicit: an independent woman, or snake for that matter, is never truly satisfied until safely confined as the mate of a male.

The story begins off the coast of Sumatra, where a Chinese man, Yee Su, hires a native from the island of Ooala to catch the enormous snake that has been stealing goats from his plantation at every third full moon. A month later, the captor receives a full bag of strange coins from the mate of an English ship bound for Singapore in exchange for the snake, whom he has named Diana. The capture and description of Diana are filled with contradictions. The snake is both a "devil" and the "queen of the Greeks." Her enormous size and aggressiveness disguise, at least for a time to the captain, her sex. She is named after the goddess of the moon and a figure who was both virgin and mother, the epitome of the unattainable ideal that women were supposed to emulate. Most important, she is captured through the primal urge of hunger in a "mysterious, godless jungle" (227), far removed from civilization. Such a setting implicitly juxtaposes the naturalness of her existence against the "unnatural" world to which she is transported and which transforms her into a captive beast.

She is sold, most appropriately, to a wild animal show and transported to the United States, which, according to the narrator, relies on "romance and drama . . . imported from every corner of the earth, duty free" (228). Exhibited in Golden's Wild-Animal Show, Diana is owned by Hester Golden, the owner, manager, buyer, and seller of the show, even though the show's legal registration belongs to the fictitious "Ed Golden." Unlike the other animals Hester acquires for a season's worth of shows and then sells, Diana has been kept because, as Hester says, "'nobody can handle Diana but me.' "'I've had men work for me trying to handle her,'" Hester explains, "'But she gets the notion they aren't right. Perhaps she don't like the way they look at me. Then she'll wait her chance to take a turn around 'em. Did you ever see a snake like her wrap herself on a man? It's—it's—oh, I never can get used to it!'" (230).

But Hester's fascinated dismay at Diana's exhibition of power over men and the reason she gives for Diana's squeeze—"'Perhaps she don't like the way [the men] look at me'"—unite Hester and Diana in a relationship that is more intimate than simply trainer and beast. When the alcoholic protagonist and ultimate hero of the story, Jack De Neill, follows two men struggling with a red box labeled "Diana, the Largest ————Alive," his curiosity overcomes him, and he walks right into the apartment of the woman who has opened the box and is stroking whatever is in it. Jack's initial focus, however, is on the woman. "Before all other physical attributes, her wonderful health clamored for notice," the narrator notes, adding:

> She had been tanned by sun and wind; she was the color of a gipsy; even her brown hair had been touched on every strand by sunlight which had left its glistening there. Under the thin material of a summer dress, there showed the muscles of her lean but powerful shoulders, and a fullness of chest and roundness of throat suggestive of exercise and happiness in the good, clean air of the out-of-doors. Like her figure, the bare forearms and well-shaped, slender hands were clean of line and beautifully molded. This rare, lean, graceful, strength in a woman, pleased the young derelict. (229)

Hester's beauty bears a striking resemblance to Diana's, and their mutual attractiveness and attraction suggest narcissism and the sexual inversion it implicitly embodies. Diana's body is "great" and "graceful," tanned, like Hester's, with the markings of soft reds, browns, and golden yellows. Both are dignified, with "a triumph of poise" (230), and later their eyes are described with the same jewel imagery of polished topaz or obsidian.

When Jack De Neill notices the snake, he faints, and Hester must drag him to her couch and arrange for him to rent the room next to hers. Her landlady, upon hearing Hester's wish, exclaims, "'It's irregular, Miss Golden, ain't it? What will they say? And you—who won't so much as let a man look at you, havin' that little use for 'em and bein' a—what is it?—a feminist, you was tellin' me!'" In a curious conflation of man and beast, Hester angrily replies to the landlady, "'It's what I'd do for a black leopard. . . . Call a doctor now; don't talk as if I was soft. Being a feminist doesn't mean having no heart. But I'm not soft, anyway. You know me. I'm hard. I'm as hard as nails'" (232). With this exchange, the inseparable connection between Hester and Diana is made, and the two, despite their difference in species, become lovers of a sort, each protecting the other, each giving herself to the other. But this intimacy also reduces Hester to a beast instead of elevating Diana to the level of humanity. Indeed, the negative connotation of *feminist* relegates Hester to a less than womanly position, particularly since she does not allow men to even look at her, just as the snake reacts when men allegedly look at Hester the wrong way. This intimate relationship between the woman and the female snake exists for their mutual comfort and benefit, and together they fight or frighten off the men who would come between them. But their designations as "feminists"— for "Diana is a feminist, too," according to Hester (233)—elevate their oddly figured relationship to an intimate confidence.

Even more important, what this loaded conversation establishes is an erotic relationship oddly constructed not only because one of the participants is a snake but also because the masculinely gendered Hester is the object of attraction for both Jack, who represents a heterosexual and antifeminist structure, and Diana, who represents the independent, feminist, and inverted possibility. Jack's introduction into the feminist world, however, is effected on that world's own terms. Although independently wealthy, Jack joins Hester's trip under an assumed name and for a common laborer's salary. But he also joins the voyage as a beast, having asked Hester to "train" him as she trained the wild animals. By lowering himself to the level of primitive "feminist" beast, Jack is ready to compete for Hester on equal terms with Diana. This odd structure is in place when the three set out for the Far East, far away from the "civilization" of the United States and into an arena that will allow for the resolution of the competition, the severing of the same-sex bond and the return of all three members to their traditionally appropriate, even "natural," environments.

After two days of sailing, Jack confronts Diana directly. "'She's another feminist,'" he remarks, "'And that is something new.'" Then, in an indictment of same-sex intimacy that carries the weight of the entire heterosexual society with it, he adds, "'It's against the rules.'" Intent on knowing if Diana could indeed be a feminist, with *feminist* clearly defined as a female who has no need or desire for a male's love, Jack directs the following romantic taunt to the silent red box that contains the snake: "'Sleep on, philosophizing lady with eyes of adamant! Dream of the jungle. Picture the moonlight clothing the fronds of giant ferns. Hear the night insects of the jungle, the chatter of moving creatures in high trees above that one on which you have coiled your beautiful body. Feel the warm breath of night from sun-bathed, glassy seas. And then, as you wake, think of some other great creature of the forest depths. Think of him. Listen, Diana! Thy beloved is here!'" Suddenly, Diana begins thrashing in her box, banging her head against the lid of the trunk, straining the hinges that held the box intact. Jack, awestruck by his own success, "half frightened at the result of his experiment, staring out in front of him as one who has seen visions," whispers to himself triumphantly, "'She thought it was him! . . . She thought it was him!'" Laughing derisively when Diana has calmed, Jack puts his anger into one word, uttered at the snake, and to all the women she represents. "'Feminist!'" he sneers (236).

Jack confronts his competition directly again with the taunting jibes of heterosexual attraction when, after he has returned from a night of drinking in the city of Fayal, he opens the lid of Diana's box and dares the "beautiful, cold lady" to come out. "'They say you will kill men who love your mistress,'" Jack taunts, and then he slaps the snake's face and cries "'So! You are a feminist? So!'" and whistles in Diana's face. With this, the snake launches herself and rolls her muscular body around Jack, treating him as a "plaything." His eyes throbbing with blood pressure and his heart feeling as if it had been squeezed upward, Jack feels Diana's embrace around his neck and knew, as the narrator relates, "This, at last, was Diana. He knew his own lips were as black as hers" (238). The snake is attributed knowledge of Jack's attraction to Hester, and her vengeance becomes a dire indictment of the violence that feminism and lesbianism were capable of perpetrating on the heterosexual social structure.

Hester saves Jack but then contradicts herself by resorting to her animal trainer's mentality to curb his "beastliness." As punishment for Jack's drunken behavior, Hester whips him, with the suggestively called "blacksnake," an animal trainer's device, until welts appear on his torso and arms. Despite the pain, Jack smiles. "'You are—fine animal trainer . . . you are very kind. . . . Thank you,'" he gasps. This odd scene of sadomasochism positions Jack in the role of beast in Hester's last, desperate attempt to exert her feminist philosophy. But her attempt fails, and she allows Jack to remain with her. Even her reason for saving Jack from Diana is hollow. She sneers, "'I would have saved anyone from Diana,'" yet Hester has not saved every man whom the snake deemed to be desirous of her mistress (238). Jack's physical punishment, although certainly painful, is an erotic act that showcases Hester's physical prowess but seemingly gives Jack sexual pleasure and Hester some enjoyment as well. With Diana locked away in her box, unable to defeat her competition because of Hester's intervention, the once-odd formulation of desire begins to right itself into a more acceptable and traditional conclusion as the supposedly staunch feminist Hester chooses Jack and the heterosexuality that he represents.

Once this psychological shift has been completed, the only thing left is for the same-sex relationship to be physically dissolved and the ousted Diana to be given over to heterosexuality as well. Having dropped off the cargo of wild animals, the steamer pushes on to Ooala at Hester's urging, so that Diana can be returned to the island on which she was captured. The change in the feminist Hester is profound—now she is interested in clothes made of beautiful fabrics and a bead necklace—in short, she has exchanged her feminism for the feminine, even surrendered her masculine independence and her belief that a woman can be "complete in herself" (239).

When the ship arrives at the island, Hester, Jack, and Diana go ashore to spend a few nights in the now-deserted plantation of Yee Su. Diana now "thrashed about with the evil sounds of great, soft, looping coils and hard skull knocking futilely against the wood." Returned to her original habitat as the defeated suitor, Diana again assumes her bestial nature. On the third midnight on shore, Jack awakes to find Hester's hammock empty and the air "reverberant with the sounds of the jungle" and "reverberant with something else—a stress of some kind; an unusual and restless spirit was abroad" (240). Startled by the empty box that should have contained Diana, Jack fears the worst and thinks the snake has killed Hester. Able to pick up the track of the snake, Jack follows the trail for three miles along the moonlight beach, where he finally finds Hester's sandal print. "When he arose, the girl herself was standing behind him. He stared at her with a face as white as the moonlight on the beach." "'Come with me,'" she said, breathing hard. "'Oh, you were right! Come with me!'" (241)

There in the sand, the narrator describes, Diana's "track was joined by another." Obviously humbled by the reunion, Hester surmises that it was the full moon which led Diana's mate to her. "'He has come for two nights. I found the trail. You were right,'" she says to Jack, "'it was her mate. Perhaps he has been waiting all these years—believing and waiting with all faith—and she, too. Behind her cold, yellow eyes there was. . . .'" Before she can describe the longing she envisioned in the snake's eyes, Hester is interrupted by the incredulous Jack. He confirms the double trail and follows it until it turns toward the jungle, where "the alang-grass was beaten down where their heavy bodies had gone into its depths. The trail ended among the festoons of vines and giant ferns." Jack's entry into the jungle is stopped by a "black ape" that leaps out of the vines and screams at the man. When he returns to Hester, he finds her crying softly. Cautious about his next move, Jack strokes her hair, and Hester "reached for his hand and pressed her warm, wet cheek against it." Jack, according to the narrator, "knew" that Hester's hands "had touched no other hand as they had touched his. They were moving softly, telling him of recognition of the great rules of the game over which philosophies cannot triumph or theories of selfish freedom made by either men or women prevail" (241). Completely subdued by the overwhelming natural impulse of heterosexual love, Hester, knowing her feminism is beaten, only wishes now that she "'wouldn't have to lose her freedom,'" although she cannot explain to Jack why such freedom might be stripped from her.

Thus, the great feminist snake was hiding her longing for a mate, and so, it can be inferred, was Hester. Returned to the wild, the primitive snake finds her mate and therefore acts according to the same natural heterosexual status quo that governs all the beasts, humans included. Hester is stripped of her independence and held captive by the emotional love from which she had mistakenly thought herself immune. Far from a civilization that corrupts and alters a woman's "central core of femininity" by allowing a woman a financially and socially independent life, Hester finally returns to her native state of feminine dependence and heterosexuality on the deserted jungle island.

It is women's freedom that has been deemed "selfish," for both Hester and the innocent Diana, stolen from her mate. In the final line of the story, the narrator comments, "For those who are true feminists can never understand." Yet, who is the "true feminist," particularly given the treatment of Hester's feminism and the result of the voyage? Can Hester, the "true feminist," never understand the selfish freedom she relishes and thus the life from which she purposely excludes herself? Are the true feminists some readers who can never understand Hester's submission to the heterosexual world? Or, in a more intriguing possibility, given the outcome of the story, can Jack be the "true feminist"? It is Jack, after all, who asks the final question, wondering if her independence was what caused Hester all the "fuss" (241). As a rhetorical question, the query also carries some genuine wonder, and Jack's inability to grasp Hester's dilemma, although failing to render him a "feminist" as Hester described the term may, in fact, render him a "feminist" according to the author. Instead of "feminist" denoting an independent woman, Jack's "feminism" may be an interest in the feminine, a recognition of the true male and female roles, and an assumption of man's authority and protection for the weaker sex, which he has finally, through the long voyage, realized.

The final blow to Hester's "feminism" is thus enacted by a manipulation of the term itself, rendering it powerless in the face of the "great rules of the game." Her submission is complete—not only has she turned Diana free to rejoin her mate, but she herself has embraced a man—and she can only wish now, rather than demand, that she "wouldn't have to lose [her] freedom." The seduction of the feminist and this strangely rendered same-sex relationship reaches its final and most inescapable conclusion. Mary Hastings and Miss Egert, at least, remained only on the fringes of the heterosexual status quo, having been thwarted in their love and returned to the comfortable social confines of spinsterhood. Hester, whose feminist beliefs were the strongest of them all and whose masculine womanhood even went so far as to assume a male economic and pseudonymic identity, is the one who falls greatest victim to heterosexuality.

The popular press offered only one venue in which the feminization and seduction of the masculine woman could occur. Sherwood Anderson's *Poor White* (1920) traces the life of Hugh McVey, uneducated and ill-bred son of a drunkard father. The text intends to contrast Hugh's innocence with the seemingly unstoppable force of capitalism and the mechanized perils of industrialization. Hugh, of course, is lost in the tide, unable to function successfully in modern life without the generosity of the townspeople, first of Mudcat Landing and then of Bidwell, Ohio, who are more often than not motivated by greed. Included in Anderson's collection of characters is Clara Butterworth, initially a personification of sex-gender confusion but ultimately Hugh's maternal protector. While away at the State University at Columbus, Clara meets Kate Chanceller, a masculine woman who has acknowledged a romantic interest in Clara. Clara's ultimate sexual expression, however, is unquestionably heterosexual and maternally feminine. "She wanted," the narrator offers, "something more than caresses. There was a creative impulse in her that could not function until she had been made love to by a man. The man she wanted was but an instrument she sought in order that she might fulfill herself" (332).

Clara Butterworth is first described as a teenager, a "tall, strong, hard-muscled girl, shy in the presence of strangers and bold with people she knew well." The only child of the widowed farmer Tom Butterworth, Clara does not have the "frail" characteristics of her mother but instead inherits Tom's physical strength. When she is seventeen, however, Clara's figure, which had been "boyish and strong," starts to change, and she begins to understand her plight as a woman: "The farmer's daughter became conscious. She knew a thousand things she had not known a month before and began to take her revenge upon men for their betrayal of her" (253).

Shortly after her awakening, Clara leaves the farm and her hometown of Bidwell to attend college. Although she boards with one of her father's married sisters, she encounters a variety of characters, including Kate Chanceller and her brother. Together, the siblings make a remarkable pair, and the description of them gives the first hint that Clara has been introduced to something other than traditional heterosexual intimacy. "The truth," confides the narrator, "was that the brother was like a woman and Kate Chanceller, who wore skirts and had the body of a woman, was in her nature a man" (262). Sometimes, such as when Kate thrust her hands into her shirt pockets "that were like the trouser pockets of a man," her appearance assumes such a masculine air that Clara has difficulty even remembering Kate is a woman. It is not only in appearance that Kate's sex and gender seem ill-matched. Clara talks to Kate "as to a man," but without the "antagonism that so often exists between men and women" (263). Even Kate herself, clearly comfortable with unconventional sex-gender pairings, recognizes that although she is "essentially a man" (281), she is neither a woman nor a man because of her nontraditional sex-gender coupling. "'Men are such fools,'" begins Kate's outspoken commentary on modern industrialized society, "'and I suppose women are as bad. They are both too much of one thing. I fall in between'" (264).

Kate Chanceller is a masculine woman, "in between" a feminine woman and a masculine man, in both appearance and independent behavior; she even "swore like a man." Such a description provides the stereotypical groundwork for her inverted sexuality. "'Men hate such women as myself,'" Kate says to Clara as she continues her harangue against modern society. "'They can't use us, they think. What fools! They should watch and study us. Many of us spend our lives loving other women, but we have skill. Being part women, we know how to approach women'" (264–65). Kate's admission of her sexuality, immediately after both the narrator and Kate herself proclaim her to be neither a man nor a woman, alerts Clara Butterworth to the possibility of embracing an alternative sexuality. Kate, at least in her own mind, makes it clear that she is interested in a relationship with Clara. Fighting her urge to condemn marriage as she walks with Clara, Kate thinks, "I want to keep Clara for myself. I think more of her than of anyone else I've ever met" (282). Clara, despite sexual naiveté, "was not unconscious of the fact that their friendship had been something more than friendship," the narrator mysteriously relates, echoing the "apparitionality," to use Terry Castle's term, of the love between Mary Hastings and Sylvia, Miss Egert and Cynthia, and Hester Golden and Diana. "Kate loved to hold Clara's hand and wanted to kiss and caress her. This inclination had been put down by Kate herself, a struggle had gone on in her, and Clara had been dimly conscious of it and had respected Kate for making it" (332).

Lillian Faderman rightly suggests that the relationship between Kate Chanceller and Clara Butterworth "is given no overt sexual expression," although "it is highly charged emotionally" (*Surpassing* 470–71). Given her profession of love for both Clara and other women and her masculine appearance, Kate clearly is characterized as the older, more worldly seducer of the naive, farmer's daughter. Clara also, however, in striking up a friendship with Kate, is given the potential of becoming an active invert, particularly since immediately after her rushed marriage to Hugh McVey, she thinks of Kate. When the marriage feast comes to an end at 2 A.M., instead of thinking of sexual consummation with Hugh, Clara thinks, "What I want above everything else is a woman" (380). She begins to "caress the memory of her one woman friend, Kate Chanceller," even though she has previously determined she wanted "something more than caresses," remembering a time when they held each other and a "strange gentle yet hungry look came into Kate's eyes." She recalls the simplicity of Kate, "who had known how to love in silence," and she wistfully realizes that if she could have been with Kate on her wedding night, she "could have come to a man believing in the possible sweetness of marriage" (381).

That Clara thinks only of Kate on her wedding night significantly connects sexual intimacy to a woman-to-woman relationship, thereby lending credibility to the expressed sexual possibility between the two former schoolmates. But Clara, portrayed as the naive woman overwhelmed by the boldly masculine Kate, still has hope for redemption from homosexuality through her marriage. Even in this initial same-sex pair, a traditional gender coupling is maintained: Kate assumes the masculine role, while Clara, whose figure and psyche have become more womanly, assumes the feminine role. Anderson, however, is unable to leave this schema in place in 1920 and instead follows the pattern of the other fictional stories that resort to a seduction of the same-sex couple by the heterosexual status quo so that the social order is restored. Clara, assigning her "creative impulse" the greatest act of fulfillment for her, realizes she needs to use a man as her instrument. A relationship with Kate, although it may be full of "caresses," cannot be reproductive, and clearly Clara is meant for maternity. Even though her marriage remains unconsummated for more than a week, when the novel ends, Clara not only has two children but, more important, has cast herself in the role of maternal protector of Hugh.

Kate Chanceller, who was so instrumental in getting Clara to "think" about her life, ceases to be an active presence in the story, even in Clara's memory, and her fate is never revealed. Certainly, Kate's disappearance after Clara's marriage emphasizes the importance of a reproductive, traditionally feminine calling. In *Poor White,* procreation is a salve to modern industrial society, which is bent on efficient, mechanical production and threatens to exclude man entirely from natural production because of the invention of machines. To permit the masculine woman to remain, either by maintaining a relationship between Kate and Clara or by giving Kate a future in the society, would be to sacrifice procreation and admit sterility, of either machine or woman, into human relations. Seducing Clara by heterosexuality, as well as giving her procreative and maternal powers, removes the threat of sterility and dismisses masculine womanhood and female sexual inversion as a viable alternative in Anderson's midwestern world.

As a result of the seduction plot, the masculine woman faced an impossible future. The possibility embodied by Mary Hastings, Miss Egert, and Hester Golden does for a time, at least, flourish in the midst of heterosexual society. The relationship between Mary and Sylvia blossoms, Miss Egert and Cynthia have numerous painting lessons, Hester Golden lives four years with the feminist Diana, and Clara Butterworth's schoolgirl crushes are allowed a finite time in which to be explored. But ultimately, women's intimacy is broken apart by the more powerful and more acceptable forces of heterosexuality. Despite its existence, the masculine woman's sexual inversion in these 1910s' stories is not allowed to survive but gives way to the traditional order of heterosexuality. Once women obtained political independence, the threat of changing and even confused sex and gender roles became too great, and the paucity of popular fiction embracing the possibility of female sexual inversion reflected the tightening of the acceptable modes of sexuality. Given the public outrage over the perceived behavior of the suffragists and the social independence of enfranchised women, masculine womanhood's challenge to traditional sex-gender pairs and its implicit sexual challenge to the heterosexual status quo could not be tolerated. The American public might grudgingly allow political emancipation, but it drew the line at gender confusion and sexual emancipation in the pages of popular press fiction, literature, and most certainly in society and relegated such a woman first to femininity and then to the heterosexuality to which they "rightfully" belonged.

Not all instances of the masculine woman and her assumed sexual inversion ended in a successful conversion to femininity and her heterosexual seduction, however. Some fictional women embodied masculinity so strongly that they could not be seduced and instead became examples of the social destruction that results when masculine women are allowed to remain in their alternatively gendered state, precisely the outcome those opposed to woman suffrage had predicted. In this fiction where the seduction fails, the women are unable or unwilling to commit to a feminine gender and thus cannot undergo the seduction that would allow them access to and acceptance by the heterosexual society. For masculine women to marry men subverts the ideal of a heterosexual coupling by suggesting masculine homosocial bonds and implying the even greater threat of male homosexuality.

In the popular press, this failed seduction plot is evident in Maddy Vegtel's story "And Years Passed," published in *Vanity Fair* in September 1926. Two schoolgirls, Claire and Betty, clothed in the white muslin dresses of the mode of 1900, the narrator explains, "one summer evening, on Lake Geneva . . . swore each other an eternal friendship." "'And,' continued Betty (the fairer of the two), 'even if we *do* marry some day, we'll never let it make any difference between us—will we, Claire?'" "'I hope it won't,' answers Claire, but 'anyhow I don't think I will ever marry. I want to be free, I want to do just what I like—and one can't ever do that with a husband.'" As the two row to shore, the narrator carefully delineates how each girl understands this undying declaration of love: "I have a friend," thought Betty; "I love somebody at last," thought Claire (113).

The story resumes more than ten years later; by now, the two women could not be more dissimilar. Betty, married and the mother of four, which she blames for her "Rubinesque proportions," lolls about on the verandah of a plantation in Java in little more than the native white cotton *kabaya*, fastened at the neck with a gold pin. Claire is fashionable, comfortably wealthy, and well-traveled, but unmarried. Now thirty years old, she is depicted as she talks with her suitor, Dennis. As they stand on their hotel room balcony in Geneva, Claire reminisces about her school days there and realizes that she "'used to talk about what I was going to do with [my life], how I always said I wanted to be free, free to do what I liked, I always said I'd never marry—and—.'" This desire for independence uncomfortably embarrasses Dennis, and so Claire stops vocalizing her memories. Betty, after receiving a letter and picture from Claire, suggests the more explicit sexual assumptions about the independent-minded Claire when she remarks, "[H]ow strange that [Claire] has never been married, but, of course, she always said she wasn't going to. Well, Claire had always been a little strange—even in those far off days . . . talking about wanting to be free, free" (113–14).

Unexpectedly, the two women later meet in The Hague at a salon. Claire is complimented by the other women at the salon for her appearance, which they characterize as "extremely 'well preserved.'" The narrator explains the reality behind this compliment: "Claire had always been thin, but now she was altogether too flat. She was smart, and her hair was cut just like a boy's. It suited her, although, of course, it was a little too extreme for The Hague, and her dress, and those pearls—not real, of course, but *chic* all the same—yes, undeniably, Claire looked younger and smarter than anyone present" (114). The narrator never offers a description of Betty's appearance and thus no judgment. Clearly, Claire's physical appearance is meant to be scrutinized, particularly given the radically unfeminine ideas she professes about marriage and personal freedom. Betty's "Rubinesque" appearance, from the only description given as she sits on the Javanese plantation, is forgivable, even laudable, since it is attributed to her motherhood. But Claire is given no such excuse; her boyish haircut and "too flat" body type are meant to signal that her personal philosophy is not only questionable but also physically detrimental. Her physique and appearance signal an alteration of her gender and more specifically, as was the case with the suffragists, are implied to be a physiological manifestation of her politics.

After she arrives home, Claire receives a long box of roses and a man's visiting card, but "she was so accustomed to receiving them" that she mechanically unties the box, all the while lost in thought with "a smile of pity for Betty still lingering on her face." Her hands touch the flowers, the narrator notes, but then "repeated once more the words, 'four children,'" and "her smile altered a little, and took on a little note of wistfulness." It is not Betty's personal appearance that has Claire so upset; Claire's distress is because of her own insistence on independence and its resulting childlessness. Betty, despite her "monstrous fat" and "unspeakable hat," has what Claire so desires and is unable to obtain, even with economic independence and colorful experiences. Betty's reflections on her chance meeting with Claire are predictably maternalistic. "Poor Claire. So she had really never married. No children, nothing. All by herself in a dreary hotel in The Hague. Well, no doubt it was Claire's own fault . . . she hadn't really changed much—I would have recognized her anywhere—only thinner, much thinner. How horrible to be thin like that for a woman, thin, no husband, no home, no children. Yes, some people seemed to have everything, and others nothing at all" (113).

Claire's shortcomings as a representative of the feminine are blatantly expounded, and it is this conclusion that is given final validity in the *Vanity Fair* story. It is Claire, who in her schoolgirl declaration of friendship with Betty, mistakes those feelings for love and ignores the love of her male suitors. It is Claire who, when in Geneva with Dennis, ignores his kisses on the balcony and reminisces about Betty and the particular night when they made their oath to each other. It is Claire whose seemingly "well-preserved" appearance evokes pity from other women and whose childlessness elicits sympathy from the less attractive but maternal Betty. It is Claire, after her chance meeting with Betty, who is left to disparage her fate and to realize that Betty, even fat and ill-clothed, has the much more desirable four children. Finally, it is Claire's beliefs in independence and freedom that are the source of all her unhappiness; her ideas have driven suitors away, perpetrated a physical change to boyishness in her later years, and left her barren. Such notions, clearly meant to mirror the quest for women's political independence and domestic freedom that had been accomplished at the time of this story, lead not only to unhappiness but also to an unfavorable, socially threatening, and certainly unacceptable gender alteration.

This strong "message" of the story is remarkable for its clarity. The schoolgirl crush loses its short-lived credibility because only Claire decides it is "love" and she is unfeminine. The suggestion of same-sex sexuality, certainly a possible assumption given Claire's politics, appearance, and marital status, is strongly linked to "radical" notions of women's independence and freedom from men—she does, after all, "do just what I like—and one can't ever do that with a husband" (78). At the conclusion of the short story, she can do nothing but continue to reject another male caller and wish for the most feminine attribute of all, motherhood. Betty's maternity and femininely proportioned body are clearly linked to primal nature—she does live on a plantation in Java—and suggest the same idea of the "naturalness" of femininity and heterosexuality that Child's "Feminist" does for Hester Golden and Diana. Although the same-sex coupling of Claire and Betty is figured initially as a sexually alternative possibility, the attachment is not long-lived at all. It does, however, serve a vital function, namely, to establish Claire as a disreputable character who, unable to embrace femininity and the heterosexual norm, must live a life of retrospective loneliness in an impersonal hotel.

In two novels of the early thirties, the failed seduction plot seems a cruel fate perpetrated by the authors, since both their masculine women make marriage plans that would rescue them from their phase of sexual inversion. Yet each woman ultimately loses the man to whom she is affianced. Floyd Dell's *Diana Stair* (1932) creates his masculine woman in Sackett, a character who is greatly overshadowed by the socialist heroine of the novel's title. Beginning her life as a nondescript "boy-girl," Sackett, in her appearance, behavior, independence, and worship of Diana, is clearly a masculine women whose object of attraction is another woman. Despite these qualities, Sackett does manage a marriage proposal from a fellow socialist farm worker, only to turn him down because she refuses to sacrifice her dedication to social causes for the sake of the feminine marriage role. Similarly, Elizabeth Willis's short novel, *Lesby*, published in *Scribner's Magazine* in 1930, depicts the title character with many of the same masculine characteristics as Sackett's, although they, too, are not enough to prevent Lesby from receiving a marriage proposal. Unable to commit to a wedding date for reasons readers can easily infer, Lesby does not endure the self-sacrificing fate of Sackett; she simply lives her life out on the family farm, thwarted in love. These novels initially provide the means for a seduction—each masculine woman is allowed a suitor who is responsible for establishing the heterosexual alliance in place of the masculine woman's sexual inversion. The attempted seduction fails here, however. Unable or unwilling to be seduced by the masculine and hence heterosexual status quo, Sackett and Lesby are clearly portrayed as politically misguided and pathetically loyal masculine women who reject the "naturalness" of feminine womanhood and heterosexual union.

When Floyd Dell's protagonist, Diana Millburn, arrives at a boardinghouse, the proprietor, Mrs. Baxter, barks out a call to Sackett, which prompts the appearance, the narrator describes, of "a boy in overalls" carrying a hammer. Sackett orders the hack driver to carry the trunk into the house. "The voice, however," the narrator carefully distinguishes, "wasn't a boy's voice, and the young lady [Diana Millburn] looked again as she surrendered her bag. A wisp of red hair straggled from under the cap, there was a friendly boyish grin on the freckled, snub-nosed face; but a bun of hair at the back of her head gave her away when she turned; despite the overalls, a girl." Still not knowing what exactly to call the gender-confusing Sackett, the narrator at first pronounces that she is a "boy-girl," as Sackett runs ahead and deposits Diana's bag on the porch. One sentence later, after her mother, Mrs. Baxter, reminds her to mind her manners, Sackett, despite the overalls, is labeled according to her biology, a "girl," and remains so for the rest of the novel (3).

Diana is formally introduced to Sackett and learns that her real name is "Evelinda" and that "Sackett" was the name of her father, Mrs. Baxter's first husband. Mrs. Baxter, obviously embarrassed by her daughter's masculine appearance, quickly tries to excuse Sackett's fashion peculiarities. "'We let her wear overalls when she's doing chores. There's no man around the place, and somebody's got to chop the kindling and weed the garden and do the chores like that—and I guess she'd rather die than wash dishes or help with the cooking.'" "'But,'" she admonishes Sackett, "'there's no excuse for those overalls when you're not working. Go and put on a dress!'" (10). Mrs. Baxter continues her confession: "'I guess it was a mistake ever to let her get in the habit of wearing overalls to do her chores in. Now she doesn't want to wear anything else. And she's fifteen, time she began to get used to wearing a corset—and she makes the most awful fuss about it. When I lace her up, she hollers till anybody going by on the street would think she was being murdered.'" Diana rescues Sackett's decidedly unfeminine dress by declaring that she, too, thinks corsets are a "'horrid invention'" and recounts how she "'took the scissors and cut the laces'" of her first corset and then how she "'cut the horrible thing all to pieces'" and "'burned it in the stove.'" "'And,'" Diana proudly announces, "'I've never had one on since.'" After Diana's proud defiances of convention and defense of Sackett's unconventional appearance, the narrator, probably without needing to, notes that Sackett looked at Diana "in gratitude and worship" (11).

So begins *Diana Stair*, a novel more about the free spirit Diana (Millburn née Stair), the feminist and socialist union organizer turned commune leader and fugitive slave protector, than about the "boy-girl" Sackett. Given Dell's political activities, including his stint as associate editor of the socialist magazine the *Masses,* it is little wonder that the novel's overwhelming emphasis is on the socially concerned Diana Stair and the causes to which she commits herself wholeheartedly. John E. Hart characterizes the novel as "an encyclopedic coverage of historical events and intellectual attitudes of the 1830's and 1840's," including "the rise of socialism and abolitionism, the exploitation of women in mills and factories, the antagonism of capital and labor, the rise of industrialism, the intellectual ferment of the Concord and Boston circles, the Bohemianism of Paris, the social idealism that emerges from Brook Farm and other such experiments" (152). Dell also was a member of the Provincetown Players, writing plays that, according to Hutchins Hapgood, were "symbolic works self-consciously representing the 'advanced' ideas of Greenwich Village: don't be staid, prudent, or traditional; be true to self. Women should be independent. Life should be a thing *really felt.*" "The sensitive Dell," Hapgood continued, "expressed the spirit of the self-conscious woman of the time, the woman who accepts herself without the conventional lies thrust upon her by man's ancient imagination" (quoted in Brittin 37–38).

Diana moves from the teaching position back to her calling as abolition orator. Then, to bring some structure to her life, she takes a job in a cloth factory and ends up organizing the workers into a union and striking against the factory's owners. She continues her life of sexual freedom, survives serious illness, has a long poem about Sappho published in a national periodical, and becomes pregnant by the lonely artist for whom she had posed nude many years earlier. Finally, she runs away from a stifling married life with a lawyer into the arms of his English brother and then to Apple Farm, a socialist community in Pennsylvania. Diana's story ends, as does the novel, with her standing trial, along with the other members of the Apple Farm community, for helping two fugitive slaves fleeing to Canada. Because of some legal maneuvering by her estranged husband, she and the others are found not guilty, and, as she receives congratulations from all, she determines that she will amend her "loose" ways and become a more respectable wife and woman. Of course, given her strong-willed nature and her belief that she is immune from harm, it is doubtful that Diana will truly settle down as a Boston socialite and not be drawn to the latest cause. Even more apparent, Diana's heterosexuality is never in doubt. She may be a "loose" woman, subscribe to free love, and become pregnant as a result of her progressive morality. She may wholeheartedly participate in the causes of unionism, socialism and abolitionism. She may espouse radical views on the role and appearance of women, all with relative impunity. But she does not reject heterosexuality, nor is she ever considered a masculine woman, as Sackett, because of her appearance, behavior, and lack of heterosexual interest, is.

Sackett plays only a small supporting role in the novel, appearing at various times in Diana's adventurous life when she needs a friend to be devoted completely to her. But Dell provides enough of Sackett and her predilections about appearance and behavior that her status as a masculine woman and female invert is ensured. Sackett's unwavering devotion to the twenty-four-year old Diana, her insistence on overalls instead of corsets, her assumption of the male's role in the household, and the elderly women's indictments of her sex-gender confusion, including her own mother's admission that she made a "mistake" in allowing her the modes of a man, clearly signal the presumption of an alternative sex-gender pairing and sexuality. Moreover, Sackett obviously serves as a foil to all the other women who inhabit Mrs. Baxter's boardinghouse, all women who had been firmly reared in the feminine tradition and have the corseted waists, wedding rings or widowed status, or coquettish reputations to prove it. Even Diana, who despite her radical views on corsets and, later in the novel, her progressive acts involving unionization of the women workers in a cloth factory and her expressions of heterosexual freedoms, was married at age eighteen (although widowed within a year) and is thus a member of the feminine and heterosexual tradition from which Sackett is established as so separate.

When Diana first arrives at Mrs. Baxter's house, Sackett hovers around Diana's room, "anxious to serve, hungry for a word, and frankly adoring." But to suggest that Diana is engaged in same-sex sexuality would discredit her power and worth in the novel. Rather, Sackett is the only masculine woman in the novel, left without a woman who is receptive to her love and forced, given the authority of Diana, to remain in her state of masculine womanhood or attempt to adhere to feminine behavior. That Sackett is in love with Diana is obvious, but Dell's clever strategy is to use this emotional awakening to attempt to turn Sackett into a woman, that is, a heterosexual who is more femininely gendered than she had ever been.

Masculine womanhood and its implied sexual inversion are precisely what Sackett, over the course of the novel, attempts to leave behind. Diana, hoping to give the young woman "some philosophy and courage with which to face the world" (37), arranges for Sackett to attend a women's boarding school. But this all-women enclave, instead of providing a safe space where woman-to-woman relationships can be experienced, serves the opposite purpose. Sackett, having already had her emotions awakened by Diana in her mother's boardinghouse, enters the school in need of not sexual experimentation but lessons in femininity and heterosexuality. Initially, Sackett is miserable away from her home and, more specifically, away from Diana. "But by Easter," the narrator informs, "she had become transformed; she had made friends among the girls, and she was imitating them in her speech and manner; she had ceased to be an awkward tomboy—actually, she was becoming young-ladylike!" (411)

When Sackett next appears in the novel, she is a member of Apple Farm. Here, she is far different from when she is first introduced in the novel as a "boy" and then a "boy-girl." Her boarding school days, as the narrator highlights, had "overlaid" her boyishness with "some feminine traits acquired through imitation of her girl friends" (537). Still, Sackett's unconventionality cannot be discarded so easily. Although fellow member Jeffrey Lipscomb wants to marry her and Diana approves, Sackett does not marry him. "'I tell him I can't marry him,'" Sackett explains, "'Because I love him too much the way he is. And if he settled down as a husband, even in a Socialist colony, he'd be different. He'd be just a good vagabond spoiled.'" Sackett's beliefs in free love also have contributed to her seemingly nonchalant attitude about marriage; in the presence of both Jeffrey and Diana, she declares that Jeffrey is her "'first lover,'" which Jeffrey interprets to mean that Sackett "'look[s] forward to a lot of other love affairs in the future,'" an interpretation Sackett does not deny. The two young lovers look to Diana to settle the dispute. Sackett implores Diana to express the same views of free love that she does, but Diana's experience has, apparently, taught her that free love is not the ideal for women, although it may be for men since "'they may feel the need of a wider experience.'" Then, in a curious gender refashioning that would seem to lead Sackett back into her masculine womanhood and ascribe to Jeffrey some feminine sexual attitudes, Sackett surmises that Jeffrey's insistence on marriage, since he has "'been looking for happiness—and now that I've found it, I want to keep it,'" is the feminine attitude toward love. The masculine viewpoint, however, belongs to Sackett, since she feels "'the need of a wider experience'" (538). It would appear from these comments that Sackett's reluctance to marry is not because she does not love Jeffrey; according to Sackett, the contrary is true. Rather, as she has done for most of her life, Sackett adopts the masculine attitude, thereby conflating and confusing her newfound femininity with her original masculinity. Such a mixture, a woman who is not entirely feminine—her masculinity has only been "overlaid" with femininity—proves to be unfit for marriage in Dell's novel, despite the notions of free love espoused by the heroine.

One additional passion characterizes Sackett as a mix of femininity and aggressive masculinity. As the conversation between Diana, Jeffrey, and Sackett continues late into the night, the talk turns to the French government's reprisals against the revolutionary workers. Eyewitnesses in the newspapers tell of prisoner massacres and burnings, all because, Sackett concludes, "'they came up out of their stinking slums and demanded of the Republic the right to work, the right not to starve, the right to have homes and not holes to live in. For that they are butchered'" (540). Sackett's fury at the wrongs, according to the narrator, reveals the ultimate reason for her reluctance to marry Jeffrey. Declaring that she "'wants to make war on those well-dressed butchers'" and wants "'the wrongs of the poor revenged in blood,'" Sackett quietly pleads that her hatred is the reason she cannot marry. "'As his wife,'" Sackett explains, "'I should not dare to let myself know what was going on in the world outside our home. I should lose my hatred. And I intend to keep it.'" Then, she implores Jeffrey to "'let [her] go when [she] can find work for [her] hatred'" (542). Her insistence on free love explains only half of her inability to marry. The other, more altruistic half, is her emotional need to serve a cause and to right the wrongs of an unjust society. In short, like the suffragist women, she desires political autonomy and independence to express her own views. Sackett's dual nature has shifted from a "boy-girl" status, a confusion of traditional sex-gender pairings to the degree that her biological sex is mistaken, to that of a woman whose sex is not in doubt, even though her gender still remains mixed since she espouses sexual and political attitudes that initially seem more akin to masculine prerogatives. She therefore remains unmarried, unable or unwilling to sacrifice her masculinity for the sake of gendered femininity and, by association, socially sanctioned heterosexuality.

Still, this failed seduction of Sackett does not signal that she retains her status as a masculine woman. Rather, she is seduced by a femininity that would tame her overt masculinism, transforming her from a "boy" to a "boy-girl" and eventually to a "girl." Unlike other masculine women during this time, Sackett requires this gender seduction because she begins not as feminine or even as a biological "girl" but as masculine and as a "boy." Before her attempted heterosexual seduction can occur, she first must be seduced to the feminine so that she can be an appropriate and acceptable object for masculine affection. But the feminization of Sackett is not complete since she is unable to commit to marriage. Sackett becomes, then, an unmarried, unmarriageable woman, seduced by the compassion she feels for the French workers and expressed in the masculine form of hatred. Sackett's seduction by femininity only serves to remove the inverted possibility from her, without rewarding her with a socially appropriate marital lifestyle. Stripped of her boyness, Sackett must negotiate the conflicting genders of masculinity and femininity, which may serve her socialist agenda but seem to deny full expression of her identity and sexuality.

Dell's presentation of a failed seduction in *Diana Stair* is hidden behind the altruistic motives of a socialist agenda and overshadowed by the charismatic title character. Not all failed seduction plots assumed secondary importance, though. Whereas Dell's novel, published by Farrar and Rinehart, had a limited audience, Elizabeth Willis's novella was distributed in a popular American magazine. In 1930, *Scribner's Magazine* held a $5,000 contest for short novels, received 1,672 entries, and then printed the five best. The large sum of prize money and the large number of entrants hoping to use the contest as a stepping-stone into literary acclaim are not nearly so remarkable as the last of the short novels published in December 1930. Editorially introduced as "the story of a powerful and able woman who ruled her father's farm," the novel, "alive with drama, the people full of human warmth and character," was titled only with the protagonist's first name, Lesby (571). There is no need to give Willis a benefit of the doubt as to the suggestive definition of the main character's name or to reserve initial judgment until after the short novel has been discussed, for both the story and its character, are exactly what is implied: namely, the "powerful and able woman" is, stereotypically, more masculine than feminine, more male than female, and, ultimately, unmarried because of reasons never given but easily inferred.

The obvious agenda of this novel becomes even more remarkable considering the delicate implications about female sexual inversion that appeared in popular writings. Willis takes no such precautions and blatantly labels her story and her heroine with the derisive appellation that is more slang for female homosexuals than a proper name. On one hand, this clear indication of alternative sexuality suggests that such an idea was not nearly as threatening as it had been earlier in the century. If Willis is able to construct a prize-winning novel around "Lesby," then female inversion must have been more accepted and widespread. On the other hand, this thinly disguised acknowledgment of a masculine woman's abnormal sexual intimacies results in the same romantic conclusions for the heroine as did the suggested inversion of Dell's Sackett, namely, a life of lonely unattachment. What may seem to be a successful rendering of the masculine woman is ultimately only a more blatant reaffirmation of her threat to the male, heterosexual status quo.

Lesby is first introduced as what she is not—the sixth child of John Croy, a man whose first five children were boys—and then for what she is, "big and husky as the best of the five who had deserted him [the father], deep-bosomed, wide-hipped, built for service." She wears "a coarse brown shirt," which she

stuffs down into her trousers, the narrator describes; as she "strode by her father's side, crushing the short stubble under her heavy boots," Lesby's "broad
shoulders [rose] several inches above John's stooped ones" (571, 72). Her skills
as a farmhand are surpassed only by her abilities in domestic work, which she
also must perform because her younger sister, Anne, is too romantically inclined to perform the mundane chores of cooking and cleaning. Curiously,
however, it is Lesby, the embodied transition from male children to the female
and feminine Anne, who incorporates the masculine into the female-sexed
body and becomes the romantic interest of more than one male farmer. Yet it
is not her skill as a cook that attracts the would-be suitors; it is, as the more
desirable Anne thinks, her exceptional farming skills. The men, the narrator
offers, echoing Anne's insights, "once seeing Lesby, their eyes never came down
the half-dozen inches to the height of an ordinary woman—for by the side of
Lesby all other women looked ordinary" (573).

A character constructed by contradiction, Lesby alternates between masculine and feminine appearance and behavior, and she is the female object of
male affections, although that is a part she does not willfully or enthusiasti-
cally assume. Her younger sister, Anne, whose emotional attachment to the
creek and cherry thicket on the land give her, at least in Lesby's opinion, an
air of foolish and unproductive romanticism, does not have the male admir-
ers that Lesby does.

Although it would be easy to dismiss Lesby as an unknowing and disinter-
ested accomplice in heterosexual desire and Anne as a jealous hysteric, the
interaction and difference between these two sisters clearly define the roles they
later play. Lesby's masculine womanhood attracts men but for the wrong reason—namely, her masculine ability on the land—which still has not led to
marriage. Anne's femininity is initially overshadowed by the alternative gendering of Lesby, but her romanticism, which is ridiculed by Lesby's decidedly
unromantic practicality, and her feminine desires, which seem to be so out of
place on the farm, eventually earn the sympathy of readers as well as Stephen
MacLaren, the man who has bought a half-share in the Croy farm. John Croy,
whose physical impotence is rivaled only by his inability to see Lesby for the
strange hybrid she really is, is made foolish in the short novel; he exists only
to provide a pedigree for his daughters and a rightful owner for his land. Finally, Stephen, about whom little information is given, does spend most of his
time with Lesby but always on the land, where both of them are masculine in
appearance and behavior. Stephen and Lesby do not assume the heterosexual
status quo, which would necessarily reduce Lesby to feminine domesticity,
something she clearly rejects, and to a sexuality she clearly does not possess.

Instead, the socially dangerous combination of masculine homosociality is introduced with their growing affection and must then, by the end of the story, be dismissed.

Stephen becomes the farming son John Croy never had. Moreover, with Stephen's arrival come two young farmhands, who free Lesby from farm labor and enable her to devote her time to domestic concerns. Despite her coarse and masculine appearance and her more than capable work on the farm, Lesby is relegated to the domestic sphere in an attempt to ready her for entrance to the heterosexual world. The second section of the short novel ends with two significant acts: first, Lesby's complicated gender is apparently untangled and remade into traditional femininity; and second, as a result, the rivalry between Lesby and Anne increases.

Stephen's half-interest in the land, however, also metaphorically reflects his level of interest in Lesby, who throughout the short novel is identified with the earth. If Stephen had bought the entire farm, he might have claimed Lesby for his own; his half-ownership allows him to remain partially unconnected to Lesby. Moreover, the half of the land that Stephen owns does not encompass the creek, cherry trees, or maple groves that are so dear to Anne. While Lesby's connection with the fields is focused on their productivity, Anne appreciates the land for its beauty, preferring to spend her time by the creek and cherry trees instead of butchering hogs or tilling the fields. Stephen's half-possession of the land, and consequently of Lesby, already signals a failed attempt at seducing the masculine woman.

Lesby's relationship and identification with the land, however, initially signify the efficacy and validity of masculine womanhood. Performing all the tasks that her male counterparts do, Lesby changes the sexual dynamics of farming. Land is traditionally thought of as feminine, and an early comment by the narrator—"Anne lay for a time listening, feeling the earth under her breathe like a sleeping woman" (573)—reaffirms this gendering and reinforces the feminine connection between Anne and the land. Although Lesby is described as masculine, she also is unmistakably female, resulting in the odd act of a masculine woman plowing the feminine earth. This odd juxtaposition suggests her figurative sexual inversion, a counter to the way that male control of nature signals men's aggressive and sexual domination. That the Croy farm should be left by default in the strong hands of a masculine woman, however, does not bode well for its fecundity. When the last of John Croy's sons decides to seek fortune elsewhere, the farm at once becomes unmanageable for the hands of a masculine woman and an impotent old man. John Croy's crippled body emphasizes that he will be unable to coax produce out of the land. Moreover, Lesby's work on the land is ultimately doomed to fail because the female-figured land is being plowed by another female figure; like a sexual union of the same kind, it is sterile.

Meanwhile, Stephen and Anne discover a mutual attraction. "'That was a picture—you layin' there asleep,'" he says to her. "'You were sleepin' while you were waitin'. . . . You were the Sleepin' Beauty waitin' for the Prince to come an' give you a kiss and wake you up. And instead of a Prince—why, a red-headed farmer fellow comes along—a stupid old fellow who wanted to kiss you awake and didn't have the nerve'" (582). His confession of a heretofore unexpressed interest in Anne sets in motion the events that will extricate Lesby from a heterosexual relationship, keep Stephen from marrying a woman he does not love, and lead Anne to her death.

Flustered and embarrassed by Stephen's articulated desire, Anne removes her shoe and throws it playfully at Stephen, who is bending over a broken plow. Stephen loses his balance and falls forward across the upturned blade of the plow. Momentarily, Stephen lifts "himself from the ground only to sink back into a sitting position where he remained bent over with both hands clutching his groin." Stephen's call for Lesby in his moment of potential castration signals her connection to this emasculating action. Lesby, having seen the startled horse running out of control, is halfway to Stephen with her emergency medical kit before Anne can even move. By the time Anne returns to the scene of the accident, Lesby is bent over Stephen washing out the wound, seemingly unfazed by its location; "[Stephen's] overalls had been rolled down and he lay naked from waist to knees." Anne, the more modest of the two, "gave one look and blushing fled." Lesby's field surgery saves Stephen's life, but it is clear that the objects of attraction have changed when Doctor Mayberry asks how Stephen came "'to do such a fool thing as fall over a plowshare in broad daylight'" (583). Instead of implicating Anne's role in the accident, Stephen replies that the horse kicked at a fly and that he fell on the blade while attempting to dodge the flying hooves.

Nevertheless, the doctor and John naively pronounce that Lesby and Stephen "'are a great pair,'" and Stephen's farming metaphor carries the weight of a marriage proposal—"'Well, Lesby, it looks like these friends of ours think we'd travel well in a double harness. Does it sound pretty good to you?'" Lesby acceptingly answers, "'Yas—pretty good. I might choose a worse mate to travel 'longside me'" (584). Their engagement, however, never results in marriage because Lesby, thrust into a role she is ill-equipped to play, postpones the ceremony time and again. Farming chores take precedence over the wedding: they must first harvest the crops, then roof the barn, and then build a silo. Lesby's first attraction remains to the female-figured land, and, unable to sever this link, she is unable to commit herself to marriage and the heterosexuality that it mandates.

To continue the farm work, Lesby takes Stephen's place in the field while he is confined to bed, signaling the reversal of roles and genders between the two who are engaged. While Lesby remains at home, their relationship is permitted to grow intimate; now, however, she readopts masculine dress and behavior, and Stephen is, at least temporarily, emasculated. He turns his attentions to the feminine Anne, who assumes the chief domestic role. Still covering for Anne's role in the accident, Stephen suggests that she retrieve the slipper to remove any suspicion if it is ever found in the field, and he then blames himself for the accident: "'I got what was comin' to me. . . . I'm not sayin' I deserve to have bled to death out there. I'm glad I didn't. I'm glad Lesby came in time to sew me up.'" Stephen's recognition of Lesby's medical expertise evokes Anne's jealous wrath: "'You want her because she's big an' strong an' can work hard. You want her because she can lend a hand when you're short o' men— she can take your place out'n the field like she's doin' right now when you're flat on your back. That's why you want her. . . . You ought to be ashamed'" (585).

Stephen offers no reply, but it is clear that Anne's explosive tirade has more truth in it than he wants to admit. When Lesby comes to see him during lunch, she now brings with her "the smell of stables and cow-lot, and for the first time in his life the odor sickened Stephen. He felt ashamed of the feeling of repulsion it had given him." Later, when Stephen returns from having retrieved Anne's slipper from the field, Lesby comes in to scold him for his activity and wrenches his boots off. "'Damn you, Lesby, you sure give me a wrench . . . you can't seem to remember I'm a man and not a steer'" (585), even though his wound has nearly castrated him. Yet it is not Stephen's identity that is questioned in this exchange; rather, it is Lesby herself who is undergoing a transformation, returning to the masculine work of the field, assuming the smells of the farm animals, and showing a decidedly indelicate and unfeminine strength that makes a man feel like a steer. Lesby has reassumed the identity she had before Stephen arrived, and Stephen, despite his decision to marry after the harvest, can only explain to Anne that he will marry Lesby because she is "'a fine woman'" and he "'couldn't find a better [one] if [he] had looked the whole province over.'" Anne replies, "'You wouldn't say no less'n that if you had picked out a Jersey cow or a mare. . . . That ain't love.'" Stephen simply responds, "'I'm going to marry Lesby after the harvest—and my reason is my own'" (661).

After the harvest, the wedding date is set for November, but clearly Stephen doubts the wisdom of his proposal, and Lesby herself puts the marriage off.

The indefinite November date becomes a more indefinite "after Christmas." Lesby's reason for the postponement was that "she wasn't ready . . . she had nothing new to wear except the bonnet . . . and she couldn't marry Stephen without a single new dud." The narrator continues to relate Lesby's excuse: "She wouldn't feel she was married at all, going about in the same old clothes she had been wearing for years. More, she had been—and still was—too busy to make anything. There was plenty of time to get married." John, naively trying to engineer a marriage, comments to Stephen, "'If I didn't know Lesby to be a brave woman . . . I'd say she was skeered o' marryin'. Don't look like she wants to give up her independence'" (666). John is closer to the truth than he could ever imagine. Lesby does not want to give up her independence, which would mean being forced to assume a feminine role in a heterosexual agreement. When Lesby begins to receive wedding presents, including a pink silk nightgown with a low-cut lace bodice and nothing but narrow straps to hold it up, she shamefully hides it far back in her drawer.

Lesby's postponements suggest that she may have been aware of the growing intimacy between Anne and Stephen and was simply trying to give Stephen an opportunity to break the engagement gracefully. But given her tell-tale first name, her dress, her mannerisms, and her comfort in the masculine world, Lesby's motives are not nearly so altruistic; they are self-protective. Readers were clearly to understand that Lesby was, as Stephen called her, "different," particularly in terms of sexuality. Lesby's comfort in her masculine womanhood and her inability to commit to marriage signify her unwillingness to accept heterosexual marriage and the heterogendered roles that heterosexuality mandated.

It is Anne who first suggests that she and Stephen "cut and run." To "make it square with Lesby," Anne continues, "'You could give her the farm—to her an' Father. We'd give un' everything. We would take only ourselves—just you an' me. That'd be fair. The horses an' cows an' land an' everything—against you. It would balance with Lesby.'" What started as a transition by Lesby from woman to animal is now completed in Anne's formulation. Lesby would be satisfied if, in return for a man and marriage, she received livestock and land, thereby dismissing her feminine desires for marriage and replacing them with masculine desires for those possessions that would make a successful farm. Anne is vehement in her argument: "'It would balance, Stephen. . . . It would balance with Lesby. She loves land. She would have married Santee for the section of land he owns if you hadn't come along. She would. She could have stood him for the land he owns.'" Stephen is torn between his love for Anne and his chivalric promise to Lesby, but only until Anne tells him, "'If you marry

Lesby, you'll be doin' her a sin—lovin' me, Stephen'" (667). Anne's invocation of sin teems with ambiguity. Stephen would sin by marrying a woman he does not love; Lesby's "sin" in marrying Stephen would be the denial of her inverted sexuality. Anne seems to know the true cause of Lesby's inability to set a wedding date, although Anne is unable or, perhaps even more to the point, unwilling to articulate it.

Before the two can elope, Anne dies. Lesby attributes it to her "'tricky heart,'" declaring that it was "'allus goin' back on her. She must've been runnin'. She never could run, even as a little un—she'd turn blue as a goose'" (667). Stephen, now truly a broken man, is unable to do anything but accept Lesby's direction. Indeed, *Lesby* is a story about the dangers of sex-gender confusion. Stephen MacLaren is a metaphorically castrated figure whose emasculation makes him a pathetic "feminine man," unable to consummate his love with Anne. Moreover, Anne's death removes all the beauty and love in the novel—the cherry and maple groves will be tainted with the memories of her. Anne, whose femininity held the best hope for reproduction and motherhood, dies before she is given the chance. Conversely, there is no indication that Lesby has learned to love heterosexually or is now willing to be married. Rather, she returns to the same existence she had before Stephen arrived, dutiful and helpful, but clearly the embodiment of a masculine woman, defiantly not heterosexual, unable to produce. Sterility ends the novel, and it is clear that a masculine woman with implied homosexuality is at the heart of the story and is implicated in the male's impotence and the feminine woman's death.

Lesby's sterility is precisely the antithesis of what a woman is to be—feminine and fertile. Her existence outside the civilized regions of the United States, in the countryside north of Montreal, further relegates the masculine woman to a nameless existence, yet another strategy of exclusion. Willis's attempted seduction of her title character was doomed to fail. Returning to the farm, Stephen and Lesby seem to reconcile themselves to working the land together, although there is no talk of marriage. She fails to be seduced by not only the feminine but also the heterosexual and is fated to live her life on a farm with an elderly, impotent father and a nearly castrated man whose only love has died. The sterility of the novella's conclusion is, finally, overwhelming, and it is Lesby, who has been refused the feminine and heterosexual seduction, who presides over a now tainted land.

Even the failed seduction plot in Dell's *Diana Stair* and Willis's *Lesby* is an important strategy for trying to get the masculine woman to assume proper social roles and sexuality: both novels encompass and therefore destroy masculine womanhood within the sterility of spinsterhood. Because Sackett and

Lesby are independent women who have the "ways of a maid and the modes of a man," their fate, and the fate of those who dare to attempt to change traditional sex and gender status, is clear. Sackett remains a conflation of masculinity and femininity and does not marry; Lesby, the sixth "son" of an impotent father, fails to be seduced by and to heterosexuality, thus anchoring a plot of heartbreak, near castration, disappointment, and death. The message embodied in the fate of the masculine woman is clear. As the psychological results of an enfranchised woman began to permeate American society, any deviations from the heterosexual and heterogendered status quo that had existed prior to the woman suffrage movement and the Nineteenth Amendment took on a more ominous threat. What was once aberration that affected only the woman in whom it occurred now caused virtual emasculation in 1930; the masculine woman certainly was a possibility, but, through these years, clearly a possibility that had become too difficult and must, in turn, be seduced by the very heterosexuality it challenged.

Notes

1. Helen Hull's writing career spanned more than fifty years, beginning with the appearance of a one-act play in the *Woman's Journal,* and included, in addition to her novels and short fiction, several books about writing and a biographical sketch of Madam Chiang Kai-shek, one of her former students. Despite being lauded by the *New York Times,* Hull's fiction, which explored the nuances of family interaction, the ramifications of women's economic status, gender differences, and class and racial tensions, was trivialized as "women's fiction" in the 1930s. For a full-length study of Hull, see Patricia McClelland Miller.

2. For a discussion of "Miss B," see chapter 1.

3. Richard Washburn Child enjoyed diverse careers, including the editor of *Collier's Weekly* (1919), U.S. ambassador to Italy (1921–24), and author of more than ten novels.

5

Marketing Mockery

Original "Sins" and the Art of Parody

I have been thinking up a new way of making you less gay and of
making myself more gay and in a *wholly new way.*
—"When Helen Furr Got Gay with Harold Moos," 1923

While the seduction plot relied on a man's attractiveness to be successful,
other authors simplified the disenfranchisement by mocking the masculine woman and the sexual inversion she embodied. A column in the October 1925 *Woman's Journal* challenged these assumptions about sex and
gender by inviting readers to ponder the question "Can a Woman Take a
Joke?" Made up of twelve brief jokes and anecdotes, the column focused
on stereotypical attitudes about women, culled from the pages of such periodicals as *Tit-Bits,* the *London News,* the *Boston Transcript, Harper's Magazine,* the *Arkansas Gazette,* and the *Toledo Blade.* When totaled, the individual stereotypes represented the anxieties of a society in which woman
suffrage and the feared masculinization and concurrent defeminization of
women had, as the antisuffragists had suggested, become a reality.

That this column of jokes appeared in a national publication of the or-
ganization devoted to achieving woman suffrage seems incongruous. Pri-
or to women's enfranchisement in 1920, the *Woman's Journal* filled its pages
with the conservative political rhetoric and activities of the National American Woman Suffrage Association. Once women were granted the right to
vote, however, the content of the magazine shifted. Articles devoted to fash-

ion, domestic chores, and personal appearance, including makeup tips, began appearing next to essays on women's role in public health, opportunities in higher education, and accounts of outstanding women involved in the public sphere. Gradually, the advocate for women's political independence became the mouthpiece echoing many of society's ideas about the ideal woman. To be sure, woman suffragists never claimed that they would abdicate their femininity or their woman's role. Neither did they suggest that the rigid confines of gender roles be scrutinized and perhaps relaxed. Once the original goal of woman suffrage was accomplished, the organ of the movement seemingly lost its focus and reverted to perpetuating conventional stereotypes about women's roles and prescribing traditional appearance and beliefs. Elaine Showalter posits that "1925 is the turning point, both in terms of legislative success and the morale of individual women. The collapse of the suffrage coalition, the factionalization of the women's movement into bitterly opposed parties, and the absence of a clearly defined female voting bloc contributed to the political decline" (9).

The twelve jokes printed in 1925 thus represented the contradiction implicit in the *Woman's Journal*. Humor aimed at women's ideal appearance—in one joke, "A visitor said to a little girl, 'And what will you do, my dear, when you are as big as your mother?' 'Diet,' said the modern child"—took its place among jokes critical of the scanty dress that some young women in the 1920s adopted. Other jokes questioned a woman's demand for attention and humorously criticized her aggressiveness when naming a child. Curiously, this critique of women was accomplished by making "man" the subject of pity, as this brief offering illustrates: "When he is born, his mother gets the attention; at his marriage, the bride gets it; at his funeral, the widow gets it." A woman is given attention at the expense of the man, who, the underlying philosophy assumes, is the proper object of notice and praise. Or, man's inability to stand up to a strong wife—"The man who hides behind a woman's skirt is less a coward than a contortionist"—is not so much his fault as hers, for being attracted to postsuffrage modernism, which manifested itself in slim-fitting dresses (41). The man's failure to control an independent wife is really her fault, both for her dominance and for her fashion choice.

Four years before the passage of the Nineteenth Amendment, *Vanity Fair* also parodied the changes caused by the women's movement in a fictitious conversation between a feminist woman, Edith, and her naive boyfriend, Walter, who has just proposed marriage. Edith declines the proposal because, she announces, she is a feminist and marriage would have negative effects on her feminism. "'Marriage will have to stop being an unnatural monopoly,'" Edith philosophizes, "'when this agreement extends to all desires and inclinations it becomes unnatural. Husband and wife should each retain their freedom'" (Strunsky 39).

One way Edith proposes to retain her freedom is to relinquish taking care of children. "'Suppose, for instance,'" Edith hypothesizes, "'that I should have children. Suppose I should decide not to bring them up myself, but to entrust them to the care of more competent people?'" The women's movement, she informs Walter, stands for "'sex-equality—economic, social, political and industrial sex equality. A movement that stands for freedom of conduct, deliverance from man-made laws and regulations'" (39). Edith's characterization of marriage and the home relegates women to a submissive role, to be dominated by her husband, and, as a result, the feminine and masculine roles of traditional society are maintained. This maintenance of the heterosexual status quo is what Edith escapes in her rejection of marriage, maternity, and domesticity.

It is difficult to determine whether it is Edith or Walter who ultimately loses the most. Walter certainly has his imagined world of marital and domestic bliss shattered by Edith's feminist philosophy, emphatically summed up by her final command to Walter, "'Dearest—you must go!'" But Walter is only ordered to leave Edith's apartment. Her insistence on freedom is a resistance to the feminine tradition; her unwillingness to marry and play the traditionally appropriate female role makes her less feminine and more masculine because of her assumption of the masculine prerogative of freedom in "economic, social, political and industrial" terms (39). Despite the uncompromising passion of Edith's beliefs, it is she, rather than Walter, who is made the extreme comical figure. Even though Walter's masculine virility is stripped from him and he is left a trembling, dismissed, and overwhelmingly confused man, he is not faulted. Rather, the blame rests with the woman's aggressiveness, just as it did in the joke about the man who hid behind the woman's skirt. Edith, her masculinity illustrated by her feminist philosophy and reinforced by her cigarette, is ultimately the absurd figure, the cause of the threatening gender confusion, the emasculator of man.

Five years earlier, Anne O'Hagan wrote four short parodies, entitled "Little Duologues on Feminism," which reflected the increasing influence the woman suffrage movement had on American social life and society's attempt to dismiss the threat of independent women through parody. Published in the March 1920 issue of *Vanity Fair,* the parodic pieces not only mocked women who wanted to usurp men's traditional behaviors but, more important, presented these absurd women as social detriments. Hester, an ardent feminist, is foiled by a narrator whose literal interpretation and extrapolation of Hester's feminist philosophy results in absurdity. "'Of course you are a feminist?'" Hester asks. "'Of course,'" the narrator answers with "carelessness," "'Was I not a veteran marcher in suffrage parades? Had I not watched with grim, silent, unavailing rage, the triumphal descent of the villages' ne'er-do-wells upon the polls, there to register their supreme wills in regard to the disposition of my taxes? A feminist? Rather!'" By the end of four incidents, however, the narrator is not quite so sure of her feminism, and she is left waiting for "an authoritative definition" of the term. In the meantime, she writes, "I cling to the old-fashioned cause, the cause of true advancement of women, which sometimes seems, to anxious eyes, to be tying a bewildering, perhaps even a dangerously down-dragging, number of tails to its kite" (37).

The first superficial "tail" tied to the kite of a woman is fashion, as recounted in "The Incident of Hester's Hair." "Young and ardent," Hester bobs her hair in the "boyish style," a style, the narrator naively notes, that is becoming to her. "'Becoming? Bosh!'" Hester says to the narrator.

> "Why should I waste time and energy—yes, and money!—on hairpins and hair washes, curling irons and transformations, when there is so much useful work to do in the world? Think of the time that man gains just in that one respect! An hour a day for dressing our hair, an hour a week for shampooing, eight hours a week—Four hundred and sixteen hours a year—five weeks! A year in every ten. Think of the knowledge, the power, women could attain in a year. No wonder man has usurped the position of the dominant sex! No wonder their wily poets have always gushed about woman's crowning glory! It's part of the masculine conspiracy to keep us down!"

The narrator, "fired by [Hester's] zeal," adds her own strategy to coiffure. "'If we women could only acquire early baldness we should come to our own at last! And man would still need to shave. That's where we'd have him. It's a magnificent strategic idea'" (37).

Duologue IV, "The Incident of Dr. Loeb's Lady Frog," follows the same rhetorical pattern. Dr. Loeb, according to Hester, has succeeded in producing "'a perfectly healthy little family of frogs without the intervention of the male principles at all. . . . Only the mother frog! Oh, it is splendid—the unnecessary sex—the male!'" Hester's glee continues: "'If in frogs, then in time in all the higher animals! The useless male—to be sloughed off as nature in her great economy sloughs off all useless things!'" The narrator, initially caught up in Hester's feminism, is quickly sobered by the thought of reproduction. "'The little frogs . . . they have gone on, I suppose, developing more little frogs?'" The answer, of course, is no, but that is no worry to Hester. "'We can attend to that when the time is ripe. It's the first step that counts—and after all these centuries of our subordination!'" A final twist on this satire comes as the two women view a man, "the husky, disgusting creature," strolling along with his hands in his pockets while his "poor" wife carries the valise and the baby. The narrator, mindful of Dr. Loeb's family of little frogs, concludes, "'Perhaps he is only trying to educate her for the glorious future. . . . Give him the benefit of a charitable doubt'" (37).

In both of these duologues, the narrator carries the words and actions of the independent-minded feminist to absurdity.[1] The desire for "early baldness" only ridicules Hester's subversiveness and presents the laughingly preposterous idea that a woman should completely and absolutely forsake the ideal of feminine appearance. Bobbed hair as a partial subversion may be acceptable; a completely shorn head is ludicrous. The same ridicule to the point of derisive absurdity colors the example of Dr. Loeb's frogs. That females reproduce even without the male frog is a seemingly acceptable outcome, but their offspring are sterile. Such reproductive independence is not to be; sexually independent frogs cannot reproduce, and by association—"'If in frogs, then in time in all the higher animals!'" as Hester says—sexually independent women cannot reproduce, and their very womanhood is questioned. This condemnation also reinforces heterosexual coupling and conversely discourages same-sex sexuality since females can reach their full potential of womanhood only through heterosexuality. Failure to reproduce, then, questions a woman's femininity: women who do not reproduce are abnormal and unnatural, just like the frogs. They are, in short, not women. The sexual necessity and authority of the male are reinforced in another way, by the example of the woman on the street carrying the valise and the baby while the husband strolls along empty-handed. Women are faced with two options: live without the benefit of men and fail to reproduce or live with the sexual benefit of men and heterosexuality, do all the domestic work, and be complicit.

Clearly, O'Hagan's duologues, like many of the popular press's offerings, exaggerated a serious and often threatening issue through humor to transform it into a topic that was safer to handle and understand. The humorist Alice Duer Miller used the same strategy but this time to point out the absurdity of antisuffragist arguments. In "Why We Don't Want Men to Vote" (1915), Miller provides five reasons that read as opposites of antisuffragist opinions on women's franchise:

1. Because man's place is in the army.
2. Because no really manly man wants to settle any questions otherwise than by fighting about it.
3. Because if men should adopt peaceable methods women will no longer look up to them.
4. Because men will lose their charm if they step out of their natural sphere and interest themselves in other matters than feats of arms, uniforms and drums.
5. Because men are too emotional to vote. Their conduct at baseball games and political conventions shows this, while their innate tendency to appeal to force renders them unfit to government. (4A:6)

Miller, in focusing on the martial and violent behavior of men and restricting men to only one sphere, knowingly and deliberately uses the same narrow reasoning as antisuffragist arguments about women. Such calculation, even though humorously rendered, does pare down the extraneous details that often hide the heart of the matter. Her emphasis on male violence, just as O'Hagan's focus on female reproduction, exposes underlying fears, specifically details the governing male and female characteristics and behavior, and reveals the dangers of masculinized women.

Vanity Fair magazine uncovered the same fears and used the same humorous method to overcome it. Its editorial policy claimed such parodic license. *Vanity Fair* "will print much humor," wrote Frank Crowninshield, the editor, in the inaugural issue, March 1914,[2] adding "it will look at the stage, at the arts, at the world of letters, at sport, and at the highly-vitalized, electric, and diversified life of our day from the frankly cheerful angle of the optimist, or which is much the same thing, from the mock-cheerful angle of the satirist" (13). This double-edged editorial policy blurred the line between satire and seriousness, making it difficult to determine where one stopped and the other began, if indeed a reader can ever be sure. In particular, such indecipherability allowed the magazine simultaneously to promote the new woman and parodically undermine her character. Such a questionable compliment was clearly evident in 1923 when *Vanity Fair* reprinted Gertrude Stein's short story "Miss Furr and Miss Skeene" from her new book *Geography and Plays* (1922) and then followed it three months later with a parody called "When Helen Furr Got Gay with Harold Moos."

In his cultural exploration of Stein and her neglect in the American marketplace, Bryce Conrad specifically cites the difficulties Stein encountered with Ellery Sedgwick, the *Atlantic* editor who refused to publish any of her work. "Your poems," Sedgwick wrote in a rejection letter in 1919, "I am sorry to say, would be a puzzle picture to our readers. All who have not the key must find them baffling, and—alack! that key is known to very, very few" (quoted in Conrad 216). Sedgwick was not the only one to criticize Stein's "Miss Furr and Miss Skeene." Edith Sitwell negatively reviewed the story in *Nation and the Atheneum* on July 14, 1923: "I hope I shall not be regarded as a reactionary, but I am bound to say that I prefer words, when collected in a sentence, to convey some sense. And Miss Stein's sentences do not always carry any sense—not even a new one. . . . Lord Tennyson," she pronounced, "could produce the same feeling of monotony with more economy of means, and with less risk of reducing his readers to the asylum" (45, 46).[3]

Stein's story of two women with more than a hint of their same-sex relationship reached a much larger audience when it was reprinted in *Vanity Fair,* thereby disseminating the potential of same-sex sexuality across a wider range. The two title characters are modeled on two midwestern women who visited Gertrude Stein's salon in Paris, Ethel Mars and Maud Hunt Squire. Although they were puritanical when they arrived, Bettina Knapp writes, "after just one year in the liberating environment of the city of lights, the change in both of them was clearly discernible: they now sported brilliantly orange hair and heavy makeup, which looked more like a mask than a face." Their seemingly fictional counterparts undergo a similar change when Helen Furr escapes her boredom and moves in with the exciting Georgine Skeene. Moreover, in the text, although Helen and Georgine are seen in the company of "dark and heavy" men, Knapp contends that "it is inferred that their [sexual] pleasures were enjoyed with each other not with the opposite sex" (93). At the end of Stein's account, Georgine Skeene leaves Helen Furr to live with her brother for two months, but Helen does not return home to her parents. Rather, she "did go on being gay" and, in fact, was "gay longer every day than they had been being gay when they were together being gay." She also becomes a teacher, "telling some about being gay," and she "taught very many then little ways they could use in being gay" (94).

Critics have disagreed about the definition of "gay" in "Miss Furr and Miss Skeene." Edmund Wilson determined that the story was about a "touching pair of left-hand gloves" ("Young and Old" 87), written in a "repetitive rigmarole manner" that was "admirably suited to render the monotony and insipidity of the feminine lives which are being narrated" ("Gertrude Stein" 62). More recent critics have been kinder to Stein and her characters, although not all read "gay" in its current usage. Catherine Stimpson, for example, determines that "Miss Furr and Miss Skeene" is a "witty story about a disintegrating relationship" between two women that has no "explicit sexual detail whatsoever" (187), while Lillian Faderman posits that the "predominantly heterosexual readers" would have read the story as "an ironic commentary on the social life of 'spinsters'" ("What is Lesbian Literature?" 54). Bettina Knapp, however, argues that "Stein's repeated use of the motif of 'being gay' . . . implies lesbianism, but also happiness and release" (94), while Marjorie Perloff simply asks, "If we interpret 'gay' as homosexual, what are Helen Furr and Georgine Skeene doing when they 'sit regularly' with the dark and heavy men?" (103). During Stein's time, Perloff continues, "the designation of 'gay' as 'homosexual' was not yet so much a known underground meaning" as one that was still known by its dictionary definition of "happy" or "good-humored" (102). Bruce Kellner, the editor of a collection of essays on Stein, writes that "Stein may be the first to have employed the word as double entendre" (230). Jayne L. Walker goes even further: "'Being gay,' the dominant motif, is repeated with variations that multiply its meanings as the text progresses. . . . 'being gay' comes to signify both a particular action and a statement of sexual identity . . . [the] interplay of repetition and difference subtly renders a process of psychological change" (80, 81). Granted, much of *Vanity Fair*'s reading public would not have understood "gay" in its now familiar definition of *homosexual,* but the possibility of attracting the attention of those who knew the underground meaning was increased by such a popular reprinting.

When the story appeared in *Vanity Fair,* the title was followed with a subtitle that concisely summarized the plot: "The Tale of Two Young Ladies Who Were Gay Together and of How One Left the Other Behind." The editorial introduction commented that the "amusing short story" was written "in one of Miss Gertrude Stein's simpler manners" and that it "should convince those readers who have hitherto been baffled by her later and more telegraphic style that she is really a writer of remarkable abilities." According to this introduction, "the style, though queer, is exactly suited to the subject, which if it were not developed monotonously could scarcely be developed at all" (55). Other Stein stories published in the popular press appeared with similar subtitles, Bryce Conrad argues, and were the magazine's attempt to "package" Stein's modernist style to "construct and prescribe" a judgment of the work's literary value "that readers would be unwilling or unable to formulate for themselves" (222).[4] He reads this "packaging" as a positive marketing strategy designed to sell not only Gertrude Stein but also modernism to a skeptical reading public and contends that Stein "undoubtedly learned much from the way that the magazine constructed her market value by emphasizing her connection to modern French painting and her wartime relief activities" (223). But beneath the faint praise of *Vanity Fair*'s editorializing prologue, the magazine's parodic response to it three months later, "When Helen Furr Got Gay with Harold Moos," challenges *Vanity Fair*'s marketing intent and provides an alternative interpretation of what "product" the magazine was selling.

To say that "Miss Furr and Miss Skeene" "is a story of how a girl from a nice home comes out of the closet, has a brief fling with a less nice girl, and thus gains the experience to carry on with her 'gay' life," according to Marjorie Perloff, "is to reduce Stein's enormously subtle work to a cartoon. The text itself remains impervious to such an easy reading for it never allows us to make secure judgments about characters and action" (103). Much of the inability on the part of the reader to decide absolutes is because of Stein's at times exasperating style. Constructing her story from a deliberately limited lexicon, Stein repeats certain words, such as *gay, regularly,* and *cultivating,* changing the meaning of the word each time it is used. As Perloff characterizes this style, "from Stein's perspective" the "best words . . . are those whose meanings remain equivocal and hence able to take on slightly different shading at each reappearance." Stein's short story is remarkable for the limited words it does use, which are, as Perloff notes, "defined only by their indefinability" (101), and for the story that is constructed from those relatively few words. Perloff fastens on the word *gay* by way of an example. First introduced in the seventh sentence of the story—"She [Helen Furr] did not find it gay living in the same place where she had always been living"—the word *gay,* according to Perloff, "strikes us at first as meaning no more than that Helen Furr is somehow bored at home. Not until 'gay' begins to undergo its series of permutations does its other meaning (inevitably prominent for the contemporary reader but surely latent in Stein's text) come into prominence" (102).

Stein's double entendres that create stylistic license transform that denotative definition of *gay* into a subversive meaning. Corinne E. Blackmer suggests that "Stein renders the contextual meaning of the 'gay' relationship between Misses Furr and Skeene so transparent that only the ingrained habit of the closet . . . could prevent anyone from perceiving this story as a coming-out narrative that assumes the existence of an articulate homosexual community" (93). Much has been made of Stein's experimentations with language and their consequent challenges to and elaborations on the modernist tradition, but might not her "permutations" here be a challenge to the traditional romance and social plot of heterosexuality? Might Stein's most successful experimentation be her ability to publish a seemingly benign short story that offers a subversive declaration of same-sex intimacy, as Zimmerman reads her "cryptic language of sexuality" and her oblique "hinting" of a lesbian relationship (*Safe Sea* 6)? Might her double entendre use of *gay*, simultaneously affirming and disaffirming the feminine ideal and the heterosexual status quo, in a popular and widely read magazine be the ultimate subversive act itself?

Such clarity of double meanings becomes more ambiguous when Stein's short story is examined in relation to its 1923 *Vanity Fair* parody. A parodic advertisement for the magazine that appeared three months after the publication of "Miss Furr and Miss Skeene" indicates that while the subversive meaning of *gay* was perhaps officially unknown, sophisticated readers might have recognized the underground meaning. Desiring a more literary form of self-promotion than simply loud or colorful advertisements, *Vanity Fair* created fictional stories that offered a sure-fire cure for boring dinner guests, uninformed husbands or wives, poor conversationalists, and generally uninteresting people. The cure, never revealed until the last sentence of the page-long piece, was, of course, a subscription to *Vanity Fair*. In October 1923, one of these clever advertisements appeared under the title "When Helen Furr Got Gay With Harold Moos" and was billed as "A Narrative Written in the Now Popular Manner of Gertrude Stein." The story in the advertisement begins where Stein's story ends and uses the same style of repetition and word play as her text. Georgine Skeen (the spelling is changed in the *Vanity Fair* parody) has left Helen Furr at the place where they had been so gay together, and Helen, according to *Vanity Fair*, "went on being gay there. She was quite gay and a little more gay than she had been when she and Georgine Skeen had been gay there together. This was because she received visits regularly from Harold Moos," who was not a "gay man" but was the "darkest" and "heaviest" and "baldest" of the men who sat regularly with Helen Furr (37).

As the story continues, Helen was "very gay" whenever Harold came to sit with her, and in fact, she was "much more gay than she had been when Georgine Skeen was living there then." Helen still, of course, "knew all the big ways of being gay and all the little ways of being gay," and she knew "all the old ways of being gay, and she thought up lots of new ways of being gay and particularly ways that Harold Moos would like to see her use in being gay." But rather than suggest that Harold was a sexual voyeur, watching Helen "being gay" with another woman, it is Harold himself who is the object of Helen's "gay" affections. She would talk "baby-talk" to him, straighten his tie, pick threads off his coat, put on and knock off his hat, all the while "always being gay" (37).

One day, when Helen was being gay and Harold "was feeling very dark and very heavy and very bald and not at all gay they were married—regularly there then." Helen went on "being gay" but could devise no new ways of "being gay," which eventually grated on Harold's nerves. After they had been married for a year, Harold, "who was not feeling regularly gay," said to Helen Furr, "'I have been thinking up a way of making you less gay and of making myself more regularly gay and in a *wholly new way.*'" With that pronouncement, Harold hits Helen over the head three times with his walking stick, which, he exclaims, does make him "already feel a little more gay." But to be "*extraordinarily* gay," he subscribes to the "gayest magazine in the world," which by this time readers have guessed is *Vanity Fair* (37).

Imitation may indeed be the highest form of flattery, but the replication of Stein's style and story for a *Vanity Fair* promotion indicates more than esteem for or amusement at Gertrude Stein's writing, particularly given how the advertisement deviated from the original "Miss Furr and Miss Skeene." If, as Conrad contends, editorially added subtitles were a means of marketing what was stylistically unpalatable or confusing, then *Vanity Fair*'s stylistic appropriation of a Stein short story, to the point of rewriting the ending Stein offered, was more than simply an attempt at profitable packaging. Specifically, what "product" was *Vanity Fair* attempting to sell? Modernism? Stein's writing abilities? If so, these goals had already been accomplished through editorial additions in Stein's reprinted "Miss Furr and Miss Skeene" when her "remarkable" writing abilities were heralded.

With its alterations and appropriations, *Vanity Fair* also seemed to be selling traditional heterosexuality. According to the magazine's subtitle to Stein's original, "The Tale of Two Young Ladies Who Were Gay Together and of How One Left the Other Behind," the story emphasizes the finite nature of the same-sex relationship and clearly articulates that such a relationship ends in loss, something Stein does not suggest. Georgine Skeene leaves Helen Furr to live with her brother for two months, Stein writes, but Helen Furr does not return to her parents. As the narrator explains, Helen "did go on being gay" and was actually "gay longer every day than they had been being gay when they were together being gay." *Vanity Fair*'s packaging, while perhaps providing a clearer representation for audiences confused by modernist style, altered Stein's subversive same-sex love story so that it would end in abandonment.

The magazine's parody three months later seems motivated by the same intent. Harold Moos knocks his "gay" wife "senseless" because her "gayness" did not please him (37). But Helen's "being gay" does not apparently include the same practices as it suggestively does in Stein's story, namely, same-sex sexuality. Rather, Helen's "gayness" consists of teasing Harold, playing silly word games with him, and acting absurdly submissive, all of which only annoys Harold, who is "not at all gay." His violent act of "regularly brain[ing]" his wife clearly signals his displeasure with her childish behavior, even though he is the recipient of such affection. So, too, his final decision, to subscribe to *Vanity Fair*, "the gayest magazine in the world," is driven by an impulse to rival his now-subdued wife in "gayness." Yet his method of exhibiting "gayness" is artificial—he attempts to regulate Helen's "gayness" by hitting her, and he attempts to instill "gayness" in himself by reading a magazine, both methods that run counter to the contemporary scientific theory that homosexuality was congenital and could not be removed physically or instilled intellectually. Moreover, Helen has been knocked unconscious, rendering her not actively "gay" as she had been but only a passive victim of Harold's aggression.

Vanity Fair's parody is, to be sure, a playful piece of clever imitation, which undoubtedly many readers enjoyed, if only to find out how a subscription to *Vanity Fair* and the personality "disorder" it was to cure were to be included in the story. But it also can be read as a comment on Stein's story. Although Helen Furr and Georgine Skeene can be "gay" together, Helen Furr and Harold Moos cannot be "gay" together, thereby reducing the definitional variety of *gay* to its underground meaning. If critics are correct in their suppositions that Stein was the first to use *gay* in a subversive way, the *Vanity Fair* copy seems to support this. If the notion that the subversive meaning of *gay* as *homosexual* was more well-known than critics have supposed and if this *Vanity Fair* story is working on that alternative meaning of *gay*, then other possibilities exist, in addition to the marketing strategy targeting the underground, but "in-the-know," homosexual reading population. Naming *Vanity Fair* the "gayest magazine in the world" would hardly seem to be a ploy from which the magazine would prosper. Yet given the level of sophistication of *Vanity Fair*'s readers and the editorial creed of the magazine, which promised to print from the "mock-cheerful angle of the satirist," *gay* is allowed to assume its dual definitions and to reach an audience that would have recognized such an entendre.[5] That there was speculation about the sexual behavior of the editor Frank Crowninshield and the "somewhat [vague] homosexual flavor" of the magazine's atmosphere (Douglas 112) only adds to the suspicion that *Vanity Fair* staffers might have recognized that *gay* might mean both *happy* and *homosexual*.[6]

Harold Moos's braining of the "gay" Helen, who, even when married, "went on being gay in all the big and little ways," illustrates the masculine and heterosexual suppression of her inverted sexuality and the inability of the heterosexual world, as represented by Harold Moos, to understand the culture and behavior of the "gay" world. At the end of the story, Helen is unconscious because Harold has decided that she must be made "less gay." Helen Furr's same-sex sexuality, which Stein presented, is reduced in the *Vanity Fair* parody to simply a phase of development, childlike and uncreative (Helen "could not think up any new way of being gay"), occurring under the influence of Georgine Skeene and away from the stability of heterosexuality (37). Georgine Skeen appears only briefly in the *Vanity Fair* advertisement, and Helen Furr, who in Stein's piece leaves her parent's house to move in with Georgine Skeene, ultimately returns to the heterosexual household presided over by Harold Moos.

Moreover, Harold Moos's transformation from just a "dark," "heavy," and "bald" man to one who has become "more regularly gay and in a *wholly new way*" has been accomplished by his subscription to *Vanity Fair*. He needs the magazine to seduce Helen Furr and win the sexual battle. The connection is clear: heterosexuality, even potency, is linked to wit, intelligence, and gaiety— all characteristics that *Vanity Fair* promised to provide its readers who sought sophistication and informed conversation. Thus, the "gayness" of Helen is ridiculed, reduced, and relegated to a short-lived experiment, ending when *Vanity Fair* pairs her with Harold Moos and she is "knocked regularly senseless" and silenced for her homosexual transgression (37).

Certainly, *Vanity Fair's* editorialized subtitles and imitative advertisements were marketing strategies intent on selling both Gertrude Stein to a skeptical American public and itself as proprietor of American good taste. But might not *Vanity Fair's* appropriations also have signaled that, in addition to Stein's belief that "the literary value of her writing was at odds with the marketplace values of American publishers" (Conrad 215), her well-known sexual relationship with Alice B. Toklas was at odds with the American public? These clever editorial introductions to and parodic alterations of Stein's short story under the guise of sales technique rendered impotent the subversive "gayness" of Stein's "Miss Furr and Miss Skeene." *Gay* returned to its positive meaning of "happy," and any alternative definitions it might have conjured were subjected to what amounts to a literary "braining." Stein, having initially introduced the same-sex relationship, was silenced by *Vanity Fair's* marketing tactics, which not only produced a belittling caricature but also offered the magazine as the "cure" for such a malady.

Other authors enacted similar literary "cures" for equally well-known female sexual inverts. In 1928, five years after Stein's "Miss Furr and Miss Skeene," the fictional portrayal of female inversion in the early twentieth century reached its zenith with the publication of four pivotal texts: Radclyffe Hall's thinly veiled autobiography, *The Well of Loneliness;* Virginia Woolf's fantasy of sex and gender change, *Orlando;* Djuna Barnes's deviously satiric *Ladies Almanack;* and Compton Mackenzie's parodic novel *Extraordinary Women.*[7] Yet this watershed only exacerbated the backlash against masculine women and female inverts both on the page and in person. With the exception of Hall's

Well, these texts deliberately satirized the image of a sexually independent masculine woman who exhibited inverted sexuality in order to decrease or dismiss the sexual threat she posed. Although they "clearly broached the same subject," the critic Adam Parkes writes, they "escaped official censure" because they "set out to make readers laugh" (434). Following the strategy proposed by *Vanity Fair*'s appropriation of Stein's story—use of characters and continuation of her plot but forcible removal of the "gay" label Stein attached to Helen Furr—and the negation of its subversiveness, the American author Henry von Rhau presented a parody of Radclyffe Hall's *Well of Loneliness,* and Djuna Barnes belittled the lives of the American expatriate Natalie Barney and her entourage.

Written as a serious endeavor to portray the life of an "invert," Stephen Gordon, Hall's *Well* relied on contemporary sexological theories to explain Stephen's actions. Havelock Ellis, writing in a commentary published with Hall's novel, praised its "notable psychological and sociological significance." Declaring it "the first English novel which presents, in a completely faithful and uncompromising form, one particular aspect of sexual life as it exists among us to-day," Ellis suggested that "we must place Radclyffe Hall's book on a high level of distinction" (n.p.). Yet Hall's earnest attempt to sympathize with Stephen Gordon was ridiculed in the American Henry von Rhau's satiric treatment entitled *The Hell of Loneliness* (1929). The American Djuna Barnes's deviously satiric *Ladies Almanack,* often sexually explicit and bawdy, thinly disguised the sex lives of expatriate women in Paris, most notably Natalie Clifford Barney, who appears in Barnes's satire as the heroic Dame Evangeline Musset. In both of these texts, as in *Vanity Fair*'s parody of "Miss Furr and Miss Skeene," the image of a sexually independent masculine woman who exhibited inverted sexuality is deliberately satirized to undermine the sexual threat she presented.

Despite Hall's earnestness, her novel provoked public outrage and moral condemnation that culminated in obscenity trials, in both England and the United States, and the novel's censure in Great Britain. Even though the judge in the British obscenity case conceded that *Well* "had some literary merit" and that such a book "might even have a strong moral influence," he contended the novel did not contain "one word that suggested that anyone with the horrible tendencies described was in the least degree blameworthy. All the characters were presented as attractive people and put forward with admiration" (quoted in Parkes 435). To make matters worse, Alan Parkes notes, the judge also concluded that "certain acts were described in the most alluring terms" (435). Making her female inverts above reproach, Hall's biographer, Michael

Baker, avers, "provoked moral censure" (220). If these virtues, Parkes argues, "had been nonexistent or at least laughable . . . *The Well of Loneliness* would have passed muster as having, if not a 'strong' moral influence, at least not a bad one" (435).

The American and English publics, however, did not have long to wait before *The Well of Loneliness* and the ensuing cult of censorship became laughable. Within five years after the 1928 publication of *Well,* four parodies appeared on the scene that took as their subject matter not simply the life of a female sexual invert but specifically Radclyffe Hall's controversial novel: Beresford Egan's *Sink of Solitude* (1928), a "Verse Lampoon" accompanied by a "Series of Satirical Drawings"; Henry von Rhau's *Hell of Loneliness* (1929); Percy Reginald Stephensen's *Well of Sleevelessness: A Tale for the Least of These Little Ones* (1929); and Robert Leicester's *Hell of Comeliness* (1933). In his introduction to Egan's *Sink,* P. R. Stephensen declared, "If ever there was an occasion for reviving the lost art of the lampoon, it is this trivial and vulgar occasion" (9).

Yet it was not simply that *The Well of Loneliness* was parodied. The swift appearance of these parodies implicitly suggested numerous cultural attitudes. That *Well* was parodied bespoke its popularity—the audience reading the parodies would have had to know the novel to understand many of the inside jokes and direct references to Stephen Gordon's life. Despite condemnation by the British home secretary and the prohibition of its publication in England, the novel fairly jumped off the shelves before it was banned, and afterward it was smuggled in from the Continent, where it also was a success. The government's censure, as Stephensen wrote in the preface of another of Egan's satires on British governance, *Policemen of the Lord, a Political Satire,* had contributed to the popularity of Hall's novel. "This is, above all, not a defence of *The Well of Loneliness,* which is a dull and insipid book," he declared. "But for the combined efforts of James Douglas [Sunday editor of the *Daily Express*] and William Joynson-Hicks [British home secretary], the book would more than probably have fallen into insignificance already. But these two simple fellows, the one with his publicity, the other with his brief authority, have made almost a martyr of Miss Radclyffe Hall. Thanks to their crusade, millions of shop, office, and mill girls have been led to ask the furtive question: What is Lesbianism?" (quoted in Brittain 97).

Henry von Rhau's limited edition, forty-page parody turned the world of Hall's *Well of Loneliness* upside down by crassly ridiculing the very sexuality Hall presented. Dedicated to "Satyrs All by Dryads Bilked," von Rhau's *Hell of Loneliness* parodied just enough specific *Well of Loneliness* events and characters—the birth of Stephen, the scene at Alec's bar, and the descriptions of

Anna and Philip Gordon and Miss Puddleton, for example—to make the connection unmistakably clear. Clearly, von Rhau's careful appropriation of Hall's
Well, turning her serious examination of a life of an "invert" in England into
a humorous rendition of a New Jersey man emasculated first by his sexually
inept parents and then by his wife when she takes a female lover, is meant as
an indictment of the female invert's lifestyle that destroys heterosexual marriage and threatens and even emasculates men.

Unlike *Well*, which begins "not very far from Upton-on-Severn—between
it, in fact, and the Malvern Hills" at the "country seat of the Gordons of Bram-
ley" (11), von Rhau's *Hell* lacks the British aristocratic air. Instead, *Hell* is set
in New Jersey, "not very far from Weehawken, between it in fact, and Hoboken" (7). Compared with the Gordons' "well-timbered, well-cottaged, well-
fenced and well-watered" property and their Georgian red brick house that
not only is "charming" but also has "dignity and pride without ostentation,
self-assurance without arrogance, repose without inertia," and "a gentle aloofness" (11) is the country seat of their vulgar counterparts, the Kugelmanns.
Their New Jersey home is, according to the narrator, "probably the most hideous house in existence," described as a "smelly, drab, damp horror." "No one,"
the narrator concedes, "could have conceived of it but an idiot and no one
could have lived in it but the Kounty Kugelmanns" (7).

Nevertheless, the house is beloved by its owner, Baron Ehrenfriedrich J.
Kugelmann, and to it, in the "early 90s," he brings his "buxom-bride—Gunikunda Schmitt of Hoboken," who can only mutter "'Phooy'" when she sees
the house. Anna Gordon, of course, is Gunikunda Schmitt's predecessor and
is first introduced as a bride of twenty, "lovely as only an Irish woman can be,"
a "slim virgin thing, all chastity" when Sir Philip Gordon first meets her. In
short, according to Hall's narrator, Anna is "the archetype of the very perfect
woman, whom creating God had found good" (11). For his part, Baron Kugelmann, whose character is already suggested in his affinity to the shabbiness
and "idiocy" of his house, treats his wife carelessly and discourteously, "load-
ing her down with carpet bags" on their wedding day "until she bent double."
Compared with the callous drunk Kugelmann, Sir Philip Gordon acts as the
aristocrat he is, "noble," with lips "well-modeled and sensitive and ardent" that
"revealed him as a dreamer and a lover" (12).

The world populated by the Kugelmanns is von Rhau's crass version of
English aristocracy; Hall's serene setting is countered with the failed aristocracy of a displaced baron who can do no better than settle in New Jersey.
Whereas Hall's purpose in establishing the best pedigree for her "invert" signals a desire for acceptance into English society and an attempt to produce a

well-bred genetic basis for "inversion," von Rhau's placement of his parody in the "smelly, drab, damp horror" of the Kugelmann estate suggests that his plea for sympathy will be for someone far different from the "invert." Furthermore, the clear patterning of Gunikunda Schmitt and Ehrenfriedrich J. Kugelmann as the opposites of Stephen Gordon's parents establishes *Hell*'s characters as caricatures, absurd to the extreme, particularly when compared with the "archetypes" of heterosexual bliss.

Von Rhau's setting, however, is not the only opposition he creates. Both the Gordons and the Kugelmanns are married ten years before having a child, but whereas the Gordons await their child with the anticipation of "complete fulfillment, the fulfillment for which they had both been waiting," the Kugelmanns do not even "know how to go about" conceiving a child, since they live, according to the narrator, "in the age of innocence" (8). Having failed to have had the facts of life explained to him by his parents, the baron accidentally finds a book, *What a Midwife Should Know,* and, having "studied it hard," is rewarded with an infant, Otto. The Gordons, despite their longing for a son, are given a daughter, "a narrow-hipped, wide-shouldered little tadpole of a baby" whom they name Stephen (13).

In addition to von Rhau's oppositional setting and characterization of the Gordons of England and the Kugelmanns of New Jersey, he connects Stephen to Otto. Stephen, after initially crying for three hours without ceasing, "as though outraged to find itself ejected into life," Hall's narrator explains, becomes "quite a well-behaved baby" with a "fine constitution" (14). Otto, whose unstoppable howling turns the night "hideous" and the day "noisome," makes life in the Kugelmann home "just hell." Baron Kugelmann's high hopes for Otto are dashed when he finds that Otto is "just like other children, only worse." Still, the baron wishes for more children, "so Otto could have lots of brothers and sisters to fight with." Baroness Kugelmann, however, refuses with a terse explanation: "'Once bitten, twice shy'" (9). Stephen, too, is to have no siblings, although unlike the baroness, the Gordons want another child, preferably the much-desired son.

Not only is the behavior of Hall's fictional infant altered, but, more important, the infant's sex is changed. This difference is crucial because at the end of the story the character with whom the reader is expected to sympathize is not, as is the case in Hall's novel, a female invert but a heterosexual man. The sex change, then, serves to shift the focus from sexual inversion as a natural right "denied" by narrow-minded heterosexual society to, in von Rhau's parody, a sexuality that denies heterosexual men their wives, friends, homes, and economic property. In short, in *Hell*, the female invert is the figurative castrator of socially acceptable heterosexual men, maligned for her intrusion and invasion into heterosexual marriage, not, as Hall's novel purports, a misunderstood social outcast deserving of society's sympathy.

The similarities between *Well* and *Hell* continue, most notably in the events involved in Stephen's upbringing. Whereas Philip Gordon's love for horses is replicated in Stephen, the baron, who loved only whisky more than horses, taunts two-year-old Otto with a rocking horse "the size of a brindle cow." He would "lift little Otto up, seize the horse's tail and rock it violently 'till Otto fell on his head, then," the narrator notes, "the Baron would roar with laughter." When Otto is five, his horse troubles worsen; he is given a "real live pony," described by the narrator as a "hideous brute—cow-hocked, spavined and wind broken" (10). Although the baron thinks it would be a "good joke" to bring the pony up to Otto's nursery, he is met with "loud lamentation," and so the wary Otto, "roaring his protests," is brought out to the stable. Otto attempts to befriend the pony, despite "every evidence of mutual distrust and dislike," but is promptly bitten on the hand and runs away; in retaliation, Otto pelts the "brute" with rocks. With this mutual display of aggression, the narrator ironically adds, "they knew they belonged to each other" (11).

Von Rhau's account of Otto's young life moves quickly. Young Otto's failure to answer "simple questions on the advantages of the bi-cameral system of government and on the theory of relativity" disappoints the baron, who labels him a "dum-kopf," boxes his ears, and then hires Miss Muddleton, a "large and rawboned" English woman of "uncertain age" (11–12), to teach him. Muddle, as she is not-so-fondly called, "always wore a monocle, a gray skirt and coat, high button shoes, a red tie and a derby hat" and is, to Otto's "childish mind," an "appalling example of repression."[8] Von Rhau's Muddle is fashioned after Hall's Miss Puddleton, herself a representation of sexual repression, although Puddle's influence is far more supportive than Muddle's. Otto himself is so "full of repression" that whenever Muddle boxes his ears, "he would dearly want to murder her" (12), although he is too weak to do so and "lacked the proper implements of slaughter" (13). Conversely, Puddle stimulates Stephen's mind with lessons from mathematics and algebra to Latin and Greek, and Stephen gazes at Puddle "in a kind of amazement" (68). Their relationship as teacher-student becomes, as the novel progresses, one of confidantes and travel companions; Stephen relies on the practical wisdom of Puddle. The relationship between Otto and Muddle, however, is not nearly so endearing or enduring as their models'; the most affection Muddle can muster is boxing the deserving Otto's ears "every few minutes" (16).

Thankfully for Otto, his emerging sexual interests, even though formed without the benefit of Freud, Ellis, and Krafft-Ebing since they were "barred from the nursery," soon focus on the Kugelmann's "maid of all work" (13), Fanny Rumpelbauch. Otto happens upon her one day as she is cleaning the nursery, listlessly flicking dust from one spot to another and "bending over." Her position exposes to the repressed Otto "a generous ankle and a fat calf encased in an ample red yarn stocking." It was, the narrator concedes, "[Otto's] first consciousness of SEX," and "it overwhelmed him" (14). Unable to do anything else, Otto lunges at "Rumpel" and bites her in the calf, not letting go until the efforts of the Kugelmann family succeed in prying him loose. Despite Otto's effort, the narrator expounds, neither "his lust nor his curiosity were appeased," and he "fretfully" wondered: "What is LIFE, what is LOVE, what is SEX" (15).

Otto's first foray into lust-driven physical interaction with another person, although ill-conceived, is nevertheless appropriately heterosexual and is another important deviation from Radclyffe Hall's *Well of Loneliness*. Stephen's first emotional feelings, too, are directed at a servant, the young maid Collins. When she first sees Collins, Stephen "knew that she loved her," which is a "startling revelation" to her. Eager for love, the seven-year-old Stephen yearns to touch Collins and extends a "rather uncertain hand" to stroke her sleeve as Collins sweeps the stairs. Later in the day, Collins returns Stephen's touch with an innocent kiss as she sets out the tea, and "Stephen stood speechless from a sheer sense of joy" (17); "she knew nothing but beauty and Collins, and the two were as one, and the one was Stephen" (18). From this moment until Collins leaves the Gordon household to marry, Stephen's world "turned on an axis of Collins" (18), and she tries to impress the maid with her heroic characterizations of Lord Nelson. Otto, as a result of his sexual awakening, is locked in the coal cellar by the baron when Fanny Rumpelbauch cleans the nursery.

Von Rhau's rendering of Otto's encounter with Rumpel clearly deviates from Hall's narration of Stephen's feelings for Collins. Von Rhau not only substitutes a heterosexual object for Otto, who despite his young age assumes the male gaze at the objectified female and the role of pursuer, but also replaces Stephen's feelings of "love" with Otto's violent expression of undisguised physical lust. Thus, von Rhau conflates Stephen's idealized romanticism with Otto's base and vulgar actions by closely paralleling the two episodes. Stephen's love is transformed into Otto's lust just as Hall's female inversion is transformed into von Rhau's heterosexuality, and readers' sympathies shift from the "inverted" Stephen, who pleads for acceptance, to the hapless, poorly raised Otto, who, at the novel's end, solicits sympathy.

Unfortunately for the females who cross his path, Otto still is unable to control his physical expressions of lust, and Connie, "a nasty fat little girl . . . with cross eyes and a running nose," is next to receive his teeth marks of passion. When Otto sees Connie, "everything else faded out," and "he trembled all over as if he were going to throw a fit, then with a bellow, he charged at Connie, flung himself upon her and bit her full on the neck like a lover." Such, the narrator avers, "was Otto's LUST." As Muddle hits him to persuade him to relinquish his grip, the "dreadful little masochist" only cries, "Harder" (22). Connie, however, is not at all dismayed by the sudden embrace and "shrieked with delight" (22–23). They are, the narrator concedes, "beautifully mated." But Connie's father breaks his daughter's heart by pouring a bucket of water over Otto, winking at Muddle and chuckling, "Boys will be boys" (23). Although he succeeds in separating the two young lovers, they are fated to meet again, after Otto returns from school at Heton.

While at Heton, Otto meets Aubrey Shivesley, who is studying to be a "bootlegger or bootician as he rather snobbishly called it" (23). They play croquet and ping-pong and sing duets, with Aubrey providing a "beautiful soprano voice." When Otto and Aubrey go to the Kugelmann home, not much has changed. The baron is still drunk, only now complaining about Prohibition; the baroness is "secretly reading Krafft-Ebing with the feeling that Knowledge is Power" (24); and Muddle still wears the same derby and high-button shoes. "Life seemed just horrid" to Otto, until he rushes to the window and sees Connie. No longer the little girl he remembered, Connie now is a "full-buttocked" and "full-breasted" woman, whose "nostrils and cross eyes betokened great promise" (25). Otto runs out of the house, and in a replay of their first passionate embrace, "he bit full on the neck like a lover," and Connie, who was "all womanly sweetness and yielding," did not "deny" Otto his lustful pleasures. The sexual consummation causes the apparently homosexual Aubrey, who has been watching his beloved Otto from the window, to attempt suicide. It also precipitates a "pretty little shot-gun wedding" between Otto and Connie (26).

Despite their premarital behavior, the young Kugelmanns do not have a child, and the nursery remains locked, "for the present at least," according to a "blushingly pretty" Connie (27). Otto, however, is not to have the experience of fatherhood. Connie one day reveals to Otto that she has "met the most wonderful person" (28), a Russian princess named Ivanova-Feodronova Kaskawisky. "'She's so magnificent, so strong, so brave, so fine,'" Connie swoons, "'she reminds me of some tall building with the wind howling 'round'" (29). Immediately after telling Otto that he is "'going to love Ivanova-Feodronova'" (30), Connie rushes to the door to welcome the princess, whom she has invited for dinner. When the princess sees Connie before the fire, she "crossed the room in masterful strides" and embraces her "in a bearlike hug" (32). She shakes Otto's hand, crushing it until he winces; he thinks "she looks like Jack Dempsey in a tailor-made suit" (33). But the two competitors for Connie have much in common. Ivanova-Feodronova "approved the sartorial perfection of Otto's dinner coat, the width of his wing collar and the cut of his tie, his charming idea of wearing rubber boots instead of patent leather gaiter-boots" (33). Otto compliments the masculine Ivanova-Feodronova "on her tailor's skill—how well he had brought out her lines—the wide strong shoulders, the flat narrow hips" (33–34). The two find that they have the same shirt-maker, wear the same size, and are "addicted to ties and handkerchiefs that matched" (34).

The masculinized Ivanova-Feodronova is the foil to Stephen's first long-term love, Mary Llewellyn, a young and naive feminine woman whom Stephen befriends while both work in the ambulance service. Adoring Stephen as her protector and falling in love with her during the war, the shell-shocked Mary presents a striking feminine counter to the masculine and self-assured Russian princess who smokes a pipe and dresses in a man's clothing. Otto has lost his wife to a female invert who seems to be more masculine than he is, and when Otto reverts back to his old fetishes of passion, she proves it. One night Otto catches a passing glimpse of Ivanova-Feodronova's "well-turned ankle, an admirably molded calf, a dimpled knee and a pleasing thigh" and, "hurtled on by uncontrolled desire," sinks his teeth into her calf. The princess, however, signaling her equality with the man, is able to knock Otto out flat with "two well-timed clips" (37). An insurmountable opponent, she differs from the victims of Otto's adolescent passionate bites, who required the efforts of many people to free them. Moreover, Ivanova-Feodronova's sexual inversion is characterized by masculine strength, able not only to steal a wife away but also to knock a husband cold.

Unable to halt the progress of Connie's and Ivanova-Feodronova's love, Otto has no choice but to watch the Russian princess move in, first to the guest room and then, a short time later, into "the big, sunny, double bedroom, so that Connie would be near her if she was needed in the night" (40). Finally, Otto is displaced altogether from the Kugelmann home, as well as his business, and spends his days at the club until the bar cuts off his credit. Otto's predicament, however, is not unique; he notices that the club is being overrun by similarly displaced husbands. "They were men who had known life, and lived it and loved it," the narrator relates in a tone reminiscent of *Well*'s narrator. "Now they were outcasts, and their horrible secret showed in their eyes" (43–44). Paralleling the club scene in the *The Well of Loneliness*, where inverts gather at

Alec's, the only place they are welcome to express their homosexual feelings, *Hell*'s scene is populated not with inverts but with the men the female inverts have displaced. Echoing the laments of Hall's homosexuals—that they are outcasts on whom Nature has exacted revenge—von Rhau's heterosexual men appropriate what in *Well* is a plea for sympathy for homosexuals, turning it, instead, into a plea for sympathy for the men who are emasculated by the women. Even their "old haunts" have become "Speakeasiettes where men were not welcome" (45); "Tony's," for instance, now is "Antoinette's." The younger generation, which in the *The Well of Loneliness* holds the promise of accepting homosexuality, is, in *The Hell of Loneliness,* belittled as self-absorbed and of no help or comfort at all to the men who have been replaced.

The future for Otto and the rest of the men is dismal. "Deeply they felt their loneliness—shunned and cast out like leperous creatures" (46), the narrator laments, just as the narrator of Hall's novel does. But von Rhau's men suffer an even greater tragedy than Hall's homosexuals when the bar bill comes due and "no one had money. They were flung into the street amid high laughter; the bartender kicked them and shewed them soundly. Then the police clubbed them" and sentenced them to six months in jail. "'They're a menace, a menace,'" says the magistrate shrilly, "'keep them apart when they get to the hoosegow.'" Only now, thrown in jail because they are unable to pay for their bar bill, do the men know "to the full THE HELL OF LONELINESS when the policeman curtseyed and took them away" (47).

Curiously, however, von Rhau follows Hall's lead in structuring sexuality and the ultimate couplings between two different genders. In *Well,* the overtly masculine Stephen Gordon becomes involved with the feminine Mary Llewellyn. Ivanova-Feodronova, likewise masculine in attire and mannerism, ultimately is coupled with the curvaceous and feminine Connie. Both novels maintain the status quo of masculinity and femininity, even while disrupting the heterosexual tradition. But whereas Hall's infamous novel attempts serious renderings of the "female invert" drawn from life, von Rhau's invert reflects the parodic backlash that excoriated the enfranchised masculine woman. Hall follows the contemporary scientific theories of inversion by seriously fashioning her women according to theorized masculine genderings, but von Rhau's characterizations are reductive and dismissive.

Just as Stein's "Miss Furr and Miss Skeene" is parodied by the *Vanity Fair* advertisement that not only ridicules the original story but transforms the subversive plot of women's same-sex intimacies into a plot of heterosexuality, so, too, *The Hell of Loneliness* transforms through parodic imitation the serious *Well of Loneliness,* reducing Hall's honest portrayal of the female invert's life to the drunken escapades of the lust-driven Otto Kugelmann. The invert Stephen, who searches for a sensitive woman to love amidst confusion, is countered by the aggressive Otto, who seems to experience only lust for the opposite sex. Hall's plea for sympathy is countered by von Rhau's, but clearly his plea is for the men of the wives who have taken female lovers. Given the aggressive masculine nature of the female invert as embodied in the representative Ivanova-Feodronova, von Rhau's intention is to portray her as an extreme, yet thoroughly plausible character. That men, like Otto and the rest who are kicked out of the bar, are unable to stand up to her and retain their status in the heterosexual status quo certainly illustrates the threat that von Rhau felt from powerful, masculine women. Much as O'Hagan's fourth duologue questioned the reproductive efficacy of the emancipated woman, so, too, von Rhau fastens on the sexual threat as recounted through Hall's *Well of Loneliness*. The hell of such loneliness, then, is that the man is emasculated by a woman who is more masculine than he. This female invert, unlike *Vanity Fair*'s Helen Furr, whose "literary brain[ing]" returned her to the heterosexual status quo, received only a mild bite on the calf by a lustful Otto. Clearly, teeth marks alone are not enough to deter her from disrupting the heterosexual society—and so she must be belittled, denigrated, and portrayed as the unstoppable force that man is unable to counter except through parody.

Djuna Barnes similarly fixes on an existing example as the subject for her parody, but unlike the others, Barnes chooses a real woman to caricature. Privately printed in 1928, *Ladies Almanack* has attracted an audience of literary scholars and historians whose interpretations seem to fall into the same trap that Virginia Woolf set for her own *Orlando*. "Yes its [sic] done," Woolf wrote in her diary, "It may fall between stools, be too long for a joke, & too frivolous for a serious book" (3:177). At the base of this tension between frivolity and sincerity is Woolf's inability to imagine what her verbal creation is, a similar conceptual dilemma posed for readers of Barnes's *Ladies Almanack*, a comical, if not malicious story of the larger-than-lesbian-life of the thinly disguised expatriate doyenne Natalie Barney.

Framing this dilemma in terms of imaginative "conceivability" is deliberate, particularly since *Ladies Almanack* mysteriously complicates the notion of "conception" when both of its texts—the written and the twenty-six pen-and-ink illustrations—are read in conjunction. The critic Ruth Vanita has suggested that the word *conception* relies on its two common meanings: the conception or thought of an idea and the conception of a child. Exploring this distinction, Vanita posits that "depending on the gender of the noun or pronoun to which the word is attached, its meaning is generally construed to be mental or physical—if a man conceives, he gives birth to an idea, a thought, a text; conversely, if a woman conceives, she gives birth to a child of flesh and blood" (20–21). The gendered difference is between creation and reproduction, a distinction that takes on massive importance given the inability of two women—and it is sexually active female inverts who populate the text of *Ladies Almanack*—to "conceive" with each other as women are supposed to do with a man.

Dame Evangeline Musset, the lesbian heroine of *Ladies Almanack,* embodies the complexity of the different notions of conception. "Developed in the Womb of her most gentle Mother to be a Boy," the text reads, "when . . . she came forth an Inch or so less than this, she paid no Heed to the Error." Instead she dresses herself in the role of male hunter and with her young dogs "set[s] out upon the Road of Destiny" (7). Musset's intuited sex is male, but that does not match up with her physical reality—"she came forth an Inch or so less than this"—and it is unclear whether Musset's sex or her shortened sexual stature is the "Error." Even more specifically, the dilemma is between physiological abnormality—a male with small genitals or a female with protruding genitals—or a social aberrance of misassigned gender.

Musset's behavior also resists easy categorization. Her father, the narrator notes, "spent many a windy Eve pacing his Library in the most normal of Night-Shirts, trying to think of ways to bring his erring Child back into that Religion and Activity which has ever been thought sufficient for a Woman" (8), namely, femininity and heterosexual desire. When he realizes that women flee from her, "snatch[ing] their Skirts from Contamination," and that her masculine sexual aggressiveness exercised in pursuit of women "would by no Road, lead her to the Altar," he asks Musset, "What am I to do?" She answers with a matter-of-fact rhetorical question: "Thou, good Governor, wast expecting a Son when you lay atop of your Choosing, why then be so mortal wounded when you perceive that you have your Wish? Am I not doing after your very Desire, and is it not the more commendable, seeing that I do it without the Tools for the Trade, and yet nothing complain?" (8). This confusion over what Musset is exactly since she does not fit the neat categories of "man" or "woman" establishes Musset's lesbian sexuality as physiological, a crucial determination because it embodies her inability to sexually "conceive" as either a creative man or a reproductive woman.

Before the generic *Ladies Almanack* even begins, Musset's presence more than confuses traditional sex-gender couplings; it dismisses them as a credible identification system. In Barnes's formulation, Musset's inconceivability appears to liberate her into a space that resists categorization, echoing Barnes's own struggle to define her sexuality. In her later years, according to Frances M. Doughty, Barnes "disavowed the world of women, denying that she was a lesbian." Interpreting Barnes's denial of the "lesbian" label, Doughty declares that "the issue is not whether Barnes was a lesbian or a heterosexual, but that she was neither" (149). Similarly, Shari Benstock wonders "to what degree was Djuna Barnes's art sexually ambivalent, shuttling between homophobia and lesbian desire, between cultural conservatism and artistic experiment" ("Sapphic" 187). Yet by Barnes's own admission, put in the same language as Woolf's generic dilemma about *Orlando,* she could not imagine herself as a lesbian, because as she demonstrated in *Ladies Almanack,* lesbian sexuality was inconceivable.

Moreover, sexual promiscuity, as exercised by Dame Evangeline Musset, clearly was foolish, superficial, and almost absurd. Karla Jay explores such promiscuity from an economic angle, focusing on the wealth that Natalie Barney lavished on many of the salonniers. Barnes was, by necessity, a recipient of Barney's largess, and, according to Jay, Barnes "was perpetually placed in the role of the beggar at the feast, the celebrant in the borrowed gown, the one to partake of others' hospitality without being able to return it in kind" ("Outsider" 184). When Barnes "depicted her wealthy friends in *Ladies Almanack,*" Jay concludes, "much of the bitterness emerged" ("Outsider" 185). Barney's sexual promiscuity was rivaled by her economic promiscuity, and despite her assistance in publishing *Ladies Almanack* (as well as subsidizing other artists' endeavors), she did not earn Barnes's respect.

Barney's Academy of Women brought together "elite women artists" who were to "nurture one another, provide supportive criticism for each other's work, and publish one another when necessary" (Jay, *Amazon* 33). But, as Jay relates, "this salon was not for everyone; Barney deeply detested the masses and envisioned herself as writing for and surrounding herself with the chosen few" ("Outsider" 185). Barnes's *Ladies Almanack* thus had a financially sinister component, repudiating Barney's obscene wealth and promiscuous spending habits by caricaturing her in the not-so-flattering character of Evangeline Musset. Barney's financial and cultural elitism is further parodied by the artistic medium Barnes chose. That Barney's "tribute" should be illustrated in a style of the common folk and available to them demeans the salon's elitism and suggests Barnes's resentment of Natalie Barney's conspicuous consumption of material wealth and women.

This tension between the common and the elite is nowhere more apparent than in the illustrations, done, according to the narrating "Lady of Fashion" in *Ladies Almanack,* with "apologies to ancient chapbooks, broadsheets, and," most notably, "Images Populaires" (3). Many of the drawings in *Ladies Alma-*

nack invite comparison with the reproductions found in a text called *L'imagerie populaire,* a 1925 anthology of French popular images that had their origins in medieval sources and changed only incrementally as they were copied through the centuries. The most obvious resemblance to this French collection is the cover illustration of the *Ladies Almanack* (see figure 10), clearly modeled after a plate entitled "Fragment de rabat de cheminée," in *L'imagerie populaire* (see figure 11). According to Andrew Field's biography of Barnes, she acknowledged this French collection as the source of her illustrations for both *Ryder* (1928)

Figure 10. Cover of Djuna Barnes's *Ladies Almanack* (1928; reprint, Elmwood Park, Ill.: Dalkey Archive Press, 1992). Reproduced by permission.

Fragment de rabat de cheminée, vers 1815. Original 32,5×34,5 cm.
La bande entière avait 1 m. 50 de long.

Figure 11. "Fragment de rabat de cheminée" in *L'imagerie populaire,* edited by Pierre Louis Ducharte and René Saulnier (Paris: Librarie de Paris, 1925), 57.

and *Ladies Almanack.* As Field recounts, Barnes showed him the "odd French albums which [she] had picked up in the bookstalls of Paris." He quotes her as saying, " 'I really shouldn't give away my secrets like this' " (125).

But tracing the source of Barnes's drawings to *L'imagerie populaire* answers only one of the questions surrounding the illustrations. More interesting is her abrupt change in artistic style. For *Ryder* and *Ladies Almanack,* Barnes abandoned the "Beardleyesque" line drawings that had accompanied her earlier poetry and journalistic writings and embraced this style of French folk art. Carolyn Burke suggests that Barnes's stylistic appropriation of the illustrations in *L'imagerie populaire* "opened a new vein of visual imagery" and inspired her with the "strong linearity, clear compositional principles, and bright, primary colors used by the eighteenth- and nineteenth-century imagiers (mass producers of graphic illustrations)" (76). Such a sourcebook, Burke continues, "offered a complete visual world, including saints and soldiers, virgins and amazons," which Barnes could then adapt to her own purpose (77).

Such explanations, however, seem too simplistic, particularly since Barnes's modern Parisian milieu would have exposed her to any number of artistic traditions and styles, all of which would have given her some type of "complete visual world." There is more at work than simply adopting various literary and artistic genres and fashioning a creative composition. By appropriating medieval and renaissance images found in French popular art to frame the satire of lesbian lives in literary Paris of the 1920s—thereby accomplishing the same historical validation that critics have suggested about her written text's reliance on long-established generic forms—Barnes's verbal and visual experiment seems to validate lesbian sexuality.

Yet it is important to note that these popular images were not an elite form; they were indiscriminately mass-produced for an audience generally unsophisticated in tastes. According to *L'imagerie populaire* editors Pierre Louis Ducharte and René Saulnier, "les imagiers eux-mêmes se sont copiés entre eux, souvent sans aucune pudeur" (the image makers often borrowed from one another, often completely without shame) (12). Moreover, the images are anonymous; the original artisan responsible for the woodcut or etching was most likely unknown. Furthermore, Ducharte and Saulnier wrote that connecting "popular" with "art" is complicating, because "toutes les équivoques possibles et en effet l'un semble s'opposer à l'autre. Qui dit art, dit création individuelle, et populaire sous-entend création collective" (the juxtaposition of these two words has caused all sorts of confusion, all possible ambiguities and in effect each word seems to be the opposite of the other. That is to say, "art" is an individual creation and "popular" is understood to be a collective creation) (9).

In his influential essay "The Work of Art in the Age of Mechanical Reproduction," Walter Benjamin suggested that beginning with the replication of the woodcut, mechanical reproduction represented "something new" because it disallowed knowledge of the original, or as Benjamin phrased it, "the whole sphere of authenticity is outside technical . . . reproducibility." He explained: "the technique of reproduction detaches the reproduced object from the domain of tradition. By making many reproductions it substitutes a plurality of copies for a unique existence. And in permitting the reproduction to meet the beholder or listener in his own particular situation, it reactivates the object reproduced. These two processes lead to a tremendous shattering of tradition which is the obverse of the contemporary crisis and renewal of mankind" (221). Mechanical reproduction, then, like the woodcuts decorating the pages of *L'imagerie populaire,* can be understood to be reproductive, although not creative. In other words, although able to be replicated, the woodcuts present nothing essentially new and are, in fact, only sterile copies of an unknown original. It is precisely this contrast between "creation" and "reproduction" that is reinforced by the illustrative style Barnes chose to accompany her verbal text, artistic reproductions but not creations. Moreover, as Adele Friedman noted in her discussion of *images populaires* and their connection to popular *chansons,* these artistic renderings "display traditional society as it was perceived from within" (766). As such, they demonstrate a fairly inflexible conformity to generally accepted ideas of order (767), even though they often present precisely the opposite view.

This topos of *le monde renversé*—or as Natalie Zemon Davis phrases it in her study of society and culture in early modern Europe, "the woman on top"—assumes not only political but sexual connotations. According to Davis, the "sexual inversion" that occurred during these carnivalesque moments consisted of switches in sex roles, often manifested by dressing or masking as the opposite sex. The primary impulse during these times, however, "was not homosexuality or a disturbed gender identity" but a finite form of "literary and festive transvestism" (129). Such "sexual inversion" is ultimately, Davis writes, "a source of order and stability." Drawing her conclusions from anthropologists and sociologists, Davis notes that in a hierarchical society a temporary turning of the world upside down can, in fact, clarify that hierarchical structure by reversing it. Even though such "inversion" can "correct and relieve the system when it has become authoritarian," such play does not "question the basic order of society itself" (130). In short, a world turned upside down can only be righted, not changed. Barnes's deliberate casting of her unconventional subject matter within the suggestive confines of not only sterile reproduction but also the trope of *le monde renversé,* even modeling some of her illustrations after the woodcuts in *L'imagerie populaire,* is, ultimately, a presentation of the "inverted" world, a definition inclusive of short-lived festivity and the early-twentieth-century sexological term for *homosexuality.*

This conclusion resounds throughout Barnes's text that finally not only indicts her subject matter but, since she is the authority of such "inversion," renders her "unnatural" as well. To pose this dilemma as a question: what does it mean when a woman gives birth to a text and how is this idea complicated when the content of that text is the sexual escapades of women who do not conceive as women are supposed to? The interrelated texts of *Ladies Almanack* provide an answer—they are ultimately a treatise on the tension between conception and reproduction that finally affirms the sterility and inauthenticity of lesbian sexuality. By fashioning the biography of Dame Evangeline Musset according to a topos that has such clear insinuations of fantasy, finitude, and disorder, Barnes signals the chaotic sexual space to which her lesbian was restricted, marginalized by, and removed from the restored social order. More specifically, her artistic appropriations of the generic traditions and the *images populaires* are, in essence, an assemblage of parts, each forcibly dismembered from its tradition, thus destroying the tradition. The woman is likewise destroyed. Not only is she condemned as a viable whole through fragmentation, but Musset's reassembling of sexual parts—a promiscuous act in and of itself—constructs a monstrous lesbian sexuality. This metonymic dismemberment, then, frighteningly reproduces but does not create the lesbian and ultimately renders her inconceivable.

In Barnes's display of the zodiac (see figure 12), the center of the circle is occupied by a naked woman, and her various physical parts, including "the dear buttock," "the kneeling knee," and "the love of life" (genital area), are each connected to the zodiac sign from which it came. Placing woman within the

ZODIAC

Figure 12. Illustration in Djuna Barnes's *Ladies Almanack*, 52. Reproduced by permission.

ancient symbol used to interpret, understand, and order the universe, Barnes apparently firmly historicizes her in the popular imagination, a conclusion other critics have reached regarding her use of the almanac tradition. However, what exactly is historicized? The dismembered lesbian body cannot be "conceived" of because all the pieces necessary to form a whole human conception are not available. Moreover, the direct references to the lesbian's sexual body parts—"the dear buttock" and "the love of life"—accentuate her sexuality, creating a woman who is not the sum of all her parts but a dismembered woman whose sex-related body parts are her identity. Placing the lesbian within the zodiac's circle and connecting the zodiac signs not with the whole woman's body but only with individual parts that emphasize her sexuality ultimately objectifies her sexuality, rendering her, at best, the sum of fragmented erogenous pieces.

The same destruction of lesbian sexuality by fragmentation is invoked when Dame Evangeline Musset playfully describes her ideal woman, an action she calls "moulding the Pot," a concept visually emphasized by the accompanying illustration of floating body parts (see figure 13). Although Musset never gets her wish "'to order our Ladies as we would, and not as they come,'" she is not dismayed and suggests the following composition culled from satirically named women who appear in the *Ladies Almanack:*

> "If I could mould the Pot nearer to the Heart's desire, I would have my Scullion's Eye lie in the Head of Billings-On-Coo, with the Breasts of Haughty on the Hips of Doll, on the Leg of Moll, with the Shins of Mazie, under the Scullion's Eye which lies in the Head of Billings-On-Coo. The Buttocks of a Girl I saw take a slip and slither one peelish day in Fall, when on her way to Devotion in the side Aisles of the Church of the *St Germain des Pres,* to lie on the back of the Hips of Doll, on the leg of Moll, whose shins are Mazie's, all under the Eye of the Scullion, Etc., and the rowdy Parts of a scampering Jade in Pluckford Place, on the front of the Back that was a Girl seen one peelish day, all under the Scullion's eye. . . . But the Hand," she said, "must be Queen Anne's, to smooth down the Dress with the rightful and elegant Gesture necessary to cover the Hip that was and the rowdy Part, etc., and the things that there were done." (65–66)

Musset's insistence on selectively piecing together her ideal lover illustrates her emphasis on parts deemed sexual or erotic—the breasts, the leg, the hips, the buttock, and the "rowdy Part"—a clear signal, like the zodiac, that the lesbian is identified by her physical sexuality. Moreover, Musset's "creation" is described as "fanciful," at best an imaginary figure who clearly does not exist and cannot be conceived of in the real world.

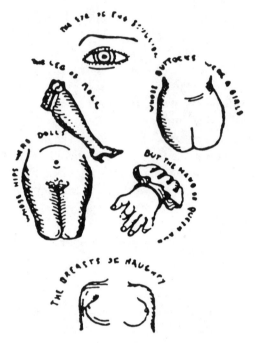

Figure 13. Illustration in Djuna Barnes's *Ladies Almanack,* 64. Reproduced by permission.

The ornamental illustration that appears on the title page of *Ladies Almanack* offers another example of the dismemberment of lesbian sexuality, again within the guise of tradition (see figure 14). Doughty reads the image as a "slightly stylized representation of female genitals, with Dame Musset, busby and all, at the entrance, appropriately enough, to the vagina" (151). By assigning sections of the image to anatomical parts, Doughty discovers the "disguise" and enjoys what she calls the "pleasure of recognition, the little self-congratulatory moment" of "getting it" (151, 152).

Yet this illustration positions the lesbian, in the form of Musset, precisely within the vagina—again, a dismembered sexual body part—suggesting that lesbian sexuality is simply genital intimacy. In the text of the *Ladies Almanack,* it is clear that Musset's physical sexual appetites far surpass any psychological or emotional benefit derived from the many women she loves. Barnes's clever frontispiece focuses the viewer's attention on this lesbian lust and carefully establishes that the story of lesbian sexuality that follows must necessarily be understood only as physical, genital pleasure.

Moreover, placing Musset squarely in the codified vagina prohibits entrance to it except by Musset herself, thereby dismissing any potential for procreation that may have existed. Patience Scalpel, the only heterosexual woman in the *Ladies Almanack* and the procreative foil to Musset's seemingly celebratory lesbian abandon, declares that her daughters "'shall go amarrying!'" "'Unless some Her puts them forth,'" Scalpel declares in support of heterosexuality, "'they themselves will have no Shes'" (13). Thus, Musset's place in the lesbian world and, specifically, in the stylized genitalia is owed to heterosexual procreative women; the history ultimately evoked, then, is where conception can exist only as the result of heterosexuality.

Barnes continues this torturous fragmentation of the lesbian's body through Musset's death at the end of the *Ladies Almanack*. Her funeral resembles Christ's procession to the cross (Lanser 44), yet by this time the reader knows that the sainthood and divine resemblance are only parodies, since the life of Dame Evangeline Musset is far from traditional sanctity. For two days, the text notes, a "wrangling" of grief is heard, and forty women shave their heads and carry the dead Musset "through the City"; then "she was sealed in a tomb for many days," while "the Women twittered about the Tomb like Birds about the Border of a Storm" (82–83). Saint Musset's body achieves its ultimate fate when "in the end they put her on a great Pyre and burned her to the Heart." But not every part of her body is destroyed. Musset's physical remains are completely consumed except for her tongue, which only flames and, the reader is told, "would not suffer Ash" (84).

Figure 14. Illustration in Djuna Barnes's *Ladies Almanack,* n.p. Reproduced by permission.

Barnes is successful at verbally and visually conflating the sacred with the profane, entombing Musset in a parallel of the Christ story yet burning her in a pagan ritual of death. Yet her tongue withstands the funeral rites; it is the phallic "tool" that signifies both her sexual masculinity and her lesbianism, her capability and her lack. Unlike other critics who read the unconsummable tongue as a "celebration of oral sexuality," Karla Jay interprets it as a "demeaning definition of lesbianism" because it focuses solely on the genital component of sexuality ("Outsider" 207). More specifically, the lesbian is once again reduced to one sexual part, dismembered even after death. The tongue, with the codified genitalia-heraldry that introduced the *Ladies Almanack,* presents the oral-genital sex that is the expression of Barnes's lesbian, a sexual entity that ultimately cannot be wholly conceived of because it is composed of only fragments. Even though Senorita Fly-About enjoys cunnilingual pleasure from Musset's immortal tongue—she "came down upon that Urn first," the text relates, "and beatitude played and flickered upon her Face, and from under her Skirts a slow Smoke issued, though no thing burned" (84)—the flaming presence of Saint Evangeline Musset's tongue, the tongue that initially secured her election to the Hall of Fame, is a disembodied symbol of promiscuity and sexual pleasure without the possibility of creation.

Having established the lesbian as inconceivable because she is only dismembered sexual parts, the strange story of the "birth" of the first lesbian in the "March" section can be read as a story of inconceivability. According to the narrator, this "is the part about Heaven that has never been told" (24); it is unknown because of its impossibility. "After the Fall of Satan," the narrator relates, all of the angels, who are identified by the twelve signs of the zodiac, gather so closely together that identities are blurred—"so close," the text reads, "that they were not recognizable, one from the other." Nine months later, their commingling produces an egg (see figure 15) that is, according to the narrator, "as incredible as a thing forgotten." It falls to the earth "and striking, split and hatched." From the midst of the egg "stepped one saying 'Pardon me, I must be going!'" who, as the narrator notes, "was the first Woman born with a Difference." The reproductive act accomplished, the angelic zodiac figures part, and, the reader is told, "on the Face of each was the Mother look" (26).

Barnes's rendition of the "birth" of "the first Woman born with a Difference" is remarkable for its emphasis on the inconceivability of the act itself. The signs of the zodiac have created this woman. Yet these zodiac signs are, in Barnes's text, directly connected to the fragmented lesbian body, a figure that is not possible. Although each angel surveyed, with the look of a "mother," the "first Woman born with a Difference," maternity is made suspect by its ano-

Figure 15. Illustration in Djuna Barnes's *Ladies Almanack*, 25. Reproduced by permission.

nymity. The egg drops from a combination of "angels" that is so blurred that individual identities are unable to be deciphered, imagined, conceived. When the woman is hatched, the mother-look is on all of her procreators, and still the reader is unable to trace maternity. This woman is simply the product of a conglomeration of the sacred and profane, of heaven's angels and the zodiac, not only masking lineage but also becoming an unrecognizable embodiment of not difference at all but sameness and indecipherability. She is born "different" but to what—the anonymous bodies of her parentage or to other women, who themselves, since they have not been "born with a difference," are all alike? The "birth" of this woman imitates the artistic reproduction and subsequent anonymous promiscuity of the French popular images themselves, since their original creators are unknown as well and now exist only as a compilation of artistic reproductions, "as incredible as a thing forgotten," as inconceivable as something inconceivable.

The anonymity inherent in these images and in the birth of the "first Woman born with a Difference" necessarily accents the idea of "conception," particularly since Dame Evangeline Musset does not simply assume the place of a saint once beatified but instead iconographically becomes the Queen of Heaven, a title heretofore reserved for the Virgin Mary (see figure 16), arguably the most pervasive *images populaire* in history. However, Musset's achievement of

Figure 16. Illustration in Djuna Barnes's *Ladies Almanack*, 16. Reproduced by permission.

sainthood before her death at the age of ninety results from a very different standard of beatification as Catholic saints. To be precise, her sainthood is contingent upon her expressed and practiced lesbian sexuality. Twelve reasons, sexual expressions really, are given for Dame Evangeline Musset's sainthood: in January, "she was found to have missed by an inch" (14); in June, when thirty years old, she "made a Harlot a good Woman by making her Mistress" (15); and in November, when eighty-eight, "she said, 'It's a Hook Girl, not a Button, you should know your Dress better'" (17).

Musset takes the place of the spiritual virgin and mother, and in the illustration she wears a crown and holds the traditional symbols of Mary, the heart and rose. Her assumption of the title of Queen of Heaven blasphemes the divine order and exchanges miraculous heterosexuality for homosexuality. Not only does Musset remain unmarried and enjoy happy, nonheterosexual, and long-lived sexuality, but she is, most explicitly, a lesbian. Moreover, according to doctrinal lore, Mary is a woman who conceives only once and does that without the benefit of sexual intercourse; she also is, Vanita notes, "rewarded and acclaimed for not mating or reproducing thereafter" (25). Such a state challenges the post-Freudian and post-Lacanian milieu in which contemporary theorists find themselves. According to Vanita, "Most feminist and gay and lesbian theorists have accepted, in one form or the other, Freud's insistence on the centrality of the penis to the male and the female imagination and/or Lacan's reading of this theory, whereby not the penis but the symbolic phallus, which nobody has but everybody wants." This acceptance, Vanita argues, "compels" theorists "to insist on the woman-affirming quality of vaginal and uterine imagery in texts," which "only reinforces the bind of woman = heterosex = reproductive motherhood" (8). Mary and by association Musset, because of their virginity (lack of heterosexual complicity), escape the bind of "woman = heterosex = reproductive motherhood" (25).

But this shift also removes any possibility of sexual reproduction at the same time it introduces the denigration of promiscuity. Musset's gender already has been questioned, ever since her birth, and she is seen as masculinely gendered but femininely sexed. Her lesbianism, which traditionally signaled a masculine sexual aggressiveness, now is incorporated into the passive status of virginity, and her heretofore unused reproductive capabilities exist simultaneously with Mary's motherhood. The Virgin becomes the lesbian, thereby removing the possibility of procreation since heterosexuality is abandoned. Mary becomes Musset, the virgin ideal of sexual chastity replaced with the lesbian's ideal of sexual promiscuity. This clever connection between Mary—her immaculate conception is rationally, reproductively impossible—and Musset—

an impossible figure herself because she has been formed from dismembered sexual parts—coupled with and reinforced by the anonymous promiscuity of the popular images and the subversive genre of parody that Barnes uses to detail the life of Dame Evangeline Musset, signals that Barnes's "slight satiric wigging" of same-sex sexuality is ultimately, and divinely, inconceivable.

In American society, woman suffrage had become a reality, and the predictive fears about enfranchised women changing their very psyche and physiology now had the opportunity to be made manifest. The jokes reprinted in the *Woman's Journal* conceived of a possibility that women would receive all the attention and act contrary to their submissive expectations. Anne O'Hagan's feminist Hester celebrated female frogs that could reproduce without a male. Gertrude Stein's Helen Furr and Georgine Skeene implied same-sex intimacy; Stein's fictional woman who appeared to embody the very worst outrage attributable to suffrage independence, female sexual inversion, elicited from that same anxious society a clever caricature that not only lightened the mood but, more important, parodically dismissed the threat. Radclyffe Hall's Stephen Gordon wanted a sympathetic reading public; Djuna Barnes's Dame Evangeline Musset desired to "mould the Pot" to her own liking. Yet the conception of women who challenged the rigid definitions of sex-gender assignments ultimately rendered them impossible. Reaction was swift—such women were not to be taken seriously and deserved ridicule. They were targets of a social derision that responded to their physical, behavioral, and sexual practices—the second generation of Dr. Loeb's female frogs were sterile, Helen Furr was made "less gay," Otto Kugelmann evoked sympathy, and Dame Musset was mockingly caricatured. Women could take a joke, as the *Woman's Journal* posited, but only if they adhered to their feminine expectations; if not, they became the joke and were disenfranchised, made unimaginable, through parody.

Notes

Portions of this chapter previously appeared in "Marketing Mockery: Original Sins and the Art of Parody," *Journal of Modern Literature* 21 (Summer 1997): 151–54, and in "The Inconceivability of Djuna Barnes's *Ladies Almanack*," *Women's Studies* 28 (1999): 503–25.

1. They also capture the future split between the old feminists, such as Elizabeth Cady Stanton and Charlotte Perkins Gilman, and the new, more radical feminists who expected sexual equality.

2. Frank Crowninshield, the driving intellectual and social force behind the success of the magazine, was editor for all of *Vanity Fair*'s life, from 1914 to 1936, when it was merged, much to his displeasure, with another Conde Nast publication, *Vogue*.

3. Sherwood Anderson, in his introduction to *Geography and Plays* (1922), was much kinder to Stein than either Sedgwick or Sitwell was. Her books, he wrote, "do in a very real sense recreate life in words. . . . For me the work of Gertrude Stein consists in a rebuilding, an entire new recasting of life, in the city of words" (8).

4. Bryce Conrad, although citing five appearances of Stein in *Vanity Fair,* does not document what they were, and so it is impossible to determine if "Miss Furr and Miss Skeene" is included in his count. He does, however, note that in all five instances, the magazine added short introductions that attempted to explain concisely what was to follow, as it did with the reprinting of "Miss Furr and Miss Skeene."

5. George H. Douglas, in his study of "smart magazines," maintains that even though the "general appeal" of *Vanity Fair* was to both sexes, the magazine "always had what might be called a slightly more masculine than feminine appeal and ambiance. A men's magazine? Too strong a term, perhaps, but, yes, a magazine to tempt the masculine fancy. It was an essence or a perfume that would doubtless never have been detected in *The Smart Set,* edited as it was by those two robustious bachelors-about-town," H. L. Mencken and George Jean Nathan (112).

6. Edmund Wilson, who wrote for *Vanity Fair* in 1920 before going to the *New Republic,* commented in his diary on the frequent speculation that Crowninshield was a homosexual. "In spite of the habit of seizing you by the arm in a way that seemed calculated to establish some kind of affectionate ascendancy," he wrote, "I do not believe that he was." Wilson did believe, however, that the atmosphere of *Vanity Fair* was homosexual and emanated from the men's fashion department, "where the regular staffers were invariably homosexual" (quoted in Douglas 111–12).

7. Interestingly, three of these texts are written by British authors; Barnes is the only American in the group, and her text follows the lives of expatriates in Paris. This is probably not coincidental, given the emergence of sexology in western Europe. These theories, coupled with relaxed social freedoms that attracted many Americans to Europe in the 1920s, as well as the memory of the Oscar Wilde trial in Britain, provided a fertile ground for authors interested in exploring alternative sexualities.

8. Muddle's appearance vaguely resembles that of the masculinely dressed Radclyffe Hall. See Rolley 54–66.

6

Distant Relations

"Put Out of Town for Gettin' Too Int'mate"

> The essential facts are that women can do men's heavy work with substantially equal output, without any disturbance of the particular industry, and, when guided by proper conditions, without detriment to their health. How far and how long they ought to do it in the emergency arising from the war is to be decided upon different grounds.
> —W. Gilman Thompson, "Women and Heavy War Work," 1919

The attempt to recapture the lost femininity of women and reverse the inversion of the sexual and political economies forced authors, who were unable or unwilling to present masculine women and their same-sex relationships as a viable and worthwhile alternative to feminine women and their heterosexual couplings, to rely on another strategy to disenfranchise the masculine woman. Plotting their fictional removal followed a pattern similar to the removal of women from the masculine realms of business and the professions that occurred throughout American society. The implicit message in this literary strategy is that some masculine women cannot even be integrated into society—that their inversion has been so complete and so much more deeply experienced that they must be banished completely. The masculine woman and her inverted sexuality are perhaps attributable to what Sherrie A. Inness describes as a "flexible" or "transcendent" "signifier" that identified a lesbian as a woman engaged in far more than "'abnormal' sexual practices; indeed, lesbianism was hinted at whenever women attempted to change the patriarchal balance of power, whether by pursuing formerly male-dominated jobs, organizing to vote, refusing to marry, living alone, fighting for women's rights, or pursuing higher education" (*Menace* 36–37).[1] Although these accounts still provide a fictional space for the masculine woman, writers placed them outside the realm of American society and forced them to exist not only in the fictional space of the story but also in the even more fictional and ambiguous space of a world outside contemporary American society.

Nowhere is this forced movement more apparent than in American life immediately after World War I, a change that was visually articulated by the *Life* cartoon entitled "The Transition Period" (see figure 17). Having been pressed into the masculine economy during World War I, women were now to return to their traditional femininity, clearly represented by the difference between the "man-tailored" work clothes and the unmistakably feminine dress. Even more telling was the middle, transitional period—she was devoid of all clothing except her shoes, suggesting to a concerned society that she had been a woman all along, that even though outer appearance might have been altered, underneath she still was feminine. Yet she had no actual physical body. This utter dismissal of the female body, captured en route from masculine to fem-

WAR   PEACE

THE TRANSITION PERIOD

Figure 17. Cartoon by Paul Reilly in *Life,* January 30, 1919, 216.

inine identity, suggested that a woman could be one or the other but clearly not both in a society at peace. Her masculine accouterments could be accounted for and even excused by the extraordinary circumstances of war—a martially induced turning of the world upside down. Yet once that society righted itself, so must women's appearance, that is, gender. To be a masculine woman once war had ended was not allowed.

During World War I, it seemed that women who had assumed men's positions on factory lines and in professional jobs had undergone some alteration in their essential composition. As a 1918 *Vanity Fair* cartoon put it, "[T]his thing of women's filling men's positions has really ceased to be a joke," particularly for the "woman-hater," a man "who simply cannot see anything in the well-known restless sex" (Conway 68). Everywhere this "woman-hater" goes during his day is populated by women, from the haberdashery to his bar to the barber. Even his dentist not only is dressed masculinely but is apparently one of the most "virulent types." That women's place in these occupations has ceased to be a joke suggests that women who worked outside the home were viewed as only temporary employees and were even laughable as they undertook to fill in for the men who had gone to fight, but that their staying power in the occupations is threatening. As evidenced by the woman dentist, should they stay too long, even their femininity will be compromised. Two different codes are operating here: the male relies on chivalry, while the woman's motivation is equality tempered with servitude, as indeed, all of the professions depicted cater primarily to the man. Although the subtitle of the *Vanity Fair* piece reads, "It's a woman's world, after all," an altogether different message is being conveyed: a woman's world outside the home is more constrained than her world inside the home; in public, her service is unwelcome.

Robert Grant wrote in "The Limits of Feminine Independence," published in *Scribner's Magazine* in June 1919, that the war had caused society to realize the true and natural places of men and women: "the world's agony and stress of the past four years has served to set once more in high light an old truth, one which, especially in the United States, was in danger of being lost sight of in the medley of other spiritual forces—namely, that man is a robust and a fighting animal. One of the effects of high-explosive carnage has been the emphasis put on the fundamental differences between the sexes which quasi-feministic propaganda had begun to discredit and confuse" (733–34). The war, in short, according to Grant, caused society to revert "automatically to primitive instincts and the habits of the tribe" (734), namely, traditional gender roles and behavior. But World War I changed the ways in which women were perceived since women assumed many of the industrial jobs that men had occupied.

Yet women's "sudden sense of usefulness," as one writer put it, during World War I was challenged once the war ended, as men returned home to the business and industrial jobs they had left ("In Behalf of the Womanly Woman" 124). Women, it was presumed, would vacate those work-force positions and return to their traditional domestic sphere. As Dr. W. Gilman Thompson indicated in 1919, the question was not whether women "can do men's heavy work"; indeed they could, even "without detriment to their health." Rather, "how far and how long they ought to do it" once the war has ended was the much more vital and threatening question (113). If women remained employed in industry and business after the war, holding the positions the men held before the war and, more important, working outside the home, the social havoc resulting from confused sex-gender roles would be considerable. As if the women's struggle to assume the masculine prerogative of voting were not enough of a social anomaly, the same women were now assuming men's places in the factories, which was even more threatening to a society already shaken by a world war.

To assist women in figuring out their true vocation, a tongue-in-cheek article in *Vanity Fair* in August of 1921 detailed six careers for young girls that "may enable the bright ambitious girl to find a life work" ("Careers" 59). The careers proposed, however, were all typically feminine, including a "professional prom girl," a "stenographer," and, should these fail, the career of marriage. According to the author, the magazine's "success editor," parents should teach their daughters to laugh and dance. "A girl with a face and a laugh can go anywhere, but a girl with a brain is automatically disbarred from nine-tenths of polite human intercourse" (76). *Vanity Fair*'s suggested careers all remanded women to traditionally feminine endeavors, placing her in the role of object to a man's affection, gaze, or authority, and suggested that women were suited for only specific types of occupations, namely, those that did not infringe upon careers deemed masculine.

Mary Alden Hopkins (1876–1960) defied *Vanity Fair*'s prescriptions for success. After breaking free from her "home circle," which she described as "monogamous, Republican, and Protestant"—"one marriage, one political party, one church"—she became a journalist who devoted many of her stories to exposés on working women and prostitutes. In an article written for the liberal magazine the *Nation* in 1927, she revealed, "For thirty years I walked primly, directing my course by the social guide-posts set up in a New England town for the direction of well-born, well-bred little ladies. Then I broke loose. My former friends consider me a sort of wild woman because I earn my own living, do not take my husband's name, and have been known to live in strange, dirty neighborhoods where the rents are lower" (41). She finally concluded,

"I don't know what woman's job in life is, any more than I know what man's job is. And I feel it is rather silly to drag sex into the matter" (45).

Replying in the *Nation,* John Collins, a neurologist, and John B. Watson, a behavioral psychologist, condemned Hopkins's "wild" life and her notion that dragging sex into the matter of employment was "silly." "The writers," Collins declared, "are all revolutionists; that is they are all feminists. There are many varieties of feminists but they all have one thing in common; enmity to privilege. Feminists want to do something in the world and to do it themselves" (144–45). Apparently for Collins, this desire to "do something" in public was the damning behavior since the "feminists" exchanged their "duty" of motherhood for the "privilege" of expressing themselves and being happy. "Until man began to sin, God had only one command: 'Be fruitful and multiply; replenish the earth and subdue it,'" Collins wrote. "Woman is becoming more and more loath to do her duty; man more and more eager to obey God's command. Flying over the Atlantic without stop, telephoning from London to San Francisco qualify under 'subdue the earth.' The woman who is willing to have ten or twenty children is almost extinct" (145).

John B. Watson was even more severe in his observations of the modern woman's quest for fulfillment, happiness, and freedom. "So many hundreds of women I have talked to have sought freedom. I have tried to find out diplomatically but behavioristically what they mean. Is it to wear trousers? Is it to vote—to hold office—to work at men's trades—to take men's jobs away from them—to get men's salaries?" he wondered. The questions Watson asked of women betrayed his nervousness; they all focused on women's assuming masculine appearance or roles. Women did not want more comfortable dress, they wanted trousers. They did not seek employment that interested them, they took "men's jobs." They did not ask for higher wages, they wanted "men's salaries" (142). For Watson, this shift in women's focus from the feminine to the masculine was clear and could be found in one distinct population—woman suffragists. "When a woman is a militant suffragist," he concluded,

> the chances are, shall we say, a hundred to one that her sex life is not well adjusted. Marriage as such brings adjustment in only approximately 20 per cent of all cases, so poorly have men and women been taught about sex. Among the 20 per cent who find adjustment I find no militant women, I find no women shouting about their rights to some fanciful career that men—the brutes—robbed of them . . . Most of the terrible women one must meet, women with the blatant views and voices, women who have to be noticed, who shoulder one about, who can't take life quietly, belong to this large percentage of women who have never made a sex adjustment. (142–43)

Mary Alden Hopkins was not the only woman who faced such derision because she chose to earn her own living and not have ten to twenty children, even if it did result in living in a lower-class environment. Many women established "girl colonies" of working women who pooled their resources to live together in the city, according to Margaret E. Sangster in a 1901 article in *Collier's Weekly*. Although Sangster clearly applauded these communities of single women, she noted that not everyone agreed with their lifestyle. The expression "bachelor girl"—a lexicological embodiment of sex-gender confusion—Sangster noted, "has crept into general usage to describe a self-supporting young woman who prizes the independence she has earned." But she also is "disliked by many fastidious people" because the term "bachelor girl" "conveys the idea of a mannish young person in whom the distinctively feminine charm has been overshadowed by the necessities of her lot, and," Sangster concluded, "it carries with it a set of unwritten protest against home influences and restraints" (16).

The social anxiety that accompanied "wild" women and "bachelor girls" went much deeper than women's entry into the economic system. Working women who could financially support themselves had assumed (out of necessity or choice) the public male position in the economic society. If women could make the economic switch from the feminine role to the masculine, the popular reasoning went, then clearly this same woman was capable of transgressing sex and gender boundaries in other areas of her life. Economic independence came to signify the much more far-reaching issue of women's sexual independence from men and, as the "girl colonies" tacitly exemplified, an emotional dependence on women.

Removal of the enfranchised woman from what were considered men's occupations also meant providing a place for these women to go. Instead of proposing a new sphere of influence for women, however, authors sent them back from whence they had come, namely, the home and all the feminine domesticity it entailed. "Egged on by advertising, which doubled in volume in the 1920s, and by the fashion and cosmetics industries," Elaine Showalter posits, "women . . . began to praise the old-fashioned 'privileges' of femininity, and the joys of 'spending the day in strictly feminine pursuits'" (13). The "new" place for the new woman was, in fact, the domestic realm where women had existed before—the fixed feminine identity that had been the hallmark of Victorian womanhood was an identity unaffected by economic independence or enfranchisement. By the late 1920s, the re-inversion of the socially gendered world was complete.

In 1928, Anne Herendeen, writing in the increasingly conservative *Woman's*

Journal, called the working mother a "Reversible Wife," a "rather exciting model which came in some years back as a by-product of the woman suffrage battle and was standardized by the war." Herendeen challenged the popular notion that this career wife could be successful in both areas, the home and the job, colorfully described by Herendeen as "pale pink clinging semi-transparent on one side (for evenings and Sundays) and sensible blue serge on the other for weekdays, nine to five." Although the "Reversible Wife" was faultlessly dressed, had impeccably behaved children, and acted as the most generous hostess, this picture was, according to Herendeen, "shameless faking." Such perfect portraits were "supposed to help the Cause of Feminism, and they do. But we promise, imply, affirm and asseverate more than anybody can ever perform," she confessed (10). In her sharpest indictment, Herendeen asserted that "an able woman can be a fairly good business or professional person and a fairly good housewife, or she can be a very efficient business woman and a quite poor housewife, or a whale of a housewife and indifferent-to-poor in her job (only in this case she gets fired)." But, she made clear, "I have never yet met in real life the prodigy of magazine and newspaper fame who is awfully good at both at the same time" (11).

Herendeen's purpose in adding a semblance of reality to a fictionalized superwoman was apparently not a malicious and belittling move. Her motivation was to propose that being a housewife was as good a career choice as any, a way of life she called "wife-ing it" (11). The argument was to view "wife-ing it" as a legitimate career path, elevating the role of housewife to the status of work done outside the home. With that suggestion, Herendeen seemingly moved the question of woman into a new arena, encompassing the economics of domesticity. Her insistence, however, on a woman's inability to be both good housewife and good career-woman undercut her more sophisticated politicking. Women had to choose either the feminine or the masculine, either "wife-ing it" or holding down a job, and these career choices were very much dependent on traditional gender roles. Since she could not be both masculine and feminine simultaneously, she could succeed in only one. Herendeen herself admitted that being a housewife—a member of what she termed "the Nameless Profession"—was "not the ideal one." Yet instead of seeing this inability to do both as a flaw in the system, she viewed it as her own weakness, "a point against me and against my vanity and my 'satiable curiosity, and not against the profession'" (45).

Less than two years later, in July 1930, the *Woman's Journal* was even more adamant in its insistence that women be removed from careers. Marian Castle, described as "one of the younger set," announced a "Declaration of Dependence," which would make her "a traitor to [her] generation, a rebel against [her] class." Tired of the "unspeakable bondage called freedom," Castle sought to renounce her place in her generation, "the war youth." "We thought that the battle was not only for liberty, but for license; not only for unconventionality but for unfaithfulness," Castle explained. "We were inexorable in pouncing upon any furtive vestiges of scruples, restraints and inhibitions. Stark realism was what we sought." But this new freedom—which gave the younger generation the right to smoke, drink, and pet and the fervor to leave their homes and set up "housekeeping flats with other bachelor girls"— proved, for Castle, to be even more confining than the life she had left (17). "Free we were," she related, "free of food that was food, of sufficient sleep in well-aired beds, of swept and sudsy cleanliness about us, of time-tested friendships and family affections" (32).

Castle's "Declaration of Dependence" involves a "serene" avowal of religion, a love of her husband and home, and a change in reading material from *The Well of Loneliness* to *Sense and Sensibility* (33). More specifically, however, her article represents the removal of women from the masculine realm—the space that permitted women to have a career—so that she might be integrated into the feminine, domestic sphere. In this return to femininity, the message is clear: enfranchised women who had assumed other "masculine" behaviors and roles were not nearly so "free" as they thought. Once Castle recognized this paradox, she removed herself from the altered sex-gender configuration she had once embodied and happily returned to the traditional roles of women, wife, and mother, without a career. So prevalent was the insistence on removing the threatening, masculinized enfranchised woman from the male homosocial and heterosexual society that by 1929, in the publication that only ten years earlier had celebrated women's political victory, women themselves were rebelling against freedoms they had earned.

Such rebellion seems to signal active independence of thought and deed. Castle removed herself from the sex-gender configuration that had placed her in the masculine realm. Yet it is difficult to separate her desire for an autonomous decision with social pressures that made the masculine woman, in appearance and lifestyle, a pariah. Bonnie Zimmerman argues that late-twentieth-century female characters who exhibit the independence of Castle's woman "exit" from the "patriarchal mainland" through suicide, madness, or, "more positively," simply "riding away." All of these are acts that, like Castle's declaration, admit some independence for the woman. Her destination "be-

yond the boundaries," Zimmerman argues, is "women's community and lesbian culture"; her coming-out journey is ultimately affirming ("Exiting the
Patriarchy" 255).

In the fiction of the early twentieth century, however, the "exit" is due not
to the masculine woman's own agency but to her forcible removal. "Any expression of sexuality that explodes the narrow bands of the permissible," Gabriele Griffin points out, "is bound to find itself fenced off, hedged about with
signs that mark and contain its difference or deviance" (2–3). In two works,
"Hallowe'en" by Thomas Beer (1923) and *Delay in the Sun* by Anthony Thorne
(1934), masculinized female inverts appear only on a holiday, and they van-
ish, either by motorcar or by forgetfulness, once the holiday has ended.
Thorne's novel even places its masculine women in a fictitious town in a country far away from the United States, apparently untouched by the rest of the
contemporary western world. Mary Constance Dubois's "Lass of the Silver
Sword," serialized in *St. Nicholas* in 1908–9, and Jeanette Lee's "Cat and the
King," published in the *Ladies' Home Journal* in October 1919, portray classic
schoolgirl crushes but in the end allow that attraction only within the confining limits of women's schools, another example of "'dysphoric' lesbian counterplotting" (T. Castle 85). Such portrayals of masculine womanhood suggest
its appearance only in an inverted, "carnivalesque" world[2]—beyond traditional
American society—and consequently reaffirm a quotidian heterosexuality in
early-twentieth-century American society.

Although it could be argued that heterosexual seduction itself is a form of
removal of masculine womanhood and female inversion—homosexuality
eradicated by heterosexuality—removal of masculine womanhood specifically
focuses on creating a separate space into which the threatening element is
placed. The short stories by Beer, Dubois, and Lee and the novel by Thorne
provide a record of not only their creative expertise but also the social currents
that informed the authors' thinking as members of American society. The
presence and fate of the masculine woman and female invert in all of these
pieces signal that women who practiced an alternative to femininity and heterosexuality were known and that their inclusion in these texts was more than
simply coincidental or accidental. Yet their place in the fiction is far from
affirming their acceptance in society. The presentation and fate of these characters suggest not the subversive success of "disguise," as Lillian Faderman has
suggested (*Surpassing* 308), but the forcible removal of the masculine woman
from the modern American world. These women are "once removed," estranged from traditionally gendered, heterosexual American society, just as a
distant relative is one relation away from being considered a member of the

immediate family. Moreover, once these masculine women and their sexual inversion are removed, the status quo is righted, and society is once again free of the menace such women embody.

Thomas Beer's literary production encompassed two distinct types of writing. Contemporary literary critics knew him for *Stephen Crane: A Study in American Letters* (1923) and *The Mauve Decade: American Life at the End of the Nineteenth Century* (1926). The American public, however, looked forward to the *Saturday Evening Post* every week in the hope of seeing one of Beer's more than 150 short stories in its pages. Central to these stories were the fictional families of the Van Ecks and the Eggs, settings based in small-towns in the Northeast, and plots relating the very real troubles, successes, and dilemmas familiar to their readers. One such story is "Hallowe'en," first published in Beer's collection of short stories, *Mrs. Egg and Other Barbarians* (1923), a book named, according to Wilson Follett in his introduction to the reprinted edition entitled *Mrs. Egg and Other Americans,* purposely "perversely." The name was "prompted more by [Beer's] impulse to preserve his credit with the kind of persons to whom he did his talking than by the ordinary lowly reader's desire for a substantial and representative body of work in permanent form" (x).

"Hallowe'en" describes an incident involving the Egg family and its well-liked, 248-pound matriarchal grandmother, Mrs. Myrtle Egg. Although the story can stand alone, it is connected to the previous short story in the collection, "Shock" (first published in the *Saturday Evening Post* on December 9, 1922), in which Mrs. Egg's son, Adam, welcomes the birth of his first child. As "Hallowe'en" begins, Mrs. Egg, returning from the hospital after seeing her latest grandchild, strikes up a conversation with Jim, one of her husband's hired men, eager to tell her news and also to complain about the Halloween party at her house that night. "'Somethin' crazy happens on Hallowe'en,'" Mrs. Egg declares as she comments on a woman walking by dressed in trousers. "'A girl with a sit-down that size,'" Mrs. Egg declares, "'had ought to be restrained by her family.'" She adds that only two women in the town can get away with altering their dress to the masculine bent, Janie Dalgleish and Sybil Sloane. Jim vaguely remembers Sybil, but before Mrs. Egg can reveal more about her other than her first husband died and her second husband was a writer who "spoke about people he knew in a place in France named Proust" (89), Sybil drives down the street in an expensive Italian car with a California license plate.

Sybil's masculine womanhood is clear. She prefers to be called Bill or Billy, not only wears but also looks good in trousers, and drives a roadster. Although she has been twice married, her second husband's knowledge of and references to Proust suggest Sybil's familiarity with the sexual freedoms of French society. Furthermore, her California license plate not only makes her an outsider in the Northeast but also suggests a Wild West freedom more open to the vagaries of human nature than the staid small town where she grew up. When Tiger, the boy working behind the soda counter, points out to Mrs. Egg that the woman sitting at the back of the shop, smoking a cigarette, came in with Janie Dalgleish frequently last summer, there can be little doubt that Sybil Sloane and Janie Dalgleish are the two characters targeted for some adventure together and that Sybil's masculine womanhood carries with it the more ominous suggestion of female sexual inversion. Sybil is elegantly dressed in a black frock that accentuates her slim, boyish body. Mrs. Egg cannot help commenting on its effect: "'if you had any hips you'd look a fool in it!'" (90). The references to Sybil's masculinity do not end with her decidedly unfeminine lack of curves. When she explains to Mrs. Egg that her estranged husband's new novel is about "an author who married a golf-playing brute of an army officer's widow," the image suggests F. Scott Fitzgerald's golf pro in *The Great Gatsby,* Jordan Baker, who represented new womanhood. As if this were not enough evidence of Sybil's, or Billy's, masculinism and inversion, Mrs. Egg casually remembers an incident in the town's recent history, when "Miss Giddens that taught music . . . was put out of town for gettin' too int'mate with a pretty girl she was teachin!'" (91). Sybil's arrival has conjured up remembrances of a same-sex history in the town, and by association, Sybil herself is indicted.

Without expressly naming Sybil Sloane an "invert," Beer successfully casts her as the masculine woman interested in same-sex intimacy. Moreover, she is assigned the role of the more experienced, sophisticated masculine seducer of Janie Dalgleish, who is trapped in an unhappy marriage after having escaped her mother, a doting, feminine woman with "little satin sofa pillows" all over the house. This seems to be a role that Sybil is comfortable in playing, but clearly her characterization is not commonplace. She comes to town on Halloween, a holiday that Mrs. Egg has already declared a time when "somethin' crazy happens." Sybil's visit is brief; she tells Mrs. Egg that she will leave that night for Cleveland. The masculinized female invert's existence in Beer's short story thus remains confined to Halloween, maintaining its obvious association to evil spirits. Sybil even seems to be dressed like a witch in her long black frock and plain black hat, sitting hidden behind a pile of toy jack o'lanterns in the soda shop. Halloween's association with sexual inversion is reinforced when Mrs. Egg's son, Adam, refuses to tell her what bothers him. Mrs. Egg assures him that in her years she has seen every kind of sexual infidelity, but Adam replies that "'there's stuff goes on you don't know nothin' like.'" Knowing of Sybil and Janie's love affair and planned escape, Adam declares such to be "crazy stuff" and clearly associated with evil. When Adam and Mrs. Egg arrive home, Mrs. Egg cannot help thinking about Sybil as they pull into the garage. There she sees her innocent young grandson, Sanderson Patch Watson, "in his red devil's costume," which obviously has conjured up for Mrs. Egg thoughts of Sybil and, by association, the "evilness" of masculine womanhood (94).

The Halloween party for the neighborhood children is a success, partly because of the appearance of Tom Dalgleish, Janie's husband, who dances with all the young girls. Adam remarks to Mrs. Egg that the Dalgleish marriage is in trouble, adding suggestively that Tom is "'out of lucks—nights.'" Mrs. Egg, commenting that she thinks "'the darn truth is Janie's afraid of men,'" blames Janie's mother, who was "too much of a lady" (96). The lack of sexual intimacy between Tom and Janie, along with Tom's emotional regression in his dances with young girls and the presumption that Janie is afraid of men, introduces the climactic event of the story—the arrival of Sybil Sloane and Janie Dalgleish, en route to Cleveland together.

Dressed in a gray traveling outfit given her by Sybil, Janie Dalgleish presents herself to Mrs. Egg and Adam. Janie's purpose in coming to the Eggs is to ask Adam to take care of Tom, because, Janie nervously announces, "'I'm running away . . . It's something I c-can't help . . . I love someone else more—more than anything. I'm running away. We can't help it. S-simply can't help it.'" Sybil's heavy bracelets clink on the porch as Janie explains that a notice has been put in the town's newspaper, stating that "Mrs. Thomas Dalgleish has started on a motor trip to California with Mrs. Sybil Sloane, formerly of Ilium." Mrs. Egg, recovering her poise, begins wrapping up sandwiches for the women and giving Janie advice to sniff camphor, since she's riding in an open car and is not a "big horse" like Sybil. Then, the two are gone, and as they drive away, the narrator carefully connects them again to Halloween and its evil imagery. The tail lights of the car shine red, just the color of Sanderson Patch Watson's devil's costume. The car goes "hurrying and hurrying, tiny and secret," past bonfires that resemble the flames of hell and past children whose masks hide their identity, just as Sybil's and Janie's identity as inverts was hidden behind marriage and small-town heterosexual expectations. The car rolls north "in the crazy wind" and is gone (98).

Despite Mrs. Egg's and Adam's solicitous treatment of the two women, the ultimate judgment of Sybil and Janie is clearly not as generous. Although some passing reference is made to the their meeting the summer before, all of the action that assigns them the sexually inverted label occurs in the present and on Halloween. Given the connotations surrounding that holiday and the connections between Halloween and Sybil's and Janie's actions, the same-sex intimacy in the story becomes evil, hidden, secret, and, like the wind that howled through the town, "crazy." Or, as the narrator emphasizes in the last paragraph of the story as the reader is left with the image of the motoring women, "the lunatic wind rattled trees and some leaves hissed on the grass" (98). Sybil, the aggressive, masculinely gendered invert, has come into town, riding, like a witch, a crazy wind. She and Janie leave the town using the same lunatic wind as their guide and momentum. As soon as Halloween has ended, children will remove their costumes and become girls and boys again, and the evil of masculine womanhood and female inversion will have left town, banished in a motorcar to wander west across the continent. The acceptable heterosexual and procreative way of life that introduced the short story is maintained, having suffered only a momentary incursion of inversion that can easily be attributed to All Hallows' Eve lunacy.

Anthony Thorne's *Delay in the Sun* (1934) relies on the same plotting strategy as Beer's "Hallowe'en"; it introduces inversion as a result of a holiday and then removes the same-sex sexuality once the holiday is over. Thorne's novel places the female same-sex possibility even further from American society because it is set in Querinda, Spain,[3] which, the narrator notes, cannot be found on a map and "is an unimportant, forgotten place, visited only by those who have lost their way—and inhabited, according to most visitors, by those who have lost their reason." Furthermore, the town is described as having "a fair amount of adultery" and "little of law or order," which the rest of Spain "does not mind since it does not know" (3). Thorne's characterization of this forgotten town en route to someplace more important initially establishes it as a venue of an inverted world, where normal rules of order and decorum are suspended, including, significantly, sexual mores. Even more significantly, Querinda is visited only by travelers who are lost, signaling as much their state of mind as an error in the travel route. As a further strategy of removal, Thorne, although American, centers his novel on nine British tourists who unwillingly are left in Querinda because of a bus strike, as if to suggest that Americans, even if abroad, could not be affected by the unnaturalness of alternative sexuality.

The novel focuses on two couples in particular, Julian and John, who, unbeknownst to John, are father and son (John), and the would-be lovers Sidney Grunbaum, who is Jewish, and Mrs. Rose Tassell, a widowed Christian. Other characters play significant supporting roles, including two young women who are traveling together. The aristocratic Jean Porteous, with an "untidy boyish thatch of raw sienna hair," is more attractive than the typist Betty Sale-Jones, who "had an air of surprised helplessness." As the descriptions continue, the reader learns that Betty is not very intelligent and, despite being a member of the working class, "doesn't seem to do anything." Additionally, she "lived alone," which, according to the narrator, "sounded so—peculiar" (76). Jean surpasses Betty in not only physical attractiveness but also activity. Preferring "mountains to men," perhaps because she is unable to socialize with men at her mother's soirees, Jean is thought to be somewhat strange. Only a few people, "mostly women," realized that Jean's social clumsiness was a defense. It was as if, the narrator muses, suggesting the larger role impulses and motivations will play in the novel, she "led a secret life" of imagination and sensitivity. Jean's description, however, is not confined only to social behavior. Unlike the feminine Betty with her "surprised helplessness," Jean has a "masculine determination," matched by an embarrassment at having to wear gowns to which dressmakers had "added despairing touches of femininity" (72). She loves competitive, fierce winter sports and driving a car at outrageous speeds, both interests signaling her status as "new woman." But her inability to understand or respond to the advances of a Scotsman who had proposed marriage to her, when coupled with her characteristics, makes her a masculinely gendered woman, while her traveling companion, Betty Sale-Jones, is feminine. Thorne's characterizations of the "couple" thus establish the foundation for a possible same-sex relationship.

As the British tourists resignedly settle in for an indefinite stay in Querinda, it is implied that Jean and Betty are a couple. They have talked about sharing a London apartment once they return from their holiday, assured of their compatibility because both are "in revolt" against their upbringings and their parents. When the nine travelers first meet for lunch together at Querinda's only hotel, the Gran Oriente, Stanley Grunbaum decides they should sit "alternative woman-man." But since there are only four men to the five women, Betty and Jean have to sit next to each other, clearly viewed by the other tourists as a couple since all the couples, including the young honeymooners and Grunbaum and Mrs. Tassell, are positioned next to each other (119–20).[4] Grunbaum, seemingly good-naturedly, shouts to Jean, "You'll have to be half a woman and half a man!" since she is seated between Betty and the young groom, Cosby. Jean, perhaps realizing the germ of truth in the comment, angrily retorts, "Don't be a bloody fool!" Moreover, the women are given one room, double-bedded and "inappropriately called a *cuarto matrimonio*." Despite Jean's resentment of having to share a bed with Betty, "who at every point of contact [seemed] to be extremely hot," she does not seem to mind when Betty lifts up the sheet and spreads it "very carefully, very gently" over Jean's body. Jean's smile at this gesture, although certainly not indicative of a same-sex sexual relationship, does provide a suspicion of intimacy between the two women, one who is "half a woman and half a man," and clearly foreshadows the events to come (71).

Querinda proves to be a magical place for these displaced British tourists and, as a result, allows or perhaps impels them to act contrary to expectations. John and Julian, who have separated themselves from the group by staying in rooms over a pub, somewhat humorously muse that the seven other travelers "were in danger from the sun" (125). Since they have been stranded, John recalls, not one of the tourists has mentioned the bus strike or the possibility of leaving Querinda. Julian's explanation of what is happening to the other tourists is likened to a grammatical event: "If you interrupt a man in the middle of his life you surprise him, so to speak, in the middle of a sentence. The sentence is incomplete. . . . Put an unexpected semicolon there. The rest of the sentence may be entirely different" (34–35). There is, however, some special power associated with the town, despite John's disavowal "to credit Querinda with the extraordinary powers of Circe's Island" and the "wonderful moment" when "the ship of Odysseus is drawn into Circe's harbour by an invisible agency" (36). Given the introductory description of the town and this suggestion that Querinda does possess some strange power over the British tourists, the geographical space of the novel provides a fantastic setting for fantastic events, such as the love between the once cynical Jewish traveling salesman Grunbaum and the widowed Christian Tassell or sexual intimacy between Jean Porteous and Betty Sale-Jones.

To advance the relationship between the two women into inversion, Thorne provides a final element of the setting. Already warned by the worldly Julian and John about the dangers of the sun in the strange town of Querinda, Jean and Betty nevertheless walk about one day with their heads uncovered, feeling the sun beat down on them. On the same day they choose to explore the old section of the town, there is a procession of the *Virgen de los Ojos Grandes* (the Virgin with the Large Eyes), led by a beautiful, young blind girl dressed all in white, whose uncanny ability to trace the steps without stumbling gives the impression that she is "in a dream, half human, half phantom, without mind" (175).

Jean and Betty, although not observers of the procession celebrating the holiday, are affected by the strange mood of the day as they cross the old bridge and seem to wander into "a town of their own, a town in which they were the only inhabitants" (159). Their remove to old Querinda gives them a feeling that they have "turned their backs on the life that they knew" and have entered a "secret town." Once there, the women enter a bullfighting ring, and Jean and Betty both climb down to the sandy floor of the arena. "'If we were children

now,'" Jean wishes aloud, "'we'd play at bullfighting.'" Assigning herself the
masculine part of bullfighter, Jean assigns Betty the role of the woman in the
front row to whom Jean would show all her "tricks." Betty, acting out of her
usual deference, suggests that no harm would come if they "play at bullfighting
now." "'Why can't we be children for an afternoon?'" she asks. At this moment, Jean, who has taken off her beret and now feels the hot sun, notices Betty
in an entirely different light, according to the narrator. "Jean glanced at the girl
beside her, at the delicate figure shining in the penetrating light through the
thin folds of her pale yellow dress that was the colour of her hair, at the pretty
smiling face of a della Robbia smooth plumpness, at the wide greyish blue eyes
that did not need the accents she gave them." Jean thinks, as the narrator relates, that "Betty looked charming today" (160). Betty, also affected by the sun,
is captivated by the graceful precision of Jean's imaginary bullfighting maneu-
vers, her eyes following her first with "amusement" and then with "admiration and wonder." The narrator suggestively cautions, however, "Playing together, [both women mock] a dangerous game. And dangerously they entered
a secret world in which they had so great a need of each other" (162).

The friendship of the two women, heretofore based on their common rebellion, has become an intimacy much deeper than parental dislike. In the
bullring, the women assume even stricter guidelines governing gender roles.
Moreover, the emotions of both women, as a result of the strong sun and holiday, are intensified, and the heterosexual model of attraction is discarded as
they recognize the previously unseen beauty and strength of each other. Certainly, the sexual possibility between Jean and Betty is anticipated by their
gendered behavior, shared room, and emotional attachment. But not until they
venture on a special feast day beyond the common, bustling center of Querinda and into the old section of the town, exposing themselves to the dangerous sun, do they allow such a possibility to become a reality. The same-sex
intimacy, however, blossoming only in these extraordinary circumstances, is
deliberately made transitory, to be hidden once the day is over. Its gamelike
status also hints that the attraction each feels while "playing" in the bullring
is only a stage of childhood, not meant to last in either the adult world of the
Hotel Gran Oriente or, more important, London.

When they return to the hotel for dinner that evening, the narrator remarks,
"How very burnt they had got, they must have been out in the sun the whole
afternoon," and then notes that they chose to sit at the corner table together,
"dreamy and distant," "withdrawn and secretive." After dinner, the "two girls
went again in search of their secret world," retracing their steps over the same
bridge and into "a town of their own." The sun, although now set, continues

to touch them, as Betty remarks that it is "like a hand on my forehead . . . burning me far more than when we were walking this afternoon. It's a fiery hand that I can almost see." That the dangerous sun's intensity burns even hotter now in the two women, in the cool evening, signals that their attraction has gained strength and probability and that the two women are metaphorically walking much deeper into their intimacy than they had in the bullring. Its synecdochal "apparitionality," as Terry Castle termed it, suggests that "the love that dare not speak its name" is, at least for this moment, audible and visible. As they hold hands and walk through the darkened town, they walk "right past the bullring without recognizing it," although "in such a night as this," the narrator comments, "the bullring might be there no longer." They draw closer together, and the shapes of buildings lose their form, and the streets "had somehow the crazy inconsequences of a dream" (207).

Jean suggests they go into the horseshoe-shaped gardens, a "charmed circle that had not been closed," a prelapsarian Edenic but also magical atmosphere. The flowers seem strange, and the moon is a "silver face mocking them from tree to tree." The flora are personified as welcoming hosts and populated by apparitions as "now and then a startled white face shone suddenly among the leaves, or a branch moved and there were petals falling." "But," the narrator notes, "no one spoke." Jean and Betty, in imagery that carries with it much sexual innuendo and perhaps even blatant anatomical description, "stopped, as though it [the garden] were a place that they had been seeking, when they came to an opening between two dark trees, and found within the green cave a bush covered in flowers that they had never seen" (208). Smelling of hyacinth, the petals of the "small flowers" shine in the moonlight "as though they were made of glass and were stiff, almost brittle." The delicacy of these flowers parallels the fragility of their attraction, despite the implication of sexual intimacy in this metaphorical garden of strange pleasures. They lie down with their fingers still linked, they lose all notion of time, and "their fingers tightened, as though in a kiss." Then, in a seeming curious tribute to female inversion, the narrator judges that "living in a garden like this, they would live forever. The trees would drop eternal fruits into their hands, the fountains would refresh them, the flowers would spread new garments overnight on the ground. They would never grow tired or old. For here there was peace and beauty and love. They would live forever, if they could live in a garden like this" (209). Clearly, however, their eternity of bliss is never to be realized because their journey to the garden has been established well outside the bounds of acceptable society. The garden exists only as a fantasy world for the two women and only as long as they still feel the sun burning their faces. What initially seems to be a positive portrayal of same-sex intimacy is reduced, finally, to a fantastic impossibility.

Before they leave the garden, the women weave flower necklaces for each other. Walking together in "profound mystery, in strange seclusion," when they return to the stone bridge that connects the old town with the new commercial center, "they felt that they must have flown there on wings from the gardens, and that their feet had not touched the earth" (209). Once they reach the marketplace and the noise of human activity, however, they lose their sense of mystery and become afraid. They let go of each other's hands, do not look at each other, talk spasmodically in halting questions, hesitate at the door of the hotel, and are indecisive about whether to eat or drink. Most particularly, the women are unable to commit themselves, now that they have returned to society, to return to their room together at the Hotel Gran Oriente. Each anticipates the sexual intimacy that the *cuarto matrimonio* represents, and now that they have rejoined the other British travelers in the marketplace of Querinda, both fear these feelings:

> gradually, as they sat talking together on the terrace . . . both realized that they were afraid to go to bed. They both knew that they were saying what came into their heads, that they could no longer say what came into their hearts.
>
> They waited, but nothing could deliver them. They waited a long time, until the scent of flowers was faint.
>
> Then Jean stood up.
>
> "Say goodnight to me. Say goodnight to me here. We can't wait—like this." (210)

Betty begins to cry at the realization that the emotional and physical fantasy has ended, and she leaves Jean to sleep on the terrace, far away from the double bed. When Mrs. Tassell wakes Jean the next morning, the flower garlands that Betty had made for her "in a distant garden" are dead, and a flat in London and a cottage in the country that Jean has been dreaming about are "perfumed with the hyacinth sweetness of a death chamber" (211).

In the light of the next morning, the magic of the previous day and night has dissipated, and Jean's once gloriously sunned face "was burning with yesterday's sun." She looked as if she had been "scalded, and there were ludicrous white patches where shadows had been" (224). Her changed skin is not the only marker of her changed attitude toward Betty and the sexual possibility. She is "apprehensive about what yesterday has done to me" and admits the possibility of bisexuality, wondering if there are "two Jeans," a realization that "she herself had discovered only last night." Having regained her masculine aggressiveness, Jean decides that she must force the issue with Betty, to determine if, in fact, the attraction still exists and is to be their fate. "Everything seemed very unreal and unstable, she was in a world of ghosts," the narrator discloses about Jean. "It seemed to her that what happened to them both last night was something beyond their control." Such a suggestion implies that had they been in control and not under the influence of the town, the sun, and the holiday, the same-sex attraction would not have surfaced. Jean, fearing the unknown more than sexual inversion, agrees to "let this strange force follow its own law—let it part them for ever or join them for ever. It was something too big for their reason, and too delicate" (230).

Betty, of course, has the same apprehensions as Jean, although she awakes to an "aching sense of loss," an "emptiness," and the assumption that she has lost Jean's friendship. Her face, like Jean's, is "burned and parched and withered by the sun" (233). Last night, "Jean had slept by her side," according to the narrator. "And in their release from the world they had gone forth together into a place in which they could wander without fear or shame." Betty realizes better than Jean the depth of the emotion and the interconnectedness of body and mind in female inversion. "What cruel tyranny of the body was this?" Betty wonders, "And how bitter an untruth that the mind could control it!" Betty blames their delay in Querinda, "this crazy old place," for stripping her of the platonic friendship she had with Jean, for giving them time to think about and desire each other. "They had found a secret world of their own," Betty remembers, and they "had walked into a garden together and made strange garlands, not knowing how heavily they would weigh in the morning . . ." (232).

When Jean enters the room, Betty sits at the dressing table applying cold cream to her sunburned face. Despite both women's apprehension at meeting for the first time since the garden, Betty's daily morning ritual makes Jean laugh, which breaks the tension and effectively dismisses their sexual attraction and their fears of it. "They had not spoken yet," the narrator relates the scene. "They had not braved the day that confronted them with yesterday's problems. They did not know yet if they would return to an enchanted garden together, or if they must each walk alone" (234). But their laughing return to their mundane relations with each other, before the Querindan sun so affected them, makes it clear that their sexual intimacy is no longer possible; the narrator suggests that the enchanted garden may be revisited only if the two women would once again find themselves stranded and affected as they have been in Querinda. The chance of repeating such a holiday is virtually impossible. As they board the bus to leave Querinda—the bus strike conveniently ends almost immediately after all the British travelers have some sort of psychological sunstroke—Betty puts her hand to her neck, as if to feel for the garland that is now only, and always was, a fantasy (286). The best that can be managed is a weak smile between Jean and Betty as they return to social decorum and heterosexual civilization.

Jeannette Foster, in her ground-breaking work, *Sex Variant Women in Literature* (1956), praises Thorne's novel as a "heartening idyll" (306), even though she terms Betty's and Jean's romance "inarticulate." She contends that Thorne "has cannily left each reader to supply what sequel best satisfies his own philosophy, but the lingering mood is distinctly one of warm tolerance and sympathy rather than disapproval" (307). Such a reading, however, fails to account for the fantasy world that Thorne constructs for his same-sex attraction; he allows this alternative to heterosexuality to exist only when the women have been severely influenced by extraordinary forces. Although Thorne's novel may not be as adamant in heterosexuality's seduction of its female inverts as other fictional portrayals are, it explicitly renders sexual inversion inferior to heterosexuality. If the "delay in the sun" had never happened, Betty's and Jean's attraction never would have been possible. Once the "delay in the sun" is over, intimacy ceases. Contrary to Foster's assertion that Thorne allows the reader to use "his own philosophy" to determine the sexual fate of the two women, the answer that Thorne provides is not ambiguous at all, given the enchanted and contrived setting. Beer's Sybil Sloane is allowed only to breeze in and out of town riding a "crazy" Halloween wind, and so, too, Jean Porteous and Betty Sale-Jones are allowed same-sex attraction only in an "unimportant" and unknown town and under extreme and carefully delimited circumstances.

Women's schools and colleges provided a similar arena in which masculine womanhood and female sexual inversion could be conveniently confined. In the years preceding and following World War I, a time that also saw the U.S. woman suffrage movement gain momentum and eventually achieve its goal, "articles complaining of lesbianism in women's college, clubs, prisons, and reformatories—wherever women gathered—became common," Carroll Smith-Rosenberg reports (280); these arenas, it was feared, permitted the female invert "to reach out to young girls" and draw them into same-sex relationships (279). According to Mary Briarly writing in *Scribner's Magazine* in November 1922, higher education was responsible, "in the brief span of two generations," for the "[metamorphosis] of woman from a timid devotee to a fearless materialist," even "though all evolutionary rules require millions of years to effect a less startling biological change" (591). Working against traditional wisdom and medical practice that predicted dire physical consequences if women exercised their minds, numerous schools began with the sole purpose of educating women, often in the same subject matter as men's. Detractors worried that these college-educated women would lose their femininity and, as John D'Emilio and Estelle Freedman note, that college would "direct women away from marriage and motherhood" (190). One unmarried graduate of a women's college even wrote an article entitled "Does the Girls' College Destroy the Wife?" for the *Ladies' Home Journal* in June 1916, which was billed as a "frank confession of why one college girl has not married." The anonymous graduate of Vassar College, a schoolteacher, wrote that she is "accused of preferring a career to wifehood and motherhood; I am charged with shirking my responsibility to society, the nation and posterity by remaining single and childless," but she attributes her "spinsterhood" not to choice but to her college education, which prevented her from being courted by eligible men. When she graduated, men "were afraid of the dollar test and bank statement," believing that they could not support a working woman since she was accustomed to independent wealth. Her move into teaching, she confessed, was to support herself, both financially and psychologically. At age thirty-five, her spinsterhood was taking firmer hold every day, "and in my heart," she lamented, "there is bitter protest against it" (27).[5]

An even earlier voice against the college education of women was that of the prominent physician S. Weir Mitchell, whose essay "When the College Is Hurtful to a Girl" appeared in the *Ladies' Home Journal* in June 1900. The magazine reprinted excerpts from Mitchell's commencement address to students at Radcliffe College four years earlier because, according to the "Editor's Note," "Doctor Mitchell speaks with an authority that is unquestioned. No medical practitioner in America can speak from a closer or longer experience with the health of American womanhood. His words, therefore, carry with them a convincing force that it would be impossible to attach to the utterances of any other man." Mitchell contended that college education was detrimental if it prohibited or superseded a woman's knowledge of domestic duties and thus undermined her success as a good wife and mother. In making this argument, Mitchell discriminated between "natural" and "unnatural" roles:

> If the higher education or the college life in any way, body or mind, unfits women to be good wives and mothers there had better be none of it. If these so affect them that they crave merely what they call a career as finer, nobler, more to their taste than the life of home, then better close every college door in the land. In thus speaking I do not refer only to the married life. A vast number of women who do not marry come to have, at some time, charge of households or of children not their own. This surely is the natural life of women. I say the like of men. It is their natural place to meet the outside cares of life, and whatever of dissipation, mistakes or indolence unfits them to endure and to labor in their proper sphere is as

much to be deprecated as is anything which makes a woman hate the duties of home or renders her as she may think superior to their claims.

A woman's identity is challenged by a college education. Mitchell rhetorically asked if there was something wrong with women graduates and suggested that education was the cause of their unmarried state. "Is it that men do not like highly educated women? Or is it that these fail to attract, not from this cause but owing to some other reasons I have mentioned? Is it not true that some college graduates are inclined to think of marriage as of a thing beneath them?" Mitchell implied that college women had lost their "naturalness." "Trust me," Mitchell intoned against masculine womanhood, "I'm right. Do not try to be men when you are women" (14).

Only four years later, the *Ladies' Home Journal* published an even more exacting caution about women's colleges, namely, the influence they seemed to have on students' emotional attachments. In a hypothetical example of a young woman's refusal to attend her brother's wedding because she would have to leave the school and hence the older (female) student on whom she had a "crush," the author Emma Walker called such attachments "foolish friendships." They are not friendships, she declared, "and they do not deserve the name. They are not even imitations." "As a rule," she continued, "this malady affects the new girls in its most severe form. The first homesickness is an awful feeling, and the most natural step is to grasp the nearest object at hand to fill up the aching void. This object is generally a girl" (21).[6]

The women's college became yet another place where the female sexual invert was removed. The premise of the women's college, that women were as capable of being educated as men were, introduced a hint of homosociality and masculinity to the women's community, but one that was to be outgrown. Same-sex affection flourishes in this setting because, as Terry Castle points out, "male erotic triangulation is either conspicuously absent or under assault. In the classically gynocentric setting of the girls' school, male characters are generally isolated or missing altogether" (226–27). Sherrie A. Inness, in her study of Progressive Era "college fiction," suggests that this genre "ultimately functions to ensure that women's homoaffectionate relationships will be confined to a location where they can be closely scrutinized by institutional and state authorities" (*Intimate Communities* 47), much like what Michel Foucault calls "anonymous instruments of power": "hierarchical surveillance, continuous registration, perpetual assessment and classification" (220)

In the first two decades of the twentieth century, fiction presented the young woman attending the all-girls' school with the freedom to express her emotions toward another student. As Lillian Faderman notes in *Surpassing the Love of Men,* "In 1908 it was still possible for an American children's magazine to carry a story in which a teenage girl writes a love poem in honor of her female schoolmate." According to Faderman's analysis, if a love poem written from one girl to another had been written after 1920, the author "would no doubt have been rushed off to a psychoanalyst to undergo treatment for her mental malady, or she would have ended her fictional existence broken in half by a tree, justly punished by nature (with a little help from a right-thinking heterosexual) for her transgression" (297).

Popular press fiction prior to 1920 was not, however, nearly so forgiving of the sexual "transgression" among female schoolmates as Faderman argues. She posits that in the early twentieth century "popular stories often treated the subject [lesbianism] totally without self-consciousness or awareness that such relationships were 'unhealthy' or 'immoral'" (298). Moreover, despite Terry Castle's conclusion that male characters were absent and Shirley Marchalonis's conviction that men were excluded as "signifiers of romance, love and marriage" and were minimized in their importance (138), women's colleges, in reality and fiction, had the unwritten but express purpose of readying young women for marriage by permitting them to exercise their emotions in an assumedly harmless outlet, female friendships. Romantic commitments were only postponed, not rejected. Marchalonis argues, partially contradicting her earlier conviction, that "the underlying assumptions" in all the stories "is that these young women are headed for heterosexual romance and marriage" (141); men, she adds, "become the symbols of reality" (138). Women's same-sex crushes were accepted, Inness affirms, "but only so long as they do not interfere with a woman's progression into 'mature' heterosexuality" (*Intimate Communities* 45). Thus, even though male characters may not figure prominently in "college fiction," their presence is the vital center within the texts because heterosexual marriage is the desired outcome.[7]

In these texts, "experimental" same-sex attraction, far from being "harmless," was severely restricted to the women's school, that is, removed from mainstream society. Mary Constance Dubois's story "The Lass of the Silver Sword," published in the children's magazine *St. Nicholas* in 1908, and "The Cat and the King," a story published in the *Ladies' Home Journal* by Jeanette Lee in October 1919, detailed the "crushes" or "smashes" of many college women at the time.[8] Both write the story of innocent and naive infatuation that a younger girl has for a older girl, but their same-sex attractions are so constricted by place, time, and social assumption and so explicitly removed from traditional American society that they are allowed no chance at survival outside these very rigidly proscribed boundaries.

Set in a boarding school, Dubois's "Lass of the Silver Sword" takes its name from a secret club, the Order of the Silver Sword, formed by the girls at the school, but the action really follows the adventures of two women, Carol Armstrong, eighteen years old, and the younger Jean Lennox, who has fallen madly in love with Carol "at first sight." Although Jean is too embarrassed or shy to tell Carol of her feelings and show her the poems and stories written to and about her, two mischievous girls, Frances and Adela, steal Jean's parcel of love writings and deliver them, wrapped in white tissue paper and a red ribbon, to Carol. "'And it's the queerest thing you ever saw!'" Adela exclaims as she brags to her schoolmates about the prank. "'She's written the greatest lot of poems and stories, and odes to—Carol Armstrong! She's dead in love with her!'" Adela, perhaps feeling some remorse, excuses herself by noting that "'we thought it was a shame for Carol not to know Jean was in love with her, and we knew wild horses wouldn't drag it out of Jean'" (213).

Jean, when she discovers the theft, immediately runs to Carol's room in the hopes of retrieving the poems and stories. But as she approaches the door, she is horrified to hear Carol's roommates, Nancy and Marion, reading the poems aloud to a pin-downed Carol and laughing with delight. "'To Carol,'" Nancy begins a poem,

> "My love has a forehead broad and fair,
> And the breeze-blow'n curls of her chestnut hair
> Fall over it softly, the gold and the red
> A shining aureole round her head." (215)

As the older girls mockingly credit Jean as "the rising genius of the twentieth century" and express their disappointment that the last verse of the poem has been scratched out, Carol breaks free from her captors and recaptures the book, laughingly imploring them to "'give me back my property!'" Jean, who by this time has managed to get on the roof because it affords a better view of the proceedings in Carol's room, is caught by one of the teachers and, as a result, is discovered by Carol and her friends. Although Carol attempts to make amends by telling Jean that she is a "genius" and that she "ought to be proud of" her poems since she herself is "proud to have such lovely things written about me," Jean grabs the book and runs away to her room she has named "Castle Afterglow." But the love is not thwarted; later that night, Carol visits Jean, and seeing that Jean has been crying, she seats herself beside "the pathetic little figure, and putting her arms around her, drew her close and kissed her." She tells Jean that she is "'glad I got the book, any way! To think I might have gone on to the end of school, and never found you out, you dear!'" As the chapter closes, with

Carol keeping watch over a now contentedly sleeping Jean in Castle Afterglow, Carol has agreed to be Jean's "best friend" and to "pet [her] up" should the homesick Jean need to talk to someone about her "troubles" (217).

Faderman reads the friendship between Carol and Jean as "totally without the self-consciousness that would be inevitable in a post-Freudian era" and determined that "there is nothing covert in their relationship" (*Surpassing* 303). The two women's popularity remains high among the other girls; as the story continues, they arrange a summer camp for all of their schoolmates to attend. However, the two girls' and their schoolmates' presumptions occur in a socially prescribed space—an all-girls' school that permitted young women to experience intense "crushes" or "smashes" on other, often older, female students. When the same women venture outside of the boundaries, either physical or psychological, of their school and are surrounded by the more powerful heterosexual social hierarchy, the same-sex prerogative disappears. Indeed, this is precisely what occurs in "The Lass of the Silver Sword." Soon after Carol's and Jean's pledge of friendship, the story shifts to the summer camp, where the girls spend their time plotting playful jokes against the neighboring all-boys' camp and striking up socially acceptable friendships with the boys. By the end of the story, Carol and Jean are still friends, but each has shifted her interest to heterosexual relationships, refuting Marchalonis's position that in the fictional women's worlds, "men are not important factors" (141).

Although Faderman claims that there is only "some vague suggestion of heterosexual interests in the story" and that "the real emotional center is the relationship between Carol and Jean" (303), this analysis holds true only for the time the girls spend in the space of acceptable same-sex possibility, the girls' school. Dubois's inverts, removed from the heterosexual structure of society, do not threaten what Inness terms the "patriarchal status quo of that era" (*Intimate Communities* 46). Despite initially flirting with the same-sex possibility, Dubois finally positions the girls in the appropriate heterosexual and feminine space. Because she has adhered to tradition and successfully plotted for her inverts' removal, Dubois and her story escape the scrutiny of Freudian analysis.

Lee's story, "The Cat and the King," offers a similar scenario, often replicated in women's colleges of the day and a subject that Lee, a professor of English at Smith College from 1904–13, might have known well. "No debutante ball, however, auspicious," wrote Martha Coman in a 1902 article for *Collier's Weekly,* "is half so thrilling as the first formal college affair. To this the eager freshman is solely invited by an upper-class girl who sends her lovely flowers, sees that her dance card enrolls a representative selection of names, and who escorts her ceremoniously to and from the function" (20). But less than ten years later, students themselves "were becoming more aware that crushes were potentially sexually 'abnormal,'" as Inness explains, quoting a Smith College student. Writing in the "Public Opinion" column in the *Smith College Weekly* in 1911, the student noted, "Very often a great deal of unhappiness is caused simply through thoughtlessness, and a girl is made self-conscious and uncomfortable in her relations to another girl with whom she is forming a perfectly normal friendship, because a report has been spread that they 'have a crush.' No one likes to be thought subject to these unfortunate disorders of the mind" (quoted in Inness, *Intimate Communities* 165).

In Lee's story, a freshman, Flora Bailey, is infatuated with a senior, Annette Osler, who serves as the captain of the team for which Flora has been selected an alternate. When Annette sprains her ankle and is confined to the infirmary, the resourceful Flora assumes the guise of "Prudence Small," whom she had found in a "curious" case study in an old medical book borrowed for "fiction purposes" (67). Imitating the same fainting spells that landed "Prudence Small" in the book, Flora lands in the infirmary right next to Annette. Two discoveries then occur: the first is that Annette is only resting for the game and will be released that day; the second is that the kindly woman doctor discovers Flora's ruse and confronts her with the case study. Instead of berating her for her dishonest behavior and her schoolgirl crush, however, the doctor rewards her with not only her release but also a part-time job in her laboratory, where she will work with Annette, who also conveniently is employed by the doctor. As one last instruction, the doctor tells Flora that she is to report immediately to Annette in the older girl's room to ready herself for the game. Rewarding Flora Bailey's dishonesty would seem to be a positive reinforcement for her attraction to the older Annette Osler, but a closer look at this story produces a different conclusion, not nearly so affirming.

Flora Bailey and Annette Osler are only two of the students in a walled college campus that is sharply contrasted with the "free" world beyond the gates. The campus is "mysterious and wonderful," the narrator relates, adding, "but there was something overpowering about it. The great walls that looked so gracious in the fresh morning light had a way of shutting one in, of hampering and binding the movements of the freshmen. There were so many things one must do and not do within the gracious walls!" One of the rules is that freshmen are never to make friends with the seniors, except by invitation— but that is exactly what Flora tries to do. The senior chosen as the object of her affection is seemingly more off limits than others because of her physical presence. On a walk at four o'clock in the morning, Flora stops at the foot of the South Parker dormitory and looks up at the tower windows, whose part-ed curtains reveal Annette, with her head bearing "a mass of reddish hair gathered carelessly, and the light that fell on the tallest peaks and gables of the college touched it with gold." To Flora, the narrator announces, "it was as if a goddess, high-enshrined and touched by the rising sun, stood revealed" (10).

The similarity between this scene and a fairy tale, with a beautiful woman locked high in an unreachable tower, is striking. The difference is that the subject who desires the feminine object is not a heroic knight but a younger girl. Such a reconstruction of subject and object, however, is not problematic because the environment in which this alternative desire is allowed expression is rigidly controlled and confined, not only by the high brick walls but also by social decorum that determined college women's friendships. Crushes were expected in the women's college environment and were dangerous only if they persisted beyond those years. The beautiful Annette Osler remains untouched by her female suitor in her protected tower. Annette remains wholly available to the appropriate male suitor once she has graduated and makes her way into the "free" world.

The location where Flora and Annette finally do meet indicates an even further condemnation of girls' relationships. Flora is allowed to imagine the possibility of loving Annette only within the college's walls, and Flora's only chance at actually talking with Annette occurs in an even more restricted arena, the school's infirmary. Thinking that Annette might have to stay for weeks in the infirmary to take care of her sprained ankle, Flora schemes a way to be admitted into the infirmary by imitating the symptoms of a case she finds in an old medical book in the school library, "The Curious Case of Prudence Small." As she read, "her cheeks glowed and her eyes danced," and she looked at the librarian, "mounted on her platform . . . like some priestess of knowledge waiting for mystic rites to begin." Taking this as her cue, Flora knocks over her chair, lifts her arms slowly, gives a long, low moan, and then "subsides gently to the floor" (67).

She "awakes" on the infirmary couch—"five minutes the book said; she judged it to be about five minutes" since she had enacted her fall in the library—to the doctor's icing the bump on her forehead that she had accidentally acquired in her fall. When informed that her symptoms—including "a little buzzing in the top of [her] head, and the soles of [her] feet . . . slightly paralyzed"—will admit her to the infirmary bed next to Annette, Flora's pulse jumps so sharply that the doctor, holding her once-limp wrist, is suspicious. In the infirmary, Flora can turn her head a little to stare at Annette, who is sleeping with "one hand tucked under her cheek, the reddish hair gathered into a quaint cap; the moonlight, touching the quiet face, made it seem like a child's" (67).

In the infirmary, Annette is as untouchable and unknowable as she was in her tower room in the early morning. The infirmary is located at the top of the building—Flora believes "she could look down on the sleeping world and off at the great clouds drifting and swinging against a blue-black sky" (67)—thereby maintaining Annette in her exalted status since she was the first patient. Flora is admitted to this "tower," but through deceitful methods. She must feign illness to know Annette, who is less than healthy. This potential same-sex relationship is therefore initially established between two women who are not thought to be physically sound, whether by their own doing or an accident. That the infirmary is the only place where the women meet in the story further indicates the place to which female inversion has been relegated, not only behind stone walls but high above the ground in an area used to care for sick students. The implication is clear: same-sex attraction is an illness. Girls drawn to those affections belong in an infirmary and must remain until cured. The *Ladies' Home Journal* had made the connection between women's intimacy and illness even more explicit in 1913, stating that one-tenth of the college women who had crushes on other women were "moral degenerates" ("Your Daughter" 16). Mothers were warned to scrutinize their daughters' friendships for signs of "crush-itis" in the hopes of saving their daughters from a "maimed soul and wrecked body" ("Your Daughter" 78).

In Lee's story, the maternal figure is played by Dr. Worchester, who possesses the ability not only to recognize Flora's deception but also to channel it into a more appropriate expression. Annette, Flora is told by Dr. Worchester, was only resting in the infirmary for the game and was actually discharged that morning. When the doctor returns to check on her youngest patient, she brings the library's medical book with her. Ashamed, Flora tells her story to the doctor, including the crush on Annette that motivated the entire episode. When she finishes, the woman of science states matter-of-factly, "'You're not looking at it sentimentally any more,'" to which Flora admits, "'I wasn't sentimental . . . not exactly sentimental, I guess. Only it's hard sometimes to tell. Your feelings get mixed up so.'" With this exchange, the doctor's concerns about Flora's sentimentality and emotional motivation are seemingly quelled, and Flora is released, but not before the doctor performs two remarkable acts.

The first is that the doctor sends Flora to Annette's tower room so that she can join the game. The second is that Dr. Worchester recognizes that Flora has a scientific mind. Dr. Worchester's recognition comes as Flora is relating her discovery of a mole's nest. "'The little roots were shiny and laid out for breakfast, as if somebody was coming back in a minute,'" Flora describes. "'And it was all still around, and the light in the sky just growing pink. It almost hurts when things are like that. You can't help but being lonely. . . . I guess it's because it's like me, inside . . . the way I am inside—all little branches and bones and shining things.'" More prodding by the doctor reveals Flora's delight in charts and diagrams and her desire to study biology and "everything that's alive." Dr. Worchester, impressed by Flora's scientific nature, invites her to work in her lab, alongside Annette, who also is her assistant because, according to the narrator, Dr. Worchester realizes that "this was the sort of thing one sometimes came on, once in an age! And the child had supposed she was playing a prank—getting to know a senior! And the books she opened were life! The doctor had watched girls come and go, reaching out to choose some nothing. And now and then it seemed to her a gentle hand reached down and touched the chosen nothing and it became shining, a crystal ball holding life in its roundness" (71).

Flora's conversion from an emotional invert to a budding scientist is the final indictment of the same-sex intimacy that was suggested early in the story. For Flora is not the only scientist—Annette is, also, and this mention by the doctor is a subtle hint that Flora's infatuation would never come to fruition: there is not room to be both a scientist and an invert. According to the narrator, who speaks for the doctor, Flora's "prank," which might have offered the potential for establishing a relationship with Annette, was not the end and important result. Rather, as the doctor knows best, the books that fascinated Flora with their diagrams and pictures of the mysterious human body and her own "network of blue veins," which reminded her of tree branches, present "life" to the young girl. Science is the suitor of both Annette and Flora. That the matronly doctor introduces them to this opportunity, however, challenges just what exactly a woman scientist is and where she can exist.

The woman scientist may be trapped within the same walls, both physical and psychological, as the invert. Working at a laboratory at the woman's college, Dr. Worchester is as confined as the seemingly misguided Flora. Her job offer to Flora, which will put her into weekly contact with Annette, casts suspicion on the doctor's motives. She gives Flora exactly what she wants, with only the meek reassurance that there is nothing sentimental about her passion for Annette. Such a move is a double indictment of the woman who threatens male authority. Written in 1915, Lee's short story was sure to be influenced by social attitudes that advised women against entering higher education, let alone medical practice, and also advised them against intimacy with other women. That Lee locks both of these social threats within the confines of a women's college clearly demonstrates the rigidly confined place and role they ought to occupy.

The girls' relationship must be severed, and the only means to do this is by substituting the emotional attraction with an intellectual endeavor, science. That is, the feminine desire for the feminine is replaced by the masculine intellectual interest in science, thereby righting the wrongs of alternative desire that Lee initially introduces between women. In the end, as Flora and Annette go off to work in Dr. Worchester's lab, they have sublimated their desire. But science also has chosen Flora, the most threatening of the girls. As the doctor notes, "a gentle hand reached down and touched the chosen. . . ." Flora, as most desirous of the feminine, must necessarily be chosen by this scientific hand so that her unnatural desires can be channeled into more appropriate ones. Flora and Annette will work together in the confinement of the lab under the counsel and supervision of the motherly Dr. Worchester. She chooses Flora and Annette, just as that "gentle hand" does, and thus steers their energy into science rather than into each other. Moreover, the two girls still remain within the women's college. Despite the removal of their attraction and its replacement with scientific inquiry, they continue to work together confined by the walls of their school, with the implication that such a partnership is impossible outside.

In both of these short fictions, the alternative sexual relationships of the schoolgirls support Havelock Ellis's contention in 1902 that women's colleges were "the great breeding ground" of female inversion. In "The School-Friendships of Girls," Ellis suggested that inversion is an "abnormality" that affected any woman who had a "crush"; according to "authorities" this entailed more than 60 percent of students at women's colleges (quoted in Inness, *Intimate Communities* 49). Inness explains that even though Ellis emphasized that not every girl with a crush would become a "congenital invert," he "makes explicit that smashes, even in the absence of genital sexuality, are abnormal and undesirable" (*Intimate Communities* 49).[9] Clearly, Dubois's and Lee's fictional statements are much stronger, completely invalidating the existence of the female invert by relegating her to a space clearly demarcated as outside the boundaries of acceptable society.

Indeed, in all four of these texts, this confinement is apparent. Despite the seemingly progressive notion of having their female characters at school, learning such typically masculine subjects as science, these women remain confined to a stringently defined space. The high walls surrounding the school in Lee's "Cat and the King" are the visible manifestations of the social barrier that kept the danger of same-sex sexuality from being expressed in mainstream American society. Thorne's Jean and Betty are moved one step beyond confinement behind brick walls. They are relegated to a foreign country to a town that does not exist on any map. Their female sexual inversion is so problematic for heterosexual society that the two women cannot reenter it until their love has dried and withered like the flower necklace. Yet it is Beer's Sybil Sloane and Janie Dalgleish who, perhaps, receive the most severe banishment. Their ability to drive off together at the end of this story does not signal they have escaped the tyranny of heterosexual conformity, "exit[ed] the patriarchy," as Zimmerman suggests occurs in later decades. Rather, they have been utterly dismissed from the comfortable confines of their small New England town, left to wander with no tangible destination. These women have, in effect, been cut off, ostracized, estranged from their own land, and, worse yet, unmistakably marked as a product of the devil's work.

"By 1921," Faderman claims, "it was necessary to place romantic friendship at a distance, where it could be attributable to the peculiarities of time and location in order to make it safe" (*Surpassing* 309). However, the textual strategies of Beer, Thorne, Dubois, and Lee, instead of providing a safe haven for the masculine woman and her sexual inversion, confine her to a carnivalesque history and thus prohibit the same-sex attraction from entering the heterosexually structured early-twentieth-century American culture. Masculine womanhood and its inverted sexuality occur in a space that is not contemporary, recognizably geographic, or, ultimately, real.

Notes

1. John D'Emilio and Estelle Freedman take a different approach to 1920s sexuality, one they read as "sexual liberalism—an overlapping set of beliefs that detached sexual activity from the instrumental goal of procreation, affirmed heterosexual pleasure as a value in itself, defined sexual satisfaction as a critical component of personal happiness and successful marriage, and weakened the connections between sexual expression and marriage by providing youth with room for some experimentation as preparation for adult status" (241). The focus of this "sexual liberalism" was clearly directed only at heterosexual practices. Inness's "lesbian signifier" can be understood to fill the space around the affirmation of heterosexual pleasure; it becomes defined by what it is not.

2. According to Mikhail Bakhtin's analyses of the medieval world, "all hierarchical precedence" was suspended (10). Once the lesbians are removed from the fictional picture, then society returns to its normal heterosexual and heterogendered structure; Bakhtin's notion of "carnival" is the often implicit setting of many of these works in which the lesbian is allowed.

3. The virtual identicality of "Querinda" with the Spanish "Querida" suggests that the novel will focus on love, or as the Spanish definition of the noun *Querida* offers, a "lover" or "mistress." (Querinda is not a Spanish word or place name that I found.)

4. Julian and John have taken accommodations above a bar in the heart of Querinda and are therefore not available to resolve the seating crisis.

5. D'Emilio and Freedman make the economic link more explicit by contending that in "a society that defined the female in terms of her maternal instincts, these 'new women' were an anomaly, living proof of the fragility of middle-class values" (190).

6. Christina Simmons, in her article in "Companionate Marriage and the Lesbian Threat," traces the implication of lesbianism at women's colleges through the 1930s. "Concerned about sources of marital instability," she writes, "reformers scrutinized single-sex education: 'the unwholesome fashionable practice of sex-segregated schools brings young people into a homosexual atmosphere.' Deprived of male contact, young girls might not learn to love men. They would develop an 'unconscious homosexuality' which would operate 'to make mating so difficult as to be almost impossible, and to make matings unsatisfactory and unstable when they . . . [were] formally achieved" (56).

7. Terry Castle argues a similar point, drawing on the triangularization of desire that Eve Kosofsky Sedgwick made so popular (see Sedgwick's *Between Men* and *Epistemology of the Closet*). "Even in works in which female homosocial bonds are depicted," Castle contends, "these bonds are inevitably shown giving way to the power of male homosocial triangularization" (73).

8. Sherrie A. Inness lists a number of texts from the 1920s and 1930s that intimated that "a single-sex institution leads to lesbianism among both students and faculty members," (*Menace* 38), including Lillian Hellman's *Children's Hour,* Mary Lapsley's *Parable of the Virgins,* Marion Patton's *Dance on the Tortoise,* Clemence Dane's *Regiment of Women,* Warner Fabian's *Unforbidden Fruit,* Carol Denny Hill's *Wild,* Christa Winsloe's *Girls in Uniform,* and Tess Slesinger's short story "The Answer on the Magnolia Tree."

9. By 1927, Marchalonis argues, "the charge that the women's colleges encouraged homosexual relationships, hinted at in the women's magazines, is overt" (153). As an example, she cites a *Harper's* article, "The Case for the Co-Educated Woman," written by Edna Yost and published July 1927. Women's colleges, according to Yost, are "unnatural" because they remove women from the presumably feminine and masculine world, making them "misfits in life." The student at a woman's college, Yost continued, "is being consciously molded and led into good habits, one of which is to be happy and satisfied for four years without the real companionship of men" (195).

7

Mundus Reversus

Femininity Found

There is such a thing as a woman, isn't there?
—Zephine Humphrey, "The Modern Woman's Home," 1926

In October 1931, when American women without voting rights were only a memory, Charles G. Shaw concluded that "life without women would be a pretty dreary business." His short *Vanity Fair* piece, reading like the confessions of a man on the threshold of knowledge, comments on the relationship between the sexes and the composition of the sexes themselves: what he likes in women and what he does not; which modern inventions have destroyed what he calls "love blossoms"; and how to be successful at love that lasts. Shaw's musings appear to be progressive: "I do not believe that marriage is necessarily the ultimate ideal of a perfect romance," nor does he believe that great love is possible without a "goodly share of heart-aches." Such confessions, however, are remarkably conservative and patriarchal. They are remarkable neither because he believes "women to be infinitely better nurses than men, just as they are less complaining patients" nor because he does not "believe women to be as efficient shopkeepers, motorists, cowpunchers, or restaurateurs." Nor are his views remarkable because he believes "that what woman has gained in 'equal rights' she has lost in feminine charm" (48). Rather, Shaw's misogyny, innocent as it may seem, is remarkable for its conventionality. Despite articulating relaxed sexual expectations and political autonomy, his essay still betrays the fear of women who are masculinized, economically independent, and more apt than not to forsake men and marriage altogether.

But this dissolution of tradition and convention was more fiction than reality, fostered by those who feared women's independence. "Suffragists," according to Peter G. Filene, "had thought that with the Nineteenth Amendment they had marked a turning point in the history of American women, only to find that history had somehow turned upon them. They had become outdated" (123). Already in the 1920s, the older generation of suffragists had given way to a new generation, "who barely noticed their heroic elders or if they did, scorned them as 'either the old school of fighting feminists who wore flat heels and had very little feminine charm, or the current species who antagonize men with their constant clamor about . . . equal rights'" (Filene 123). As with gender and economic reversals, this generational split secured not only gender and economic reversals but also marriage; woman's traditional place was secure and, although perhaps under the scrutiny of revolutionaries, basically impervious to radical forces.

The *Woman Citizen* only solidified the feminine and domestic role of women with an article by Zephine Humphrey in June 1926. Humphrey, the reader is told, "recently read her first advanced feminist book," Alice Beal Parsons's *Woman's Dilemma,* and is concerned with two related questions: "But is there such a thing as a Woman?" and "Must we be standardized?" Humphrey's queries are curiously like those of other writers who, before ratification of the Nineteenth Amendment, cautioned nervously against the dissolution of traditional sex-gender assignments. "I found myself anxiously wondering," Humphrey confesses, "if Mrs. Parsons was going to leave to woman any peculiarly feminine attributes at all, save the physical function of bearing children." Parsons devotes chapter after chapter to proving that women are not inferior to, or very different from, men in endurance, variability, mental and physical efficiency, ingenuity, intelligence, coordination, "all the traits required by our modern life." "This equality" is true, Humphrey carefully notes, because "she established [it] by quoting precise scientific tests." Humphrey admits she is convinced: "No, woman is not handicapped except by tradition and habit; yes, her nature is almost interchangeable with that of man; certainly, she is fitted to share the full work of the world. What then? Why, let her do it." Yet she distrusts scientific tests and wonders what has happened to the once clearly defined feminine gender. Her concern is that women are being equated with men, taking on their characteristics, being subsumed by the masculine gender. "But," she nervously muses, "after all, there is such a thing as a woman, isn't there?" (22).

This was not a new question. Popular opinion had long recognized these changes and often disparaged what the emerging woman was becoming. "Alas! the woman of today is not beautiful enough to meet the test. Her loveliness is not Hellenic. It is not even Academic," Ettore Marroni had written in *Vanity Fair* more than ten years earlier. "The sedentary feminine creature of Nineteen-Sixteen is kept alive by hypophosphates. Look at her emaciated grace, her skin-and-bones fragility, we wonder whether the Venus of Milo wasn't after all too muscular? The modern woman is like modern art—she is a stimulating, baffling, nerve-wracking, grotesque sort of creation at best" (75).

Despite Marroni's lament at the "baffling" modern woman, women's independence did provoke a positive response in some areas. "Women never dressed with such comfort and healthfulness as at present," the editors at the *Woman Citizen* exclaimed, "and the world has gained one great advantage from the fact that legs are no longer a mystery, but can be spoken of in polite society." Moreover, fashion changes gave women more choices than they ever had before: "sensible, healthful, beautiful clothes." Now, the editors admonished, a woman must exercise good judgment in selecting the proper clothes to fit her figure ("What Not to Wear" 17) and her activity schedule. Compared with "the bicycle girl in enormous bloomers, the tennis girl, in a stiff white shirt waist and a heavy skirt that hid her ankles," and "a bathing girl in a voluminous garment very discouraging to Channel swims," the figures of 1927 were "extremely skimpy on yards around or down, of course—and how right that they should be! These girls were dressed to live comfortably the outdoor life that makes for health and strength. The result was taste and beauty . . . we wouldn't see young girls return to the old days for anything!" ("In Praise of Girls' Clothes" 29)

As the sporting woman's physical exertions became more strenuous, her clothing became less restrictive. Susan Cahn argues that this athletic woman "represented both the appealing and threatening aspects of modern womanhood. In a positive light, she captured the exuberant spirit, physical vigor, and brazenness of the New Woman" (43). Yet many American men and women were puzzled by this change in behavior and feared, among other things, that women's figures would be ruined for the latest fashions, exposing what one writer in the *Woman's Journal* described as "thin, sunken chests, protruding shoulder blades, splay backs and thrown-out stomachs" ("Fashion and Figure" 23). The athletic female was an anomalous derivative of women's political enfranchisement: women's athletic activity and athleticism, traditionally masculine endeavors, were physical manifestations of suffrage. As a result, critics of women athletes thought "strenuous athletic pursuits endangered women and threatened the stability of society" because these women "would become manlike, [adopt] masculine dress, talk, and mannerisms" (Cahn 43). As Cahn posits, "These fears collapsed into an all-encompassing concept of 'mannishness,' a term signifying female masculinity" (43).

It was assumed that women were the weaker sex, as the uproar over athletic women demonstrates, and writers were often reduced to begging the question "How weak is the weaker sex?" ("How Weak Is the Weaker Sex?" 15). The suggestiveness of this question implicitly accentuates the social debate surrounding women athletes' sexual expression. "Controversy centered around two issues," Cahn explains, "damage to female reproductive capacity and the unleashing of heterosexual passion." Strenuous athletic activity either would cause the reproductive organs to decay or even atrophy or would give women "strength and energy which would make them more fit for bearing and rearing children" (43). Cahn argues that the controversy "presumed heterosexuality" because the milieu of popular sports was "heterosocial." "The image of the athlete as beauty queen and the commercial atmosphere that characterized much of working-class sport," she concludes, "ensured that the sexual debate surrounding the modern female athlete would focus on her heterosexual charm, daring, or disrepute" (45).

In what *Vanity Fair* described as "a scurrilous and dyspeptic treatise, misogynic and libelous but not devoid of the mad, bad germ of truth" (71), Paul Gallico, a frequent contributor and sports writer, characterized "athletic ladies" as "muscle molls" in a 1931 article entitled "Muscle Molls—You Can Have Them." Using the term *molls* was derogatory, Cahn acknowledges, because in its only other usages, "the word 'moll' referred to either the female lovers of male gangsters or to prostitutes" (45). Gallico unflatteringly describes his "molls" as "strong and virginal young animals with red cheeks and lips adorned only by nature, who induct fresh air into their bosoms in great gulps, who perspire freely when it is hot and get chapped when it is cold, whose woolen stockings are filled with large bunches of muscles, who pack the shoulders of a welterweight prizefighter, and who, when they shake hands, look you squarely in the eye and exhibit their teeth as they mash your metacarpals and mangle your phalanges" (71). Later, Gallico concludes that "permanent devotion on the part of the madonnas to any one of the violent sports leaves indelible records upon their already absurd female figures, until they wind up actually looking like a Picasso abstract or a pair of Chirico horses which is something you would not wish on your worst enemy." Overall, "with very few exceptions," Gallico writes, "the sportswomen who populate our headlines are a knobby, leggy, weatherbeaten, unattractive lot and this is just to notify you that, as far as I am concerned, you can have them" (71).

A month later, Janice Taylor presented a "retaliatory composition" to Paul Gallico's "Muscle Molls" in which she wonders "just what good ARE [male athletes]?" (104). Not only are they "largely a collection of good-natured imbeciles, beautiful and dumb public gladiators who should never be permitted to doff their tennis flannels or football suits or other picturesque costumes, and attempt to mingle on terms of equality within intelligent people" (49), Taylor declares, but they become, once their glory days have ended, "paunchy, triple-chinned and loggy, forever reminding one of their better days and forever promising they will get in shape again, some day . . ." (104).

It is difficult, given the excessive style and exaggerated content of these two companion pieces in *Vanity Fair*, to ignore the potential for parody. The points of ironic argumentation, nevertheless, are revealing. Gallico attacks athletic females on the basis of how sports activities affect females' physical appearance. By engaging in the masculine endeavor of exercising the body, women lose the physical attractiveness that makes them women. Instead, they resemble an abstractly disproportionate piece of modern art or a prizefighter and are, at least for Gallico, his "worst enemy." To be a woman is to be attractive, according to Gallico's formulation, and to be attractive is to distance oneself from athletics. Gallico contends that the gender distinctions and their traditional sex-gender pairings have been confused, resulting in new creatures who are "absurd female figures," with the sex of a female and the masculinely gendered athleticism of a male.

Taylor, in her retort to Gallico, makes no such gender assumptions. Her male athletes maintain the stereotype and have muscles in all the appropriate places, making them overtly virile, albeit "dumb," unable to converse about or focus their attention on anything but themselves. More interestingly, man's participation in athletics does not result in the formation of a new creature. He remains a physically realistic and identifiable male, just less intelligent. Gallico and Taylor thus demonstrate how traditional male and female roles have been altered by modern activities. Males are simply adding to their physical prowess but losing some mental capacity. Females, however, are thoroughly changing. A diminished intelligence and increasing number of chins do not compromise his maleness, but a woman's athleticism removes her from the category of woman and reduces her to a sexual anomaly precisely because she transgressed traditional gender expectations.

Yet sexuality, although not overt in these two pieces, clearly is implied, particularly when another piece by Gallico is examined. In "Once a Lady Athlete, Always a Lady Athlete," published in *Vanity Fair* in August 1933, Gallico tells the presumably fictional story of a young male reporter infatuated with a female golfer. Despite the warnings of older, more experienced reporters, the naive Lony Randall loses his heart to Anya Tenniel, a "beautifully formed" golfer who "could drive a golf ball 230 yards with a smooth, graceful swing" (40). Ultimately, Randall is asked by Tenniel to balance a golf ball on his nose so that she can drive it off in a stunt event. Smitten, he agrees, ends up with a nose bloodied (but unbroken), and, angered and humiliated, goes after Tenniel with a golf club hoping to "'[b]end this over [her] goddamn head'" (48b). That Randall should have known not to get involved with the woman athlete is clear from Gallico's fictive voice of reason, Ben Whittaker, veteran tennis writer for the *Sun*. "'A lady athlete is a lady athlete,'" Whittaker explains. "'They're all screwy, or they wouldn't be athletes. They would be working in an office, or making some guy a home, instead of batting around the country, knocking the covers off tennis balls or flicking a little white pill over pasture land.'" Later, Whittaker's indictment is even more harsh when Randall asks him, "'What the devil have you got against lady athletes?'" Whittaker answers, "'They ain't women. . . . Once a lady athlete, always a lady athlete. Some of 'em look like women, dress like women, act like women—but they ain't. If they were, they wouldn't be athletes'" (40).

Whittaker's succinct pronouncement that "lady athletes" cannot be women because they have forsaken feminine submissiveness or domesticity reflects the rhetoric of female sexual inversion that sexologists had posited about masculine women in general. Mannish behavior was clearly linked to female inverts, and athleticism was clearly understood to be masculine. That Lony Randall's hoped-for love affair with Anya Tenniel goes nowhere also suggests that the "lady athlete," because of her masculinity, is not interested in, or available to, the heterosexual possibility. With the American public's increasing familiarity with sexologists' theories of sexual inversion in the late 1920s and early 1930s, Cahn posits, "the assertive, muscular female competitor roused increasing suspicion," and "women athletes—known for their appropriation of masculine games and styles"—began to be scrutinized "for signs of deviance" (46). Ben Whittaker's pronouncement that Anya Tenniel was not a "woman," with all the feminine accouterments attached to that label, was a coded message of female sexual inversion.

A woman's loss of her feminine appeal as she pursued athletics and molded her body to the "cult of boyish form" was met with carefully calculated resistance ("Fashion and Figure" 23). The vision of the masculine woman gave way to a picture of femininity in which feminine curves were replaced, or as the *Woman Citizen* of July 1927 phrased the return: "it would seem . . . that the day of the beanpole type of beauty is passing." This reemphasis on "the curves

Nature intended" brought back an ideal of feminine beauty and castigated the mannish-looking woman's body as "as neither safe nor normal" ("Return of Curves" 29).

The traditional sex-gender pairing, the feminine woman who closely resembled the ancestral Victorian woman, once again became the ideal. Nowhere was this changing construction of womanhood more apparent than in the "College Girl of 1930." Writing in the *Woman's Journal,* Jeanette Eaton revealed "a New Model of Student who Combines Feminine Charm with a Real Respect and Desire for Learning," a "composite portrait of the college maid today [that] has little resemblance to one taken twenty-five years ago" (5). In the early 1900s, college girls' fashion styles emulated those of college boys, Eaton explains, as did their college songs, customs, and manners. Scholarship was not taken seriously, and "the average girl was encased in a hard shell of immaturity" (5–6). But in 1930, Eaton is struck by the "charm" of the college women's voices and manners. "They have an essentially feminine air," she declares, and the women "no longer try to copy men" (6, 7). Women once more adopt those feminine qualities that much of society feared had been lost irretrievably as a result of the woman suffrage movement. Filene details one manifestation of the return to the Victorian ideal: the rise in home economics classes at women's colleges. Mount Holyoke students, he notes, agreed that such a curriculum may be "a little out of keeping with our cultural atmosphere," but they wanted a course in "plain everyday cooking, taught from a scientific point of view" (128). A Smith student's response was even more succinct: "No man can eat Latin" (quoted in Filene 128).

To support the premise that being a wife and mother was the greatest calling a woman could undertake, the *Woman's Journal* provided a fictional example of what would happen should a married woman sacrifice her marriage for her career. "The career woman," according to Christina Simmons, "threatened men because her independence or her intellectual interests suggested she might refuse to take care of men or do without them altogether" ("Modern Sexuality" 30). There can be no doubt in Helen Louise Walker's "Kept Husbands" (1926) that a woman's independent economic status caused the demise of her marriage and had potentially damaging consequences for her young child. In the story, Lowell Medford's femininity and commitment to maternity are immediately challenged; not only does she have a good job and salary, but she "worked until about two weeks before" her baby was born and "came back to the office an amazingly short time afterward." Needless to say, "she was doing amazingly well then and took her work very seriously" (12). Her husband, Fred, is unable to stick with anything long enough to make a living, let alone surpass her in earnings; after Lowell tells him that she cannot take care of him any longer, he deserts her to go find himself. Eventually, Fred succeeds as a writer in California; but it is not until Lowell, who has been injured in a car accident, telegraphs him that she "need[s] him" (43), that he returns and all is structurally righted.

Clearly, Lowell's success has economically emasculated Fred, who leaves because he is unable to keep pace with his career-driven wife. Despite Fred's insecurities, however, he is not ridiculed, nor is Lowell's business success heralded; certainly, these initial sex-gender reversals—Fred is feminized, and Lowell is masculinized—are detrimental to family and social structure, and the wife's business acumen is destructive to her innocent child, who, the reader is led to believe, is neglected by his career-driven mother. That this possibility was threatening to women in 1926 is clear by the story's ending. Lowell and Fred must resume the genders—and gender-specific behavioral roles—that traditionally were assigned to their sex for the story to end happily. Such a normalizing switch is precisely what happens: Lowell's "need" for Fred wins him back, masculinizing him by her weakness. Although Lowell does not promise to abandon her career, she is clearly convinced of the validity of feminine submissiveness as she recovers from her illness under Fred's care and renewed virility; the Medfords return to the ideal gendered structure of heterosexual society.

The indictment of the "wife-with-career" became even stronger as the century progressed. In October 1930, Pauline Mandigo, writing for the *Woman's Journal,* presented the dilemma as a clear and inescapable choice: "Marriage is the basic problem of the modern woman as it was of her forebears. Certainly it is the most primitive and personal one, for Eve is still Eve even in the twentieth century. . . . But her attitude toward life is complicated by a conflict between the native instinct and the desire to make use of the new opportunities education has given her." The dilemma of the modern woman is, in short, "how to make marriage, motherhood and a personal career equally successful" (14). Helen B. Phelps's illustration that accompanied Mandigo's article provided a visual representation of a career woman's choice—either "lonely old age" or marriage and motherhood (see figure 18). The very visual structure of this choice clearly signals that the modern young woman is faced with a false dilemma: both a career and marriage/motherhood are not possible, yet spinsterhood—and all that it signifies, including a rejection of the feminine, reproductive responsibility and role—is not a viable option. As Sue Shelton White, southern leader of the National Woman's Party asserted, "Marriage is too much of a compromise; it lops off a woman's life as an individual. Yet the

If at a marriageable age the modern woman has established herself in business or profession, she will sooner or later face the alternatives of a lonely old age or marriage

Figure 18. Illustration by Helen B. Phelps in the *Woman's Journal,* October 1930, 14–15.

renunciation too is a lopping off. We choose between the frying-pan and the fire—both very uncomfortable" (52).

Among possible improvements offered by Mandigo is the practice of the "true partnership" of marriage, that is, "to put it baldly, no woman expects a man to bear his and her children, but she does expect him to join hands with her in proving as a fact the long accepted theory that the maternal function is an economic as well as a social asset; and that a mother need not be deprived of her opportunities in a material sense just because such activities must be interrupted during the creation of a new member of society" (15). Moreover, employers could create more day nurseries or nursery schools to accommodate their employees who also happen to be mothers. But Mandigo's suggestions were wildly optimistic and a woman's choice of marriage or career was much more complicated than the illustrator Helen B. Phelps's "Wife-with-Career" would have us believe. Marriage mandated adherence to the traditional feminine role and, consequently, to the heterosexual status quo. But if a woman chose a career, she was forsaking more than a husband. Her very "core of femininity" was challenged; her economic, political, and social independence was disparaged, and she became, because of her assumption of male prerogatives, a masculine woman whose heterosexuality was, at the very least, questioned.

Belief in women's ability and desire for independence increasingly became linked to female sexual inversion, which was no longer constructed as a "beautiful house" but now assumed the lonely and pitiful aspects of old age or disillusionment. Constitutionally, women were given the right to vote, but socially, such independence did not abolish the fear it provoked. Women's autonomy in marriage and divorce, economic independence, and freedom of sexual movement all signaled a complication to the paradigms of feminine woman-hood, masculine manhood, and heterosexuality.

In many ways, the complications about sex, gender, and sexuality from the late nineteenth century to 1930 remained complications throughout the twentieth century and even today. The return of femininity to women after 1930 was briefly interrupted by World War II, when women again were pressed into what had been male employment. Rosie the Riveter was very much like her forerunners during World War I, engaged in work that she performed willingly, then removed from the factories once the men returned and relegated again to her domestic sphere. Not until the second wave of the feminist movement in the 1960s and 1970s did women en masse challenge the gendered behavior associated with, and assumed to be, their role. By this time, the masculine woman who engaged in same-sex intimacies had been long underground.[1] Although the late-twentieth-century American society was far more relaxed about sex and gender roles—unisex clothing perhaps the most visible marker of sex-gender fluidity—such acceptance did have limits. Indeed, some of the same strategies that were employed to disenfranchise the masculine woman in the early twentieth century are still at work today.

Although women's right to vote is constitutionally ensured and women's participation as politicians has increased, the words and the struggles of the suffragists and antisuffragists are still close at hand—as are the strategies social commentators and fiction authors used to express their fears and attempt to disenfranchise the women whom they considered masculinized. When a woman began to be identified as a masculine woman because of her insistence on political enfranchisement and when, as a result, her sexual expression became "the most aggravated form of viraginity," she became too much a reflection of a social world turned upside down. Authors, hoping to prove the pen mightier than the suffragists' word and intent on maintaining the traditional genderings of men and women, were left no choice but to find some way to maintain the social status quo and to answer Zephine Humphrey's question in the affirmative: "Yes, there is still such a thing as a woman." Labeling the masculine woman aberrant, seducing her to heterosexuality, parodying her into absurd oblivion, and removing her from any semblance of modern American society were the tactics they employed in defining "woman." Such strategies heeded the call of the Reverend Stearns, who charged, "Yours it is to determine whether the beautiful order of society . . . shall continue as it has been" (quoted in Welter 26). The alternative—a broken world composed of independent women, no "absolute sex," female sexual inversion, and women such as Phoebe Dole, Mizpra Newcomber, Lesby Croy, Ivanova-Feodronova Kaskawisky, Lady Evangeline Musset, and Flora Bailey—was certainly the "chaos of disjointed and unsightly elements." Although the possibility of masculine womanhood and sexual inversion remained and, indeed, continued to be expressed, the verbal and visual rhetoric rooted in the woman suffrage movement clearly disenfranchised her both before and after the ratification of the Nineteenth Amendment.

Note

1. Two texts provide such an analysis, as well as first-person accounts: *The Persistent Desire: A Femme-Butch Reader,* edited by Joan Nestle, and *Boots of Leather, Slippers of Gold: The History of a Lesbian Community,* by Elizabeth Lapovsky Kennedy and Madeline Davis.

Works Cited

"Alice Mitchell Insane." *New York Times,* January 31, 1892, 1.

Ames, Lucia T. "The Bostonians." *Woman's Journal,* March 18, 1886, 82–83.

Anderson, Sherwood. Introduction to *Geography and Plays,* by Gertrude Stein, 5–8. New York: Haskell House, 1967.

———. *Poor White* (1920). In *The Portable Sherwood Anderson,* edited by Horace Gregory, 119–436. New York: Viking, 1949.

Baker, Michael. *Our Three Selves: The Life of Radclyffe Hall.* New York: William Morrow, 1985.

Bakhtin, Mikhail. *Rabelais and His World.* Translated by Hélène Iswolsky. Bloomington: Indiana University Press, 1984.

Banner, Lois. *American Beauty.* New York: Alfred A. Knopf, 1993.

Barnes, Djuna. *Ladies Almanack.* 1928. Reprint, Elmwood Park, Ill.: Dalkey Archive Press, 1992.

———. *Ryder.* Elmwood Park, Ill.: Dalkey Archive Press, 1990.

Barnett, Avrom. *Foundations of Feminism: (A Critique).* New York: Robert M. McBride, 1921.

Barry, Richard. "Why Women Oppose Woman Suffrage." *Pearson's Magazine,* March 1910, n.p.

Beer, Thomas. "Hallowe'en" (1923). In *Mrs. Egg and Other Americans,* edited by Wilson Follett, 87–99. New York: Alfred A. Knopf, 1947.

Benchley, Robert. "Sex Is Out." *New Yorker,* December 26, 1925, 16.

Benjamin, Walter. "The Work of Art in the Age of Mechanical Reproduction." In *Illuminations,* edited by Hannah Arendt; translated by Harry Zohn, 219–53. New York: Schocken Books, 1969.

Benson, Elizabeth. "The 'Outrageous' Younger Set." *Vanity Fair,* September 1917, 68+.

Benstock, Shari. "Expatriate Sapphic Modernism: Entering Literary History." In *Lesbian Texts and Contexts: Radical Revisions,* edited by Karla Jay and Joanne Glasgow, 183–203. New York: New York University Press, 1990.

———. *Women of the Left Bank: Paris, 1900–1940.* Austin: University of Texas Press, 1986.

Bishop. "The Mannish Maid." In *Gay/Lesbian Almanac,* by Jonathan Katz, 314. New York: Harper and Row, 1983.

Bissell, Emily P. "A Talk to Women on the Suffrage Question." Presented at the New York State Association Opposed to Woman Suffrage, 1909. Hatcher Library, University of Michigan.

"A Bit of Fun." *Woman's Tribune,* 15 June 1907, 44. Reprinted from *Punch,* n.p., n.d.

Blackmer, Corinne E. "Lesbian Modernism in the Shorter Fiction of Virginia Woolf and Gertrude Stein." In *Virginia Woolf: Lesbian Readings,* edited by Eileen Barrett and Patricia Cramer, 78–93. New York: New York University Press, 1997.

Bloch, Iwan. *Sexual Life in Our Time in Its Relations to Modern Civilizations.* New York: Allied Book, 1908.

Bolt, Christine. *The Women's Movements in the United States and Britain from the 1790s to the 1920s.* Amherst: University of Massachusetts Press, 1993.

Briarly, Mary. "The Man, the Woman, and the University." *Scribner's Magazine,* November 1922, 591–95.

Brittain, Vera. *Radclyffe Hall: A Case of Obscenity?* New York: A. S. Barnes, 1968.

Brittin, Norman. *Edna St. Vincent Millay.* New York: Twayne, 1967.

Brown, Olympia. *Democratic Ideals: A Memorial Sketch of Clara Bewick Colby.* N.p.: Federal Suffrage Association, 1917.

Buckley, James M. *The Wrong and Peril of Woman Suffrage.* New York: Fleming H. Revell, 1909.

Burke, Carolyn. "'Accidental Aloofness': Barnes, Loy, and Modernism." In *Silence and Power: A Re-Evaluation of Djuna Barnes,* edited by Mary Lynn Broe, 67–80. Carbondale: Southern Illinois University Press, 1991.

Bushnell, Horace. *Women's Suffrage: The Reform against Nature.* New York: Charles Scribner, 1869.

Butler, Judith. *Bodies That Matter: On the Discursive Limits of Sex.* New York: Routledge, 1993.

———. *Gender Trouble: Feminism and the Subversion of Identity.* New York: Routledge, 1990.

Cahn, Susan K. "From the 'Muscle Moll' to the 'Butch' Ballplayer: Mannishness, Lesbianism, and Homophobia in U.S. Women's Sport." In *Lesbian Subjects: A Feminist Studies Reader,* edited by Martha Vicinus, 41–65. Bloomington: Indiana University Press, 1996.

Camhi, Jane Jerome. *Women against Women: American Anti-Suffragism, 1880–1920.* Brooklyn, N.Y.: Carlson, 1994.

"Can a Woman Take a Joke?" *Woman's Journal,* October 1925, 41.

"Careers for Young Women." *Vanity Fair,* August 1921, 59+.

Caricature: Wit and Humor of a Nation in Picture, Song and Story. 8th ed. New York: Leslie-Judge, 1911.

Carpenter, Edward. *The Intermediate Sex: A Study of Some Transitional Types of Men and Women.* New York: Mitchell Kennerly, 1912.

Castle, Marian. "I Rebel at Rebellion." *Woman's Journal,* July 1930, 17+.

Castle, Terry. *The Apparitional Lesbian: Female Homosexuality and Modern Culture.* New York: Columbia University Press, 1993.

Catt, Carrie Chapman. Introduction to *The Woman Citizen: A General Handbook of Civics, with Special Consideration of Women's Citizenship,* edited by Mary Sumner Boyd, 8–9. New York: Frederick A. Stokes, 1918.

Chauncey, Jr., George. "From Sexual Inversion to Homosexuality: The Changing Medical Conceptualization of Female 'Deviance.'" In *Passion and Power: Sexuality in History,* edited by Kathy Peiss and Christina Simmons, 87–117. Philadelphia: Temple University Press, 1989.

Child, Richard Washburn. "The Feminist." *Cosmopolitan,* February 1915, 227–41.

Chopin, Kate. *The Awakening and Selected Stories of Kate Chopin.* New York: New American Library, 1976.

Collins, John. "Half-Confessed." In *These Modern Women: Autobiographical Essays from the Twenties,* edited by Elaine Showalter, 144–47. New York: Feminist Press, 1978.

Coman, Martha. "Playtime at Girls' Colleges." *Collier's Weekly,* April 12, 1902, 20–21.

Comstock, T. Griswold. "A Case of Sexual Perversion of 'Urning' (A Paranoiac)," *New York Medical Times,* September 1892, n.p.

Conrad, Bryce. "Gertrude Stein in the American Marketplace." *Journal of Modern Literature* 19 (Fall 1995): 215–33.

Conway, Gordon. "A Woman Hater's Day." *Vanity Fair,* September 1918, 68.

Crowninshield, Frank. "Editorial." In *Vanity Fair: A Cavalcade of the 1920s and 1930s,* edited by Cleveland Amory, 13. New York: Viking, 1960.

Cudlipp, Thelma Grosvenor. "A Grand Old Party." *Vanity Fair,* August 1920, 34.

Dana, Charles L. Letter to Alice Hill Chittenden, president of the New York State Association Opposed to Woman Suffrage. In *Case against Woman Suffrage,* n.p. N.p.: Man-Suffrage Association, n.d.

Davis, Natalie Zemon. *Society and Popular Culture in Early Modern France: Eight Essays.* Stanford, Calif.: Stanford University Press, 1975.

Davis, Pauline Kellogg Wright. Editorial. *Una,* June 1853, n.p.

Davis, Sara DeSaussure. "Feminist Sources in *The Bostonians.*" *American Literature* 50 (January 1979): 570–87.

DeKoven, Marianne. *A Different Language: Gertrude Stein's Experimental Writing.* Madison: University of Wisconsin Press, 1983.

Dell, Floyd. *Diana Stair.* New York: Farrar and Rinehart, 1932.

D'Emilio, John, and Estelle Freedman. *Intimate Matters: A History of Sexuality in America.* New York: Harper and Row, 1988.

Deutscher, Penelope. *Yielding Gender: Feminism, Deconstruction, and the History of Philosophy.* London: Routledge, 1997.

Doane, Janice L. *Silence and Narrative: The Early Novels of Gertrude Stein.* Westport, Conn.: Greenwood, 1986.

"Does the Girls' College Destroy the Wife?" *Ladies' Home Journal,* June 1916, 27.

Doughty, Frances M. "Gilt on Cardboard: Djuna Barnes as Illustrator of Her Life and Work." In *Silence and Power: A Re-Evaluation of Djuna Barnes,* edited by Mary Lynn Broe, 137–54. Carbondale: Southern Illinois University Press, 1991.

Douglas, George H. *The Smart Magazines: Fifty Years of Literary Revelry and High Jinks at Vanity Fair, the New Yorker, Life, Esquire, and the Smart Set.* Hamden, Conn.: Archon Books, 1991.

Dresner, Zita Zatkin. "Carolyn Wells." In *Dictionary of Literary Biography,* vol. 11, *American Humorists, 1800–1950,* edited by Stanley Trachtenberg, 556–59. Detroit: Gale Research, 1982.

Dubois, Mary Constance. "The Lass of the Silver Sword." *St. Nicholas: An Illustrated Magazine for Young Folks.* Serialized January 1909–October 1909.

Ducharte, Pierre Louis, and René Saulnier. *L'imagerie populaire.* Paris: Librarie de France, 1925.

Duggan, Lisa. "The Trials of Alice Mitchell: Sensationalism, Sexology, and the Lesbian Subject in Turn-of-the-Century America." *Signs* 18 (Summer 1993): 791–814.

Eaton, Jeannette. "The College Girl of 1930." *Woman's Journal,* May 1930, 5+.

Egan, Beresford. *The Sink of Solitude.* London: Hermes, 1928.

Ellis, Havelock. Commentary. In *The Well of Loneliness,* by Radclyffe Hall, n.p. New York: Anchor Books, 1928.

———. *Sexual Inversion.* 3d rev. ed. Philadelphia: F. A. Davis, 1915.

———. "Sexual Inversion in Women." *Alienist and Neurologist* 16, no. 2 (1895): 141–58.

Ellmann, Richard. *Oscar Wilde.* New York: Alfred A. Knopf, 1988.

Evans, Sara. *Born for Liberty: A History of Women in America.* New York: Free Press, 1989.

Faderman, Lillian. *Surpassing the Love of Men.* New York: William Morrow, 1981.

———. "What is Lesbian Literature? Forming a Historical Canon." In *Professions of Desire: Lesbian and Gay Studies in Literature,* edited by Bonnie Zimmerman and George E. Haggerty, 49–59. New York: MLA, 1995.

Farwell, Marilyn. "Toward a Definition of the Lesbian Literary Imagination." *Signs* 14 (Autumn 1988): 100–118.

"Fashion and Figure." *Woman's Journal,* February 1928, 23.

Field, Andrew. *Djuna: The Life and Times of Djuna Barnes.* New York: Putnam, 1983.

Filene, Peter G. *Sex Roles in Modern America.* Baltimore: Johns Hopkins University Press, 1986.

Flax, Jane. "Postmodern and Gender Relations in Feminist Theory." *Signs* 12 (Summer 1987): 621–43.

Follett, Wilson. Introduction to *Mrs. Egg and Other Americans,* by Thomas Beer, vii–xxv. New York: Alfred A. Knopf, 1947.

Foster, Edward. *Mary E. Wilkins Freeman.* New York: Hendricks House, 1956.

Foster, Jeannette. *Sex Variant Women in Literature.* Tallahassee, Fla.: Naiad, 1985.

Foucault, Michel. *Discipline and Punish.* Translated by Alan Sheridan. New York: Pantheon, 1977.

Frederick, J. George. "The Man Problem in the Woman Movement." *Woman Citizen,* August 27, 1921, 8+.

Freeman, Mary E. Wilkins. "The Long Arm" (1895). In *Victorian Tales of Mystery and Detection: An Oxford Anthology,* edited by Michael Cox, 377–405. New York: Oxford University Press, 1992.

Friedman, Adele. "Stereotypes of Traditional Society in French Folksongs and Images Populaires." *Journal of Popular Culture* 10 (Spring 1977): 766–74.

Fulton, Valerie. "Rewriting the Necessary Woman: Marriage and Professionalism in James, Jewett, and Phelps." *Henry James Review* 15 (Fall 1994): 242–56.

Gallico, Paul. "Muscle Molls—You Can Have Them." *Vanity Fair,* May 1931, 71+.

———. "Once a Lady Athlete, Always a Lady Athlete." *Vanity Fair,* August 1933, 40+.

Garvey, Ellen Gruber. *The Adman in the Parlor: Magazines and the Gendering of Consumer Culture, 1880s to 1910s.* New York: Oxford University Press, 1996.

Gilman, Charlotte Perkins. "Turned" (1911). In *The Charlotte Perkins Gilman Reader,* edited by Ann J. Lane, 87–97. New York: Pantheon Books, 1983.

Grant, Robert. "The Limits of Feminine Independence." *Scribner's Magazine,* June 1919, 729–34.

Green, Anna Katherine. *The Leavenworth Case.* 1878. Reprint, Upper Saddle River, N.J.: Literature House, 1970.

Greening, H. C. "Giving the Freaks a Treat." In *Caricature, Wit, and Humor of a Nation in Picture, Song and Story,* 8th ed., n.p. New York: Leslie-Judge, 1911.

Griffin, Gabriele. *Heavenly Love? Lesbian Images in Twentieth-Century Women's Writings.* Manchester, England: Manchester University Press, 1993.

Gubar, Susan. "Blessings in Disguise: Cross-Dressing as Re-Dressing for Female Modernists." *Massachusetts Review* 22 (Autumn 1981): 477–508.

Habegger, Alfred. "*The Bostonians* and Henry James Sr.'s Crusade against Feminism and Free Love." *Women's Studies* 15 (1988): 323–42.

Halberstam, Judith. *Female Masculinities.* Durham, N.C.: Duke University Press, 1998.

Hall, Radclyffe. *The Well of Loneliness.* New York: Anchor Books, 1928.

Harbert, Lizzie Boynton. *Out of Her Sphere.* Des Moines, Iowa: Mills, 1871.

Hart, John E. *Floyd Dell.* New York: Twayne, 1971.

Hawkins, Mike. *Social Darwinism in European and American Thought, 1860–1945: Nature as Model and Nature as Threat.* Cambridge: Cambridge University Press, 1997.

Herendeen, Anne. "Wife-ing It." *Woman's Journal,* November 1928, 10+.

Hokenson, Jan. "The Pronouns of Gomorrha." *Frontiers* 10 (1988): 62–69.

Holland, Robert Afton. "The Suffragette." *Sewanee Review* 17 (July 1909): 272–88.

Hopkins, Mary Alden. "Why I Earn My Own Living." In *These Modern Women: Autobiographical Essays from the Twenties,* edited by Elaine Showalter, 41–45. New York: Feminist Press, 1978.

"The House That Jill Built." *Life,* February 27, 1913, 424.

Howard, William Lee. "Effeminate Men and Masculine Women." *New York Medical Journal* 71 (1900): 687.

———. *The Perverts.* New York: G. W. Dillingham, 1901.

———. "The Sexual Pervert in Life Insurance." *Medical Examiner* 16 (July 1906): 206–7.

"How Weak Is the Weaker Sex?" *Woman Citizen,* September 1925, 15+.

Hughes, Charles H. Hughes. "Erotopathia—Morbid Eroticism." *Alienist and Neurologist* 14 (October 1893): 531–78.

Hull, Helen R. "The Fire." *Century Magazine,* November 1917, 105–14.

Humphrey, Zephine. "The Modern Woman's Home." *Woman Citizen,* June 1926, 22+.

"The Ideal Woman." *Vanity Fair,* August 1926, 53, 90.

"In Behalf of the Womanly Woman." *Scribner's Magazine,* July 1920, 123–24.

Inness, Sherrie A. *Intimate Communities: Representation and Social Transformation in Women's College Fiction, 1895–1910.* Bowling Green, Ohio: Bowling Green State University Press, 1995.

————. *The Lesbian Menace: Ideology, Identity, and the Representation of Lesbian Life.* Amherst: University of Massachusetts Press, 1997.

"In Praise of Girls' Clothes." *Woman Citizen,* June 1927, 29.

Jablonsky, Thomas J. *The Home, Heaven, and Mother Party: Female Anti-Suffragists in the United States, 1868–1920.* Brooklyn, N.Y.: Carlson, 1994.

James, Henry. *The Bostonians.* 1886. Reprint, London: John Lehmann, 1952.

Jay, Karla. *The Amazon and the Page: Natalie Clifford Barney and Renee Vivien.* Bloomington: Indiana University Press, 1988.

———. "The Outsider among the Expatriates: Djuna Barnes' Satire on the Ladies of the *Almanack.*" In *Silence and Power: A Re-Evaluation of Djuna Barnes,* edited by Mary Lynn Broe, 184–94. Carbondale: Southern Illinois University Press, 1991.

"Jealousy the Motive." *New York Times,* January 29, 1892, 1.

Jordan, and Davieson. "Practical Observations on Nervous Debility and Physical Exhaustion: To Which Is Added an Essay on Marriage with Important Chapters on Disorders of the Reproductive Organs." Synopsis of lectures delivered at the Museum of Anatomy, 1625 Filbert Street, Philadelphia, 1871. Hatcher Library, University of Michigan.

Katz, Jonathan. *Gay/Lesbian Almanac.* New York: Harper and Row, 1983.

Katz, Leon. Introduction to *Fernhurst, Q.E.D., and Other Early Writings,* by Gertrude Stein, ix–xii. New York: Liveright, 1971.

Kellner, Bruce, ed. *A Gertrude Stein Companion: Content with the Example.* New York: Greenwood, 1988.

Kennedy, Elizabeth Lapovsky, and Davis, Madeline. *Boots of Leather, Slippers of Gold: The History of a Lesbian Community.* New York: Routledge, 1993.

Knapp, Bettina. *Gertrude Stein.* New York: Continuum, 1990.

Knight, Denise K. *Charlotte Perkins Gilman: A Study of the Short Fiction.* New York: Twayne, 1997.

Koppelman, Susan. "About 'Two Friends' and Mary Eleanor Wilkins Freeman." *American Literary Realism* 21 (Fall 1988): 43–57.

Kraditor, Aileen S. *The Ideas of the Woman Suffrage Movement, 1890–1920.* New York: Columbia University Press, 1965.

Krafft-Ebing, Richard. *Psychopathia Sexualis with Especial Reference to the Antipathic Sexual Instinct.* Translated by F. J. Rebman. Brooklyn, N.Y.: n.p., 1908.

Lamos, Colleen. "Sexuality versus Gender: A Kind of Mistake?" In *Cross-Purposes: Lesbians, Feminists, and the Limits of Alliance,* edited by Dana Heller, 85–94. Bloomington: Indiana University Press, 1997.

Laner, Mary Riege, and Laner, Roy H. "Sexual Preference or Personal Style? Why Lesbians Are Disliked." *Journal of Homosexuality* 5 (Summer 1980): 339–56.

Lanser, Susan Sniader. "Speaking in Tongues: *Ladies Almanack* and the Language of Celebration." *Frontiers* 4 (1979): 39–46.

Lee, Jeanette. "The Cat and the King." *Ladies' Home Journal,* October 1919, 10+.

Le Gallienne, Richard. "The Modern Girl—and Why She Is Painted." *Vanity Fair,* January 1924, 27+.

"Lesbian Love and Murder." *Medical Record* (New York), July 23, 1892, n.p.

Lester. "Past, Present and Future." *Life,* April 17, 1913, 771.

Lorber, Judith. *Paradoxes of Gender.* New Haven, Conn.: Yale University Press, 1994.

"Lovelorn Girls." *Denver Times,* July 6, 1889, 6.

Lumsden, Linda J. *Rampant Women Suffragists and the Right of Assembly.* Knoxville: University of Tennessee Press, 1997.

MacLane, Mary. *I, Mary MacLane: A Diary of Human Days.* New York: Frederick A. Stokes, 1917.

———. *The Story of Mary MacLane.* Chicago: Herbert S. Stone, 1902.

Macy, John. *About Women.* New York: William Morrow, 1930.

"Mad Infatuation." *Aspen Times,* May 11, 1889, 4.

Mandigo, Pauline. "Wife-with-Career." *Woman's Journal,* October 1930, 14+.

Marchalonis, Shirley. *College Girls: A Century in Fiction.* New Brunswick, N.J.: Rutgers University Press, 1995.

Marroni, Ettore. "An Afternoon with the Faun." *Vanity Fair,* April 1916, 75.

Marshall, Susan E. *Splintered Sisterhood: Gender and Class in the Campaign against Woman Suffrage.* Madison: University of Wisconsin Press, 1997.

McComas, Henry C. "The Eternally Feminine Mind." *Scribner's Magazine,* October 1926, 428–33.

Miller, Alice Duer. "Why We Don't Want Men to Vote?" 1915. Reprint, *New York Times,* September 30, 1990, 4A:6.

Miller, Patricia McClelland. "The Fiction of Helen Rose Hull." Ph.D. diss., University of Connecticut, 1989.

Mitchell, S. Weir. "When the College Is Hurtful to a Girl." *Ladies' Home Journal,* June 1900, 14.

"Mitchell Murder Case." *New York Times,* February 28, 1892, 9.

"A Most Shocking Crime." *New York Times,* January 26, 1892, 1.

Nestle, Joan, ed. *The Persistent Desire: A Femme-Butch Reader.* Boston: Alyson Publications, 1992.

Newton, Esther. "The Mythic Mannish Lesbian: Radclyffe Hall and the New Woman." *Signs* 9 (Summer 1984): 557–75.

O'Hagan, Anne. "Four Little Duologues on Feminism." *Vanity Fair,* March 1920, 37.

Parkes, Adam. *Modernism and the Theater of Censorship.* New York: Oxford University Press, 1996.

Perloff, Marjorie. "Six Stein Styles in Search of a Reader." In *A Gertrude Stein Companion: Content with the Example,* edited by Bruce Kellner, 96–108. New York: Greenwood, 1988.

Phelps, Helen B. "Wife-with-Career: The Modern Woman's Choice." *Woman's Journal,* October 1930, 14–15.

Porter, Edwin H. *The Fall River Tragedy: A History of the Borden Murders.* 1893. Reprint, Portland, Maine: King Philip, 1985.

"Ps-s-t Nix Lady Nix! You're Not My Kind of Valentine." In *Gay/Lesbian Almanac,* by Jonathan Katz, 314. New York: Harper and Row, 1983.

Pyrhönen, Heta. *Murder from an Academic Angle: An Introduction to the Study of the Detective Novel.* Columbia, S.C.: Camden House, 1994.

Quebe, Ruth Evelyn. "*The Bostonians:* Some Historical Sources and Their Implications." *Centennial Review* 15 (Winter 1981): 80–100.

Rappaport, Doreen. *The Lizzie Borden Trial.* New York: HarperCollins, 1992.

Reichardt, Mary R. *A Mary Wilkins Freeman Reader.* Lincoln: University of Nebraska Press, 1987.

———. *A Web of Relationship: Women in the Short Stories of Mary Wilkins Freeman.* Jackson: University Press of Mississippi, 1992.

Reilly, Paul. "The Transition Period." *Life,* January 30, 1919, 216.

"Return of Curves." *Woman Citizen,* July 1927, 29.

Rogers, Lou. "Mrs. Voteless Citizen." *Woman Citizen,* July 28, 1917, cover.

Rolley, Katrina. "Cutting a Dash: The Dress of Radclyffe Hall and Una Trowbridge." *Feminist Review* 35 (Summer 1990): 54–66.

Ross, Edward Allsworth. *Changing America: Studies in Contemporary Society.* New York: Century, 1912.

Rubin, Gayle. "Of Catamites and Kings: Reflections on Butch, Gender, and Boundaries." In *The Persistent Desire: A Femme-Butch Reader,* edited by Joan Nestle, 466–82. Boston: Alyson Publications, 1992.

Sangster, Margaret. "Girl Colonies." *Collier's Weekly,* April 13, 1901, 16.

Scharnhorst, Gary. *Charlotte Perkins Gilman.* Boston: Twayne, 1985.

Sedgwick, Eve Kosofsky. *Between Men: English Literature and Male Homosocial Desire.* New York: Columbia University Press, 1985.

———. *Epistemology of the Closet.* Berkeley: University of California Press, 1990.

Seidel, Kathryn Lee. "'Art Is an Unnatural Act': Mademoiselle Reisz in *The Awakening.*" *Mississippi Quarterly* 46 (Spring 1993): 199–214.

Shaw, Charles G. "On Love and the Girls." *Vanity Fair,* October 1931, 48.

Shaw, J. Bradley. "New England Gothic by the Light of Common Day: Lizzie Borden and Mary E. Wilkins Freeman's 'The Long Arm.'" *New England Quarterly* 70 (June 1997): 211–36.

Showalter, Elaine, ed. *These Modern Women: Autobiographical Essays from the Twenties.* New York: Feminist Press, 1978.

Simmons, Christina. "Companionate Marriage and the Lesbian Threat." *Frontiers* 4 (1979): 54–59.

———. "Modern Sexuality and the Myth of Victorian Repression." In *Gender and American History since 1890,* edited by Barbara Melosh, 17–40. London: Routledge, 1993.

Sitwell, Edith. "Miss Stein's Stories" (1923). In *Critical Essays on Gertrude Stein,* edited by Michael J. Hoffmann, 45–46. Boston: G. K. Hall, 1986.

Smith-Rosenberg, Carroll. *Disorderly Conduct: Visions of Gender in Victorian America.* New York: Oxford University Press, 1985.

Stanton, Elizabeth Cady. "Educated Suffrage." *Collier's Weekly,* April 12, 1902, 9.

Stearns, Jonathan F. "Female Influence and the True Christian Mode of Its Exercise: A Discourse Delivered in the First Presbyterian Church in Newburyport, July 30, 1837." Newburyport, Massachusetts, 1837.

Stein, Gertrude. *The Autobiography of Alice B. Toklas.* New York: Harcourt, Brace, 1933.

———. *Fernhurst, Q.E.D., and Other Early Writing.* New York: Liveright, 1971.

———. *Geography and Plays.* 1922. Reprint, New York: Haskell House, 1967.

———. "Miss Furr and Miss Skeene." *Vanity Fair,* July 1923, 55+.

———. *Three Lives.* Norfold, Conn.: New Directions, 1933.

Stephensen, P. R. Introduction to *The Sink of Solitude,* by Beresford Egan, 6–10. London: Hermes, 1928.

Stevens, Hugh. *Henry James and Sexuality.* Cambridge: Cambridge University Press, 1998.

Stimpson, Catharine. "The Somagrams of Gertrude Stein." In *Critical Essays on Gertrude Stein,* edited by Michael J. Hoffman, 183–96. Boston: G. K. Hall, 1986.

Strunsky, Hyman. "Marriage and Feminism: A Somewhat Speculative Forecast." *Vanity Fair,* January 1916, 39.

Symonds, Julian. *Bloody Murder: From the Detective Story to the Crime Novel.* 3d rev. ed. New York: Mysterious Press, 1993.

Taylor, Janice. "Male Athletes—Just What Good ARE They?" *Vanity Fair,* June 1931, 49+.

Thompson, W. Gilman. "Women and Heavy War Work." *Scribner's Magazine,* January 1919, 113–16.

Thomson, Rodney. "Militants." *Life*, March 27, 1913, 616.

Thorne, Anthony. *Delay in the Sun*. Garden City, N.Y.: Doubleday, Doran, 1934.

Vanita, Ruth. *Sappho and the Virgin Mary: Same-Sex Love and the English Literary Imagination*. New York: Columbia University Press, 1998.

Vegtel, Maddy. "And Years Passed." *Vanity Fair*, September 1926, 113–14.

Vicinus, Martha. "'They Wonder to Which Sex I Belong': The Historical Roots of Modern Lesbian Identity." In *The Lesbian and Gay Studies Reader*, edited by Henry Abelone, Michéle Aina Barale, and David M. Halperin, 432–52. New York: Routledge, 1993.

von Rhau, Henry. *The Hell of Loneliness*. 1929. Reprint, Washington, D.C.: Guild, 1964.

Walker, A. B. "Am I Losing Weight, or Are These Your Trousers, Jane?" *Life*, February 20, 1913, 368.

———. "If the Styles Were Reversed." *Life*, April 17, 1913, 778.

Walker, Emma E. "Crushes among Girls." *Ladies' Home Journal*, January 1904, 21.

Walker, Helen Louise. "Kept Husbands." *Woman's Journal*, November 1929, 12+.

Walker, Jayne L. *The Making of a Modernist*. Amherst: University of Massachusetts Press, 1984.

Watson, John B. "The Weakness of Women." In *These Modern Women: Autobiographical Essays from the Twenties*, edited by Elaine Showalter, 141–44. New York: Feminist Press, 1978.

"The Ways of a Maid with the Modes of a Man." *Vanity Fair*, May 1914, n.p.

Wegener, Frederick. "'A Line of Her Own': Henry James's 'Sturdy Little Doctress' and the Medical Woman as Literary Type in Gilded-Age America." *Texas Studies in Literature and Language* 39 (Summer 1997): 139–80.

Weir, James B. "The Effect of Female Suffrage on Posterity." *American Naturalist*, September 1895, 815–28.

Wells, Carolyn. "The Beautiful House." *Harper's Monthly Magazine*, March 1912, 503–11.

———. "The Girl of To-Day." *Harper's Magazine*, April 1922, 685–86.

———. "The Last Straw." In *Caricature: Wit and Humor of a Nation in Picture, Song and Story*, 8th ed., 84. New York: Leslie-Judge, 1911.

Welter, Barbara. *Dimity Convictions: The American Woman in the Nineteenth Century*. Athens: Ohio University Press, 1976.

"What Is a Good Wife?" *Woman Citizen*, January 1926, 18+.

"What Not to Wear—A Study." *Woman Citizen*, March 1925, 17.

Wheeler, Marjorie Spruill, ed. *One Woman, One Vote: Rediscovering the Woman Suffrage Movement*. Troutdale, Ore.: NewSage, 1995.

"When Helen Furr Got Gay with Harold Moos." *Vanity Fair*, October 1923, 37.

White, Sue Shelton. "Mother's Daughters." In *These Modern Women: Autobiographical Essays from the Twenties*, edited by Elaine Showalter, 46–52. New York: Feminist Press, 1978.

Willis, Elizabeth. *Lesby*. *Scribner's Magazine*, December 1930, 571–683.

Wilson, Edmund. "Gertrude Stein" (1931). In *Critical Essays on Gertrude Stein*, edited by Michael J. Hoffman, 58–62. Boston: G. K. Hall, 1986.

———. "Gertrude Stein Young and Old" (1952). In *Critical Essays on Gertrude Stein*, edited by Michael J. Hoffman, 85–88. Boston: G. K. Hall, 1986.

"Woman and Man." Review of *The Nature of Woman*, by J. Lionel Tayler. *New York Times*, March 30, 1913, 175.

Woolf, Virginia. *The Diary of Virginia Woolf*. 5 vols. Edited by Anne Oliver. New York: Harcourt Brace Jovanovich, 1977–84.

"Your Daughter: What Are Her Friendships?" *Ladies' Home Journal*, October 1913, 16+.

Zimmerman, Bonnie. "Exiting from the Patriarchy: The Lesbian Novel of Development." In *The Voyage In: Fictions of Female Development*, edited by Elizabeth Abel, Marianne Hirsch, and Elizabeth Langland, 244–57. Hanover, N.H.: University Press of New England, 1983.

———. *The Safe Sea of Women: Lesbian Fiction, 1969–1989*. Boston: Beacon, 1990.

Index

Freedman, Estelle: on cross-dressing, 15, 64; on the new woman, 189n5; on sexual liberalism, 188n1; on women's colleges, 178
Freeman, Mary E. Wilkins, 6, 66, 68–80
Friedman, Adele, 146–47

Gallico, Paul: "Muscle Molls—You Can Have Them," 193–94; "Once a Lady Athlete, Always a Lady Athlete," 8, 194–95
Gender: cross-gendering, 60–64; and femininity, 12–15; and homophobia, 29n3; and masculinity, 2, 12–15; and sex, 12–15; and sexuality, 3–4, 16–17
Gilman, Charlotte Perkins: and suffrage, 29n6; "Turned," 4–5, 20–24
"Giving the Freaks a Treat" (Greening), 31–32
Greening, H. C., 31–32
Griffin, Gabrielle, 166

Halberstam, Judith, 1–2
Hall, Radclyffe, 7, 131–33
"Hallowe'en" (Beer), 7, 166–70
Herendeen, Anne, 163–64
Homosexuality: relation to gender, 12–15, 29n3; relation to sex, 3–4, 12–15
Homosociality, 17–18
Hopkins, Mary Alden, 161–62
Howard, William Lee: *The Perverts*, 5, 52–57; "The Sexual Pervert," 25–26
Hull, Helen R., 87, 89–92
Humphreys, Zephine, 8, 190–91, 199

images populaires, 143–47
Inness, Sherrie A.: literary criticism of, 158–59, 180, 183, 187; on women's colleges, 189n8

James, Henry, 5, 47–52
Jay, Karla, 143, 152

Kennedy, Elizabeth Lapovsky, 14, 16
"Kept Husbands" (Walker), 8, 196–97
Krafft-Ebing, Richard von, 15

Ladies Almanack (Barnes): discussion of, 7, 132, 141–56; illustrations in, 144, 145, 148, 150, 151, 153, 154
Lamos, Colleen, 14
Lanser, Susan Sniader, 151
"Lass of the Silver Sword, The" (Dubois), 8, 166, 180–82

Lee, Jeanette, 8, 166, 180, 182–88
Lesby (Willis), 6, 105, 111–18
L'imagerie populaire (Ducharte and Saulnier), 7, 143–47
"Long Arm, The" (Freeman): discussion of, 68–80; relation to Borden murder case, 68; relation to Mitchell murder case, 68–71
Lorber, Judith, 13–14

Mandigo, Pauline, 197–98
Marchalonis, Shirley, 180, 189n9
Masculine women: and aberrancy, 60–81; and heterosexual seduction, 82–118; historical perspective of, 2–4, 15–16; illustrations of, 16, 26, 33–34, 43–44, 83; parodies of, 119–57; and social removal, 158–89; and suffrage, 43; and viraginity, 1, 5
"Miss Furr and Miss Skeene" (Stein), 7, 124–28
Mitchell, Alice, 68–71
Mitchell, Alice Duer, 123–24
Mitchell, S. Weir, 178–79
"Modern Woman's Home, The" (Humphrey), 190–91, 199
"Muscle Molls—You Can Have Them" (Gallico), 193–94

Newton, Esther, 16, 29n4

O'Hagan, Anne, 121–23
"Once a Lady Athlete, Always a Lady Athlete" (Gallico), 8, 194–95
"On Love and the Girls" (Shaw), 190–91

Perverts, The (Howard), 5, 52–57
Phelps, Helen B, 198
Poor White (Anderson), 6, 99–102

Q.E.D. (Stein), 17

Sex, 12–15. *See also* Female sexual inversion; Gender; Homosexuality; Masculine women; Sexology
"Sex Is Out" (Benchley), 2, 11–12, 14–15
Sexology: connection to woman suffrage, 2, 5, 24–25; historical construction of, 64; and masculinized women, 44–47; and sexual inversion, 44–47, 62–63; and the "third sex," 33
Sexuality. *See* Gender; Sex; Sexology; Women
"Sexual Pervert, The" (Howard), 25–26
Sex Variant Women in Literature (Foster), 26, 177

Laura L. Behling teaches in the English Department at Gustavus Adolphus College in St. Peter, Minnesota.

Typeset in 10.5/13 Minion
with Bernhard Modern Condensed display
Designed by Dennis Roberts
Composed by Jim Proefrock
at the University of Illinois Press
Manufactured by Thomson-Shore, Inc.

University of Illinois Press
1325 South Oak Street
Champaign, IL 61820-6903
www.press.uillinois.edu